Montana
Fly Fishing Guide

THE LYONS PRESS
Guilford, Connecticut
An imprint of The Globe Pequot Press

Montana
Fly Fishing Guide

by John Holt

Volume II
East of the Continental Divide

Drainages

Beaverhead
Big Hole
Blackfeet Reservation
Clarks Fork of the Yellowstone
Gallatin
Jefferson
Madison
Marias
Milk
Missouri
Musselshell
Red Rock
Smith
Stillwater
Yellowstone

The Lyons Press is an imprint of The Globe Pequot Press.

Originally published in 1996 by Greycliff Publishing Company, Helena, Montana

Printed in Canada

10 9 8 7 6 5 4 3 2

The Library of Congress Cataloging-in-Publication Data is available on file.

ISBN 1-58574-529-4

For Dad and Rich

ACKNOWLEDGMENTS

This project wouldn't have been possible without the input of countless people, including members of the Montana Department of Fish, Wildlife, and Parks, the guides and outfitters of Montana, and the individuals quoted in these volumes. It wouldn't have been possible without the work of George Holton in compiling massive amounts of stream and lake data while with the Montana Department of Fish, Wildlife, and Parks; without the example of Dick Konizeski (who initially traveled these waters in his books); an understanding Jim Pruett of Pruett Publishing Company; Glenda Bradshaw, Stan Bradshaw, Bek Meredith, Marcy Chovanak, and Gary LaFontaine of Greycliff Publishing Company; friends Jake How, Tony Accerano, Tim Joern, and Bob Jones.

John Holt donates 10 percent of his royalties to benefit the Montana environment.

TABLE OF CONTENTS

Volume II—East of the Divide

Moral: Humility and open-mindedness sometimes catch far more fish than all the wise guys.

— Robert Traver
Anatomy of a Fisherman

INTRODUCTION

Montana offers all of us who love to fly fish more than a little bit of everything. For trout there is a touch of heaven on earth. For a large number of other gamefish and panfish there is also surprisingly fine angling.

From classic rivers holding trophy rainbows and browns to high country wilderness lakes filled with unsophisticated native cutthroats, on out to high plains reservoirs and their own wind-swept version of our sometimes arcane pursuit, the land presents several lifetimes of angling experiences. Those who live here and are lucky enough to fish over a hundred days a season admit that they will see, at most, maybe a quarter of the water lying out there.

With so much to fish, and so little time to do so, the need for a guide written strictly for fly fishers becomes clear. Other guides are available, many giving much sound information and advice. But there is not a guide on the market written specifically for fly fishers, who, as a whole (admittedly, there are a number of twisted souls out there), are not overly intrigued by the idea of fooling a catfish on a stinkbait imitation (size 2, 4X long hooks work best).

Concise, accurate information for fish fishers dedicated to catching trout 99 percent of the time (chasing bass with deer hair poppers or northern pike with saltwater patterns has a certain, esoteric appeal occasionally) is not available. For out-of-state visitors, where to start can itself be a frustrating, mind-numbing dilemma. For those fortunate enough to live in Montana, information regarding quality waters waiting quietly over the next range of mountains or hiding in some out-of-the-way coulee provides the impetus to expand one's angling horizons.

I am one of the fortunate ones who lives in Montana and has the opportunity to fish 100-plus days a season. All the same, I doubt that I have fished a quarter of the waters that will be mentioned in these guides. Obviously, other reliable sources were consulted for information. Each river, stream, creek, lake, pond, reservoir, and ditch mentioned in both volumes of this guide has been cross-checked with the latest data available from the Montana Department of Fish, Wildlife, and Parks. Additonally, dozens of guides, fly shop owners, fisheries biologists, and hard-core anglers have been interviewed about the current state of trout chasing affairs.

Does this mean that every water holding good numbers of fat trout (or bass or pike) is mentioned in this book? Hell no. There are so many unnamed lakes and streams tucked away in the mountains that even fish and game personnel do not have data on many of them.

What the reader will find in here are listings and descriptions of hundreds of waters worthy of an angler's effort. Divided into sections by drainages, major rivers are described in detail at the opening of each section.

Tributaries and lakes that provide quality angling are then covered (in varying degree) in alphabetical order in each drainage section. Information includes the type of water, species present, abundance and size range of the fish, any fly pattern that is locally important, and other pertinent facts. Specific insect hatches may also be discussed.

All other waters too small to offer quality fishing, too small to sustain heavy pressure, closed for the most part to public access, or just plain lousy fishing, are listed alphabetically with brief comments at the end of the chapter. These conclusions are often a matter of opinion, of course (almost any spot can be challenging and fun for the angler with the right attitude). For example, many tiny creeks hold a couple of decent fish that are fun to locate and fool, but that's it. The rest of the stream holds three-inch dinks that would drown if they connected with a size-14 Adams. That is why each of us should fish where our curiosity leads us. That's part of the magic of fly fishing—finding trout where no one else has. In Montana this can be almost anywhere.

One of the best ways to navigate in unfamiliar territory is by using United States Geological Survey (USGS) topographical maps. These show in detail important features, including rivers, streams, tiny creeks, lakes, ponds, mountains, forests, dams, swamps, buildings, roads, etc. Anyone who can read a highway map can read a topo. They are an inexpensive means to finding waters discussed in the guides.

Because there are literally hundreds of topo maps for Montana alone, it would be cumbersome and costly to own them all. By ordering both the *Montana Index to Topographic and Other Map Coverage* (an easy-to-use pamphlet that shows all maps of Montana and in itself contains some fairly good maps of the state) and the companion *Catalog of Topographic and Other Published Maps* (giving names, dates, and prices of maps currently available), you can decide what maps to order with marginal effort; or if you are hopelessly addicted to maps and the treasures they reveal like I am, kiss an evening goodbye. Larger scale maps are also listed. The address to order these is: USGS, Box 25286, Federal Center, Bldg. 810, Denver, CO 80225. An excellent new publication for small scale topographic maps that shows major highways, public access sites, and other points of interest is the *Montana Atlas and Gazetteer* by DeLorme Mapping. You can order it by calling toll-free 1-800-874-4171, or look for it in book stores.

There are also sections dealing with subjects ranging from stream etiquette to travel arrangements to fishing gear positioned after the chapters on river drainages.

This information is not crucial to catching trout, but it does contain some intrinsic value that may make a trip easier and more enjoyable.

And because every river or lake can be destroyed in the course of a season by logging, agriculture, mining, or simply overuse by anglers, environmental problems affecting specific waters will also be mentioned. The fly fishing community absolutely must become involved with preserving and even enhancing the world-class trout habitat of Montana. If we do not, it all truly will be gone in the future. Sending a check to your local Trout Unlimited is nice but not enough anymore. Personal commitment is needed. To me that is one of the possible benefits of these guides—some new people will be introduced to what Montana has to offer fly fishers. Those that would destroy these fine waters in service of the almighty twisted dollar only listen to the heat generated by the outraged aggregation of an angry mob—in this case one clutching fly rods and wearing waders. I would much rather work a stream with an angler who shares my love of rivers and fish than watch helplessly as chainsaws and D-9s rip the guts out of both water and trout.

The environmental comments are not a declaration of doom. They are a call to join in these battles. The good news is that although some of these battles are temporarily lost, more are being won. Not only are waters being protected but many damaged fisheries are rebounding in productivity. The fact is that fly fishing for trout in Montana is better than it was twenty years ago—and with the help of people inside and outside who care about this state it will be even better twenty years from now.

Even with the swelling of our dedicated ranks, there is still a lot of unfished (or lightly fished) water. And fishing on crowded waters like the Madison is still superb. The action would be even better if everyone exercised the maximum degree of courtesy and common sense. Learning to share the resource will be a valuable skill in the future.

Admittedly some lakes, especially those with brook trout, are overpopulated and produce stunted fish. Keeping a few of these for a campfire dinner may actually improve the health of the system. But for anyone to keep a trophy brown from the Beaverhead or a trophy rainbow from the Missouri is both selfish and destructive. Catch-and-release with barbless or debarbed hooks is the only way to travel most of our waters anymore.

Still, the bottom line with fly fishing is the feeling of a large fish running for freedom as the rod bends double and the reel's drag buzzes toward mechanical breakdown. That's all this book is really about . . . the water, the trout, and the angler.

Fall on the Beaverhead
Photo by John Holt

B E A V E R H E A D   R I V E R

The Beaverhead is the type of river that humbles even the most skilled anglers all too frequently; but then there are other times when the rainbows and browns pounce on any fly drifted by their noses. The amount of light, as much as anything, seems to control the fishing. A bright sun is tough; to find rising trout after late June, fish early or late in the day or on overcast days.

Tuck casts, mending the line in the air, pinpoint accuracy to tiny pockets that fly by in an instant, maintaining steady contact with a couple of down-deep nymphs—all of these skills are needed to fool the big trout holding in the river. And once hooked, bringing the fish to net is another matter.

The river features a difficult array of undercut banks, thick weed beds, runs, riffles and deep pools. This water can be as challenging as fly fishing gets in Montana, or anywhere else for that matter. As a friend of mine once said after a tough October outing, "If you can catch fish on the Beaverhead, you can catch them anywhere."

There is an "old" way and a "new" way to fish the river. The Beaverhead's reputation for large trout was built with the old style, chuck-and-duck methods. Anglers hammered large, weighted streamers, or two big Girdle Bugs, tight to the bank. The leaders were short, minimum 15-pound test, and when the fisherman either hooked the overhanging willow branches or a very big trout he just leaned back and hoped that something would come out of the tangles.

"It's not really a Woolly Bugger, Yuk Bug, and Girdle Bug river anymore," says Tim Tollett. "You can still catch big fish that way, but the trout see those flies so much that they become extremely wary.

"Even when somebody's home in a good hole and you make a perfect cast and retrieve, the trout won't always take."

State fisheries biologist Dick Oswald agrees, saying that pattern selection has become more varied and the size of the flies has gone way down. "The overall trend in the last nine years has been from crude fishing with Girdle Bugs and 15- to 20-pound tippets to smaller nymphs and finer leaders. The big, ugly stuff used to hold sway, but it is not very often that you do well with that approach now."

So is the old way ever worth trying? On overcast, windy days the fish still seem to get silly and will chase the big flies. The most popular patterns for this method are the simplest ones to tie and the

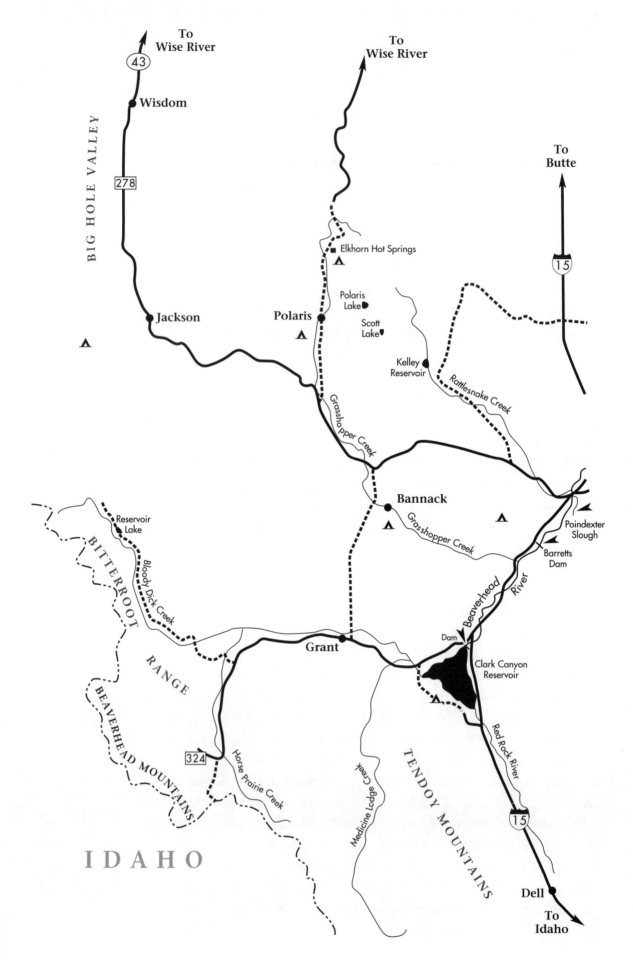

BEAVERHEAD RIVER

To Wise River

43

Wisdom

278

BIG HOLE VALLEY

To Wise River

To Butte

15

Elkhorn Hot Springs

Polaris Lake

Jackson

Polaris

Scott Lake

Kelley Reservoir

Rattlesnake Creek

Grasshopper Creek

Bannack

Grasshopper Creek

Poindexter Slough

Barretts Dam

Reservoir Lake

BITTERROOT RANGE

Bloody Dick Creek

BEAVERHEAD MOUNTAINS

Grant

Dam

Beaverhead River

Clark Canyon Reservoir

324

Horse Prairie Creek

Medicine Lodge Creek

TENDOY MOUNTAINS

Red Rock River

15

Dell

To Idaho

IDAHO

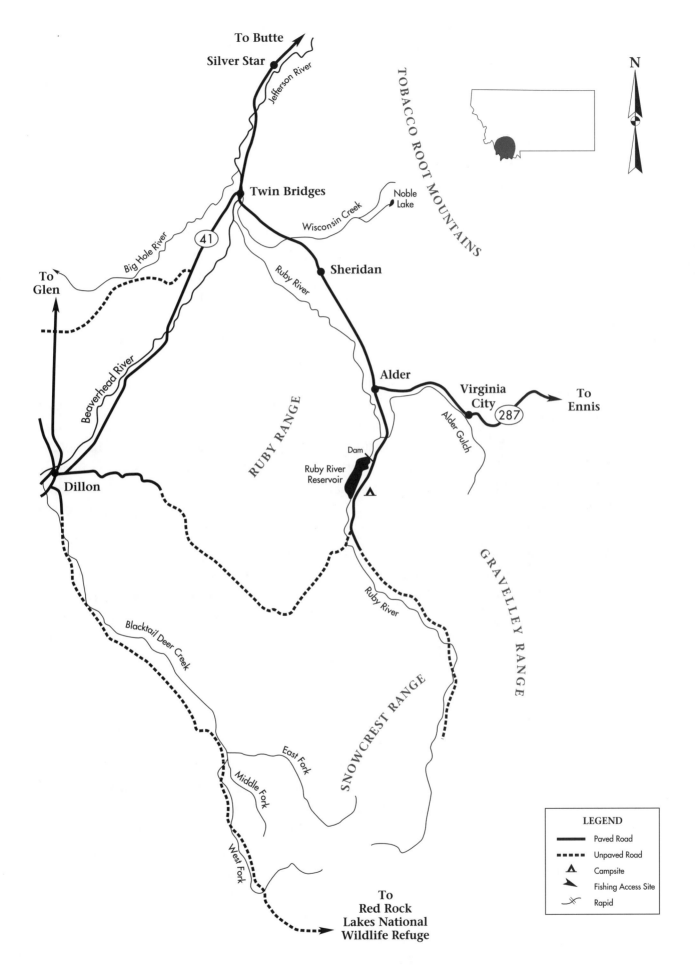

reason is plain—this is not for the timid. You have to slam the flies back into the cover cast after cast, expecting to lose a dozen or so flies in a day.

The new way uses nymphs that at least generally imitate the predominant insect forms of the river. Some of the best patterns are the Partridge & Peacock, Red Squirrel Nymph, Hare's Ear, Dark Olive Brown Flashback, *Callibaetis* Nymph, Little Beaverhead Stone, George's Brown Stone, Bead Head Pheasant Tail, and Deep Sparkle Pupa (especially as the tail fly on a two-fly dropper rig) in sizes 10 through 16. It's also possible to do well with larger patterns, such as T's Crane Nymph, that imitate the abundant cranefly larvae of the river.

The modern style of blind fishing the Beaverhead still focuses on those overgrown banks and the deeper pools. The key is a dead drift instead of an active retrieve. The problem is the dead part of the drift. It "ain't" easy and it "ain't" pretty. Whether wading or floating downstream in a boat, you are always casting across the swift water in the middle of the river. You have to mend a big, upstream belly of line to get any kind of drift.

With a river current greater than five miles per hour, running against tight corners and through swirling holes more than ten feet deep, fishing from a boat can be really frantic. There isn't much time to plan the cast and drift. You get a quick glance ahead to find the next pocket, and then you have to throw the fly almost instinctively dead tight to the bank.

Your casts have to angle downstream. You can't wait until the line is on the water to mend—you have to loop the big, upstream belly while the line is still in the air. There are probably at least one or two lead twist-ons on the leader to make the nymphs get down quickly. There's probably a big strike indicator, which hinges the leader and catches air. And remember, the casts have to be dead accurate. All this adds to the casting excitement for angler and guide alike.

Leave the 3-weight rods at home; 6- and 7-weight rods are more practical. Weight-forward and shooting taper lines predominate around here. The leaders run from 7 to 12 feet. A 3X tippet is nice for feel, but a good fish will smoke this like it's a spider web. But if you go larger than 3X, you lose contact with the flies and has trouble detecting the strikes.

POPULAR NYMPHS
Bead Head Pheasant Tail
Brown Flashback
Dark Olive Brown Flashback
Deep Sparkle Pupa
George's Brown Stone
Hare's Ear
Little Beaverhead Stone
Patridge & Peacock
Red Squirrel
T-Crane's Nymph

Sound like fun?

The Beaverhead can be a great dry fly river, but three factors control the fishing. The light conditions, the intensity of the hatches, and the rate of water flow all determine how many fish come to the surface. For most of the summer, during a normal year, the only chance the angler has to find feeders is either early, from daybreak to 6:30 a.m., or late, from 8:00 p.m. until dark. And even then, it takes a heavy hatch to get the trout interested in the surface.

The flow of the river is controlled entirely by Clark Canyon Dam. The water is delivered from Clark Canyon to Barrett's Diversion for irrigation. During a hot, dry summer, like 1994, the Beaverhead roars bank full down to the diversion because the fields need a lot of moisture. Below the diversion, it can be reduced to a trickle. But during a cool, wet summer, like 1993, the river above Barrett's runs low and very fishable because the fields get enough water from nature.

During almost any year the river offers excellent dry fly fishing before the irrigation season begins in the spring and after the irrigation season ends in the fall. There's always a lull in irrigating during August, too—the ranchers stop watering so that they can get their first cutting of hay.

Even during the heaviest flows there's the chance to catch large trout on dry flies in the huge backwaters on the Beaverhead. These are scum-covered, swirling eddies that collect bits of vegetation, occasional logs, lots of foam, and uncountable dead or dying insects. The trout sit in these reverse currents and sip insects for hours. These spots can't be fished effectively from a boat; you have to know where the eddies are on the river. You can creep up to one and work fussy trout for hours.

Dick Oswald says, "The weather makes or breaks you. One day I hid in the willows during a real goose drowner—thunder, lightning, wind, rain. In the two hours after this storm I had some of the best fishing ever. I suppose if somebody really studied this, they would figure it out, but I haven't."

Like most tailwaters the Beaverhead has a "small community" of insects. This means that there aren't many different species of mayflies, caddisflies, stoneflies, and two-winged flies, but the ones

POPULAR DRY FLIES
CDC Caddis
Elk Hair Caddis
Emergent Sparkle Pupa
Flame Thrower
Goddard Caddis
Little Olive Trude
Little Yellow Trude
Olive Serendipity
Sparkle Dun

9

Bigg's Special (Sheep Creek)

While the Bigg's Special is not a river fly, it is perhaps the deadliest pattern around for the big rainbows and browns of Clark Canyon Reservoir when the damselflies are active. This pattern has worked in lakes with damsel hatches throughout the West. The Bigg's Special works from ice-out until freeze-over.

No weight is necessary on the fly itself, but a sink-tip line is often required for fishing deeper water. After casting, let the fly sink for fifteen seconds, then give it a couple of easy, short strips. Rest the fly for a few more seconds and repeat the process. You will know when a fish hits this number.

It is so easy to tie that you can crank out a dozen while watching reruns of the Rockford Files.

BIGG'S SPECIAL

Hook: 4–10 (long, curved shank—such as the Tiemco 5262)

Tail: two wraps of brown hackle (tied full like a heavy, dry fly hackle)

Body: dark olive chenille

Wing: 4 to 6 barbules of mallard flank feathers

that are there occur in incredible numbers. The outbreaks of huge hatches must be experienced to be believed. A fly on the surface is often lost in the thundering herd of emerging, breeding, egg-laying, and just plain dying bugs.

The important hatches include mayflies such as the Blue-Winged Olive (especially since they appear spring and fall during low water), the Pale Morning Duns, Tricos, *Callibaetis*, and Little Blue-Winged Olive; caddisflies such as the Grannom, Long-Horn Sedge, Spotted Sedge, and Little Sister Sedge; the smaller stoneflies such as the Little Olive Stone and the Little Yellow Stone; and one great two-winged fly, those monstrous parodies of mosquitoes, the Cranefly.

The hatches of craneflies, those semi-aquatic larvae that live in the soft, muddy edges, can be phenomenal. The Beaverhead, with its overgrown banks, provides the perfect habitat for this insect. On summer mornings, at the first glow of dawn, the adults fly and lay eggs, skimming the surface. The trout roll and jump for these big, size 6 to size 10 flies. A matching orange fly, maybe a variant-style pattern, such as the Flame Thrower, or even a Hewitt Skating Spider, draws the same kind of splashy, heart-bumping strikes.

The popular emergers and dry flies on the Beaverhead contain a mix of proven standards and new inventions. The Elk Hair Caddis, Goddard Caddis, and Emergent Sparkle Pupa are standard for the

caddis hatches—the CDC Caddis is finding a place among that famous trio. The Sparkle Dun and the Parachute are the main styles for adult mayflies—no single emerger has caught on for the river, maybe because it is so hard to float and see a flush fly on this turbulent water. Little Yellow and Little Olive Trude patterns match the stoneflies. The Olive Serendipity is a popular midge imitation.

Clark Canyon Dam to Barrett's Diversion—Clark Canyon Reservoir was completed in 1964 and the tailrace of this concrete dam is the beginning of the Beaverhead. The releases, although they fluctuate widely, now insure adequate flows of cold water. Moisture patterns in this part of Montana have been capricious in the past few decades, to say the least, but enough precipitation normally falls to fill the reservoir partially if not brim full.

Under so-called "ideal" conditions, starting in May the rate of flow rises to around 500 to 700 cubic feet per second (cfs) compared to the winter rates in the 200 to 250 cfs range (some dry winters see flows dropping down into the 35 to 50 cfs range). During the peak of the irrigation season in June and July the releases rise to 900 to 1,100 cfs, but drop for the haying season in August to 600 to 700 cfs.

The Beaverhead doesn't lie in a valley surrounded by towering mountain ranges like many of the quality streams in the state. It flows through irrigated pastureland. Rolling hills studded with rugged rock outcroppings flank the river.

The Bureau of Reclamation, which controls Clark Canyon Dam, has guaranteed a minimum flow of between 35 cfs and 50 cfs in the winter months. Even with this "generous" allotment, the river still loses many large fish during dry years.

Dick Oswald believes that at least 140 cfs is needed to maintain winter populations. During the long drought cycle, Clark Canyon has gone into the winter, more often than not, drawn way down, and the heavy snows that would recharge the system have failed too often.

Regulations designed to mitigate the problem include the imposition of a three-fish limit with only one fish over 18 inches and only one rainbow. Previously there had been a five-fish limit with one over 18 inches in possession, and the sight of bait fishermen hauling away trophy browns on stringers was not uncommon.

These regulations might change soon because the state biologists have found trout infected with Whirling Disease in the river. This parasite, which strikes rainbows harder than browns, hasn't had a great impact on fish populations yet, but the river will be monitored closely. Brown trout make up 70 percent of the catchable-size trout and rainbow trout constitute the remaining 30 percent in the upper river.

Water flow is still the most important factor for fish populations. After a series of good winters there are literally tons of trout present in every mile of water. A general figure would be 2,500 pounds of browns and 1,500 pounds of rainbows per mile. Dick Oswald, not totally at ease with using these numbers, prefers to cite 550 trout of 18 inches and up per mile.

"The river has an incredible capacity to bounce back from bad periods," says Dick Oswald. "During electro-shocking surveys in the spring and fall, I handle a hell of a lot of fish between five and ten pounds and a few of the bizarre monsters up to fifteen pounds in the upper river."

Barrett's Diversion to Dillon—Because of the rather gentle topography surrounding the Beaverhead drainage, the river is almost totally dependent on releases from the dam to maintain adequate flow and temperature for the fish. The effects of runoff and summer snowmelt are not as dramatic here as on other rivers in the Rocky Mountain West.

Twelve miles below Clark Canyon Dam Barrett's Diversion siphons off as much as two-thirds of the water in the river. The effect of less flow, leaving the fish to freeze in the winter and bake in the summer, depresses both the number and size of the trout. And there are fewer rainbow trout down here, making only 5 percent of the population by the time the river reaches Dillon; the rainbows virtually disappear below town.

This is not as depressing as it sounds. The stretch from the Diversion to Dillon is the favorite water on the Beaverhead for many fly fishermen. This section is easily wadeable, whereas the upper river is mostly float fishing. There are good hatches of pretty much the same insects as the upper area, and the trout rise well when the bugs are out. There's the occasional big fish here, but most of the browns are 10 to 16 inches. The trout are so much more accessible on this portion that the numbers caught during a typical day can be much higher—20 to 30 fish on the water below the Diversion versus 6 to 10 fish on the water above it.

The fish are primarily brown trout, and that means casting close to or into cover. The banks are much more open down here. Some sections were riprapped for the highway; even natural sections have as much grass as trees on the banks. Bulky, attractor dry flies, such as a Humpy or a Madame X, pounded into the notches of the boulders, or buggy nymphs, such as a Zug Bug or Gray Nymph, washed against the rocks, can pull fish out all day long. If the riprap sections don't produce, small streamers, such as a Muddler or a Brown and Yellow Matuka, work consistently in areas with standing clumps of willows, with deep shade and dark water against the bank. And if the trout won't cooperate during the heat of the day, there are plenty of whitefish in the riffles and pools that will take any small nymph.

But the real fun here comes with the dependable rises every evening during the summer. This is great caddisfly water. The Spotted Sedge (size 12 or 14, with brown wings and a yellowish body) and the Little Sister Sedge (size 16 or 18, with tan wings and light ginger body) start flying as soon as the heat of the day fades and build in numbers until dark. The trout feed on all stages—an Emergent Sparkle Pupa works for the emerging insect, the Elk Hair Caddis works for the clumsy, mating adults that fall on the currents, and the Diving Caddis matches the egg-layers that go underwater.

Dillon to the mouth of the Ruby River—In the words of Ryan Sandborne (who has never really escaped the 60's), "The river below town gets really funky. It's really sucked low and it gets too warm most of the summer for good fishing. There is some irrigation return as you move downstream, but that water is not only warm, but over-fertilized and murky.

"I'll come down here in the fall, when the river runs clearer, and fish streamers for the browns. It's real lonely, which is nice, and I get a good fish every so often. The biggest ones are in the 4- to 5-pound range, but those don't come every day. The way to cover this section is with a canoe, getting out and concentrating on the mouths of some of the spring creeks. The access isn't good otherwise and I won't see many wading fishermen on a day's float."

Mouth of the Ruby River to the Big Hole River—If there is a "sleeper" section this is it. The Ruby River (a fine tailwater stream in it's own right) enters the Beaverhead three miles above Twin Bridges. The cold, clear, and constant flow of the Ruby sparks a jump in trout populations. Some of these fish, the browns still predominating, are very good size.

Bulky, attractor dry flies, such as a Humpy or a Madame X, pounded into the notches of the boulders, or buggy nymphs, such as a Zug Bug or Gray Nymph, washed against the rocks, can pull fish out all day long.

The trick is to avoid high flows of the irrigation season and rainy periods. Either one of these situations mucks up the water, turning the river to brown soup. It wasn't always this way on the lower Beaverhead. The river used to run cleaner, if not crystal clear, through Twin Bridges. The banks are so eroded now by cattle that any flush of water washes dirt into the flow. The state biologists in this region are studying this problem and might be able to work with the ranches to stabilize the stream margins.

This is dry fly heaven when the water is fairly clear. The best months are September through November. Until the first frosts, grasshopper imitations, anything from a Joe's Hopper to a Dave's Hopper, pull up fish. With the overcast days of fall, and the start of the Blue-Winged Olive hatches, the browns take positions in every good feeding lane and rise with that nose, back, and tail sequence from 1:00 p.m. to about 3:30 p.m.

The Beaverhead offers something for most fly fishermen. The upper water demands long, hard days, usually from a boat, for the chance to catch trophy trout. The section below the Diversion, easily waded, is more consistent fishing for smaller trout. Anyone who wants to be alone on a stream can explore the lower river. A visitor, to do justice to the river, should spend a minimum of five days in the area. Anyone who tries to figure out this stream by himself the first time is going to have some long, frustrating hours. On the Beaverhead, more than on most rivers in the state, a guide is a good investment. But even for the devoted do-it-your-selfer, the truly masochistic, the trout are here and waiting.

Fishing Waters in the Beaverhead Drainage

Alder Gulch (and the Virginia City Dredge Ponds): Alder Gulch runs right beside Montana 287 east of Virginia City. The creek has some rainbows and brookies, but it is small and brushy. The many dredge ponds dotted along the stream course provide much more interesting action for larger fish up to several pounds. Low profiles, long leaders, and small nymphs are most often successful, but there are hatches (including a consistent *Callibaetis*) on the ponds, and dry flies come into play on occasion. Always watch the head of any pond, too, where the creek enters—hatching stream insects drift down into the still water and trout line up to sip on these lost souls. The ponds are not the most aesthetically pleasing fly fishing in the world, unless you really like mine tailings and dredge holes, but they are challenging spots.

Blacktail Deer Creek: Near its mouth this stream suffers all the typical degradations of a ranchland stream, the cattle-pounded banks, the herbicide and waste runoffs, and the water extractions, but a few miles above Dillon it becomes a great-looking, quality stream. There are still erosion problems with the soft dirt banks, and Blacktail muddies quickly with even a modest rain (and should be avoided at these times) even in the upper stretches, but there are lots of deep holes connected by gentle runs. The stream is filled with brookies, fat and beautifully colored fish up to 14 inches, with some rainbows and the occasional fat brown running up from the river.

County Road 202, just south of Dillon, follows the stream most of the way, right up to the headwaters in the Snowcrest Range. There's good access outside of town. What works in the Beaverhead works here, but with less effort. Bright streamers, such as the classic Mickey Finn, do wonders with the brookies if the water is at all cloudy. With clear water conditions, simple upstream presentations with dry flies or nymphs take fish from runs and pools. The most notable hatches are the early June caddis flights.

Blacktail Deer Creek, like many small streams, requires a cautious approach. Photo by Eileen Clark

Bloody Dick Creek: Bloody Dick has superb brook trout fishing for fish up to a foot or so in world-class mosquito country (.28 gauges recommended). Access is spotty; your best bet is west of Clark Canyon

Reservoir from Horse Prairie Creek. It is extremely overgrown and difficult to fish in some stretches; other parts of the stream are more open, meadow terrain. Guess which sections have the biggest trout? Some rainbows and mountain whitefish also swim here.

Clark Canyon Reservoir: This is a quality, big-fish water planted with several hundred thousand rainbows each year. These rainbows, some browns, and plenty of battling carp regularly reach weights of over five pounds. This is one of the best places in the state to wear your arm out playing big trout at certain times of the year. When it's hot, it's hot.

Dick Sharon listed some of the prime areas of the lake:

a. The inlet areas of both the Red Rock River and Horse Prairie Creek, especially in the spring and fall.

b. The east side of the lake (the highway side) at the Willows Beach. The rainbows, looking for spawning areas, cruise the long gravel flat in the spring.

c. In front of the Lone Tree Campground there's another long flat that extends to the west, attracting rainbows in the spring until the water level of the lake drops and exposes the bottom.

d. The south side of the big island is a good midsummer spot, but the trout hold deep during midday and it takes a sinking line to reach the 8- to 15-feet-deep holding water.

e. At the west side of the dam the trout congregate during the summer at the 15-foot level.

f. A quarter mile off Lookout Point is always a good area for blind prospecting.

The fish that are growing well, reaching 14 to 15 inches as two-years-olds, are the Eagle Lake strain of rainbows. These trout are stocked in such huge numbers, and they're such aggressive feeders, that they actually make it harder for anglers to take the bigger rainbows and browns. The trick when the schools of young fish are grabbing everything is to use larger flies on the bottom. The 4- to 8-inch tiddlers will keep tapping big streamers, such as a size 2 Clouser

Minnow, Olive Zonker, or Silver Crystal Flash Woolly Bugger. It's hard for the angler not to strike, but the smaller fish following the fly attracts the bigger fish and this is one of the best ways to hook a trophy specimen. Just keep retrieving until something yanks hard.

There is an old road that heads out from the south and offers easy access for float tubers and boaters to bays and submerged brush along the southeastern shore near the inlet of the Red Rock River. This is the prime area for insect hatches—at ice-out it's midges; by June the damselflies are emerging; the *Callibaetis* mayflies show up for most of the summer; there's a spotty hatch of Tricos, but the spinner fall attracts gulpers from August through early October.

There's a method that started in the late 80's in the western part of Montana. It has spread to most of the large reservoirs of the state. It's effective on all stillwater fisheries, but there's something about it that makes big waters less intimidating. At Clark Canyon, in the Red Rock inlet area, it outfishes any other technique "by far" according to Dick Sharon.

The angler ties a tuft of indicator yarn on the end of his 9 feet, 4X leader. Behind the indicator he attaches another piece of leader material with an improved clinch knot. This leader material will be finer than the tippet, 5X or 6X, and can vary in length from 1 foot to 8 feet, depending on the depth of the trout. A nymph, such as a Hare's Ear, Flashback Callibaetis, Brown Bear Black, Feather Duster, Twist Nymph, or Bigg's Special (all favorites on Clark Canyon), hangs straight down from the indicator and disappears immediately with any take.

It's an easy way to fish from a float tube or a boat. The angler casts downwind and does nothing. On breezy days the chop in the water makes the indicator move up and down, and below the surface the hanging fly is doing the same thing. This is bobber fishing, in its purest and simplest form, but the natural movement of the fly tantalizes the trout.

There are other good locations, many of them, on Clark Canyon Reservoir, but on this 5,000 acre (in rare years when it reaches full pool) lake, cutting the water down to size is a necessity. There are tons of trash fish here, also. Keep an eye on the winds, usually from the north to northwest. They can make life in a float tube a difficult and dangerous proposition.

East Fork Blacktail Creek: You reach this one by dirt road up in high, sage-brush country. Some nice brook and rainbow trout hang out in the pools and beneath the banks. There are also cutthroats and mountain whitefish. Hoppers in the summer heat are nice fun.

Grasshopper Creek: This stream is like a little Beaverhead. It has most of the same hatches, the mayflies (Blue-Winged Olives, Pale Morning Duns, and Tricos) and the caddisflies (Grannom, Spotted Sedge, and Little Sister Sedge), and when the water is clear and the trout are rising, a decent match takes more fish than a general fly. The Sparkle Dun for mayflies and the Elk Hair Caddis for the caddisflies are standards. Of course, grasshopper imitations work well here all summer, but the smaller, size-8 to -12 patterns are better for the 10- to 16-inch fish than the monstrous imitations. The only problem with this creek is that it muddies immediately and badly with the slightest rain, and runs so turbid that it even discolors the entire Beaverhead once it joins with the main river.

Grasshopper takes its time flowing down through open, hay and sage flat country, on past the ghost town of Bannack, alongside some mining areas, through a dozen miles of canyon, and then into the Beaverhead. The upper reaches are about twenty feet wide with undercut, grassy banks. Some brown trout of size move up from the river into this stretch, providing good fall action on streamers. The resident trout do well all year, including rainbows and brookies. Don't worry about the rattlesnakes. They're too busy fighting off the mosquitoes.

Horse Prairie Creek: Horse Prairie flows through private, posted pastureland down to Clark Canyon Reservoir. Some big browns and rainbows move into the lower reaches. "If you're not careful," Dick Sharon says, "you can get your butt kicked by a moose real easy here."

Kelly Reservoir: This one lies above 7,000 feet west of Dillon and is reached by a real bad road up Rattlesnake Creek. To the native Montanan a road like this is the reason companies make four-wheel-drive trucks. Nonetheless. It's popular and good fishing for 7- to 11-inch brookies and rainbows.

Medicine Lodge Creek: Medicine Lodge empties into Horse Prairie Creek above Clark Canyon Reservoir after running down a valley beneath the Beaverhead and Tendoy mountains. The access is limited but attainable for the brookies and rainbows that sometimes exceed a foot in length. It's followed by a gravel road.

Noble Lake: Take the Wisconsin Creek Road right outside of Sheridan and hook into the Noble Creek Road for another exciting day of four-wheeling. The lake sits at 9,000 feet in a moonscape cirque, a piddling 8 acres but 55 feet deep. Don't bother casting towards the middle. The Yellowstone cutts, up to 16 inches, hang close to the edge. A float tube helps here.

Poindexter Slough: Extremely well known, particularly by spring creek fanatics, it's a classic; and, thanks to the efforts of the Nature Conservancy working with the Montana Department of Fish, Wildlife, and Parks (FWP), it's available to everyone. It's easy to find—I-90 passes directly over it right outside Dillon.

There are deep holes and narrow channels surrounded by thick beds of aquatic plants that wave gently in the clear currents. During the summer the hummocks of watercress get so thick that they force the water out of the streambed. The fish can graze in this salad for scuds anytime, but they quickly focus on the surface during the hatches.

The fishing is good in all seasons. There are no crowds, and when midges are on the water, a Halo Midge Emerger for the pupa or a Griffith's Gnat for the adult usually works. Caddisflies abound here. The early Grannom caddis, also known as the Mother's Day Hatch, doesn't wait for May. In a warm year it is going well by mid-April. A dark Elk Hair Caddis is an effective match for the egg-layers. Some of the species of small, spring creek caddisflies are very important here —the Speckled Peter has a concentrated emergence during late June; the Weedy Water Sedge shows during June and July; the Little Sister Sedge peaks in July but stays around all summer; the midsummer Grannom becomes very important in August; and the Vari-Colored Microcaddis may be only a size 22 insect, but in the fall it is so abundant that the trout feed on emergers readily. It seems that with all of these small caddisflies, the trout lock onto the emerging, pupal stage. The Emergent Sparkle Pupa, in the right colors and sizes, works well.

Terrestrials are important all summer—a tribute to the lush meadows of this protected area—and not only grasshopper patterns, but beetle and ant patterns, make good searching flies.

Blue-Winged Olives hatch well in both in the spring (April 10th through May 10th) and the fall (September 10th through October). The Pale Morning Duns and the Tricos—the latter with a wonderful, 9 a.m. spinner fall during August and September (best matched with a Black Clear Wing Spinner)—are important mayfly species. But the highlight of the season for the matching-the-hatch fanatic can be the Tiny Blue-Winged Olive, a size 24 insect that appears in such great numbers that it overwhelms other emergences, and during this "masking hatch" the fish are selectively taking the small flies and ignoring the more obvious, larger ones. The trout demand an exact imitation of the adult, a Sparkle Dun or a Duck Butt Dun.

When in doubt on Poindexter (and other spring creeks) strap on a Pheasant Tail, Brassie, or Brown Tear Drop—streamlined-and-weighted nymphs that will sink quickly even in sizes 16 through 22—and work the seams between the weed beds. A scud pattern, a size 14 to 16 Olive on this stream, is the main choice in a bigger fly.

Two things have made Poindexter tougher fishing in recent years. The rainbows are gone, probably wiped out by Whirling Disease (confirmed in the stream). That leaves only browns, and even their numbers are down drastically. There are still plenty of 10- to 18-inch fish, adequate numbers of 18- to 22-inch fish, and even a smattering of true brutes, but the angling pressure has increased on the stream. These trout see a tremendous number of flies. There are no second chances at this ballpark—use 14-foot-plus leaders tapered to 7X or 8X, delicate presentations, and the right fly for consistent results.

Polaris Lake: Polaris is a deep, 11-acre hike-in lake at over 8,000 feet (and at this elevation there are no easy walks). It's over 4 miles of steep trudging up the Lake Creek drainage. Go to the town of Polaris up Grasshopper Creek to hit the trailhead. The reward for the rough climb is the chance at rainbows and Yellowstone cutthroats up to 24 inches, but these are selective and spooky fish. They might take a small Olive Woolly Worm if it's not cast too rambunctiously. A more consistent producer is a tiny midge pupa imitation, something like a size 20 Black Serendipity, retrieved slowly, on a fine tippet.

Reservoir Lake: Reservoir Lake is up the Bloody Dick road (Forest Route 181), an easy 19 mile drive on improved gravel. There's also a nice Forest Service campground on this 40-acre lake at over 7,000 feet. It's worth bringing in a float tube or a cartop boat. There are steep dropoffs around most of the shore, and during the day deep techniques, with sinking lines and weighted nymphs, are productive for brookies to a foot or so. But there's also a shallow, weedy shelf at the upper end, and in the morning and evening, trout cruise and rise well in this water.

Dick Sharon says, "Reservoir Lake is an exceptional spot for fast action, and a Hair-Wing Black Ant always seems to be a good fly here."

Ruby Reservoir: When it's at full pool, it's 1,000 acres of water behind an earthen dam six miles south of Alder on Montana 287. Unfortunately, in the fall of 1994 it was drained down to "no pool," right to the sediment-laden dregs, and when pushed out through the dam into the Ruby River this poisonous soup killed thousands of trout in the river. The bright side (if there can be one) of this disaster is that the state and the irrigators reached agreements to prevent this from happening in the future. The new rules will help both the river and the reservoir, but it will take a couple of years for the lake to come back.

The reservoir is stocked with rainbows, and there are big browns and some cutthroats that work their way down from the upper river. Also, there are lots of suckers in the reservoir, which the browns gorge on. A large streamer (like a 3/0-or-so Hair Sucker), imitating these beautiful trash fish, worked deeply and slowly, is very boring, unless a huge brown nails the thing. There are roads around most of the water, which even during a good year is drawn way down for irrigation in the summer, exposing big mud flats that create wonderful breeding habitat for all sorts of flies.

Ruby River: It was called the Passamari by the native tribes, and the Stinking Water by the early white pioneers. The Ruby heads in the Snowcrest and Gravelly Ranges. The upper stretches (followed by the Upper Ruby Road) offer good fishing for rainbow and cutthroat trout to a foot, along with some browns. The fish run a few inches larger below the confluence of Warm Springs Creek (which adds the smelly, sulphuric flow that taints a small section of the river). Between the end of the Forest Service land, north to the Ruby Reservoir, the river travels through private land and fee fishing is increasing in "popularity."

Below the reservoir the Ruby (followed by Ruby River Drive) is a perfect stream for big brown trout as it winds, bends, and twists through a wide-open valley. There are miles of undercut willow and grass banks, logjams, gravel runs and sandy-bottomed pools. The "rip and strip" tactics of the Beaverhead, with a big streamer or a pair of Girdle Bugs on a short, 20-pound test leader, work on the over-grown sections of the Ruby, but with excellent populations of aquatic and terrestrial insects in or around the river, this also a fine wet fly and dry fly stream.

The early Grannom, a size-14 to -16 caddis with gray wings and a dark green body, starts emerging and egg-laying in early to mid-April. The spring Blue-Winged Olive pops at the same time. The run-off, moderated by the dam, is brief, if there's any at all, and hatches stay important through the late May to early June period. The caddis flights are heavy, with the Spotted Sedge and Little Sister Sedge appearing in late afternoon and early evening through the summer and into the fall. The fall Blue-Winged Olive, lingering into November if the weather holds, is another highlight on the river.

What's the most exciting fishing? "The Ruby is known for its exceptional grasshopper action," Dick Sharon says. The valley has everything necessary for great hopper conditions. It's dry, even drier than Montana's prevalent, semi-arid climate. The fields, expanses of generally flat grassland,

Brown trout are the main fare on the Ruby.
Photo by Steve Oristian

give the hoppers plenty of room and food. The warm summer winds off the hills blow the insects into the stream. During good-weather years, the fish begin keying on natural grasshoppers by late June, and keep watching for them until the hard, killing frosts of October.

The Ruby has been hurt in recent years. There is the continual problem of overgrazing in the upper river. In the fall of 1994 the Ruby Reservoir was drained into the river and caused a massive fish kill. In the spring of 1995 state biologists found Whirling Disease in the trout population. Even with these assaults it's still a wonderful fishery.

Unfortunately, the area is being bought up and then subdivided into "vacation" or "retirement" lots and access is all but gone on the Ruby. If you know someone who lives here or are willing to pay a stiff fee, you'll find fine action for browns of a couple of pounds or larger. If you are like most of us, you'll have to gain access from county roads and you can plan on getting plenty of grief working the river, even if you obey the state's stream access law. This river is becoming a playground for the wealthy "elite," although there are still a few gracious landowners along the stream course.

Sawtooth Lake: A 500-foot wall towers over the lake, the bare rock along the ridge jagged like saw teeth. This 16-acre lake is up Clark Creek in the Pioneer Range west of Dillon at 8,500 feet. It's beautiful and lonely, the perfect wilderness hideaway for nice golden trout that, as always, are tough to catch.

Larger goldens are primarily benthic (bottom) zone feeders that take advantage of available populations of caddis larva, midge larva, and mayfly nymphs at times, and that is when they can be caught consistently, although it means digging out the Hi-D lines and twist-ons. At other times they ingest daphnia, smaller than any hook, and then they are all but impossible to catch.

Scott Lake: Take Forest Route 192.2 to the Upper Rattlesnake Trail northwest of Dillon, hike the 1½ miles over to Estler Lake (poor fishing), and then struggle the 2 miles up the inlet stream to Scott Lake. You'll find beauty, solitude, and some healthy Yellowstone cutthroats, and possibly some rainbow/cutthroat hybrids, up to 24 inches if the lake hasn't frozen out. It receives periodic plants and there are usually nice fish here. Ask questions before hiking into this lake, unless the beauty and solitude are enough for you.

Other Waters

Barton Gulch Creek: Too small.

Blue Creek: Too small.

Buffalo Creek: Too small.

California Creek: Too small.

Carter Creek: Too small.

Clark Creek: The outlet of Sawtooth Lake. There are small brookies and cutthroats, but the bonus here is the occasional golden trout down from the lake. The goldens won't be big, but they are always worth a look. For some reason the goldens don't respond to dry flies as well as cutts and brooks do—try small nymphs.

Coal Creek: Too small.

Cottonwood Creek: Too small.

Dad Creek: Brookies and cutthroats. It's a tributary of Medicine Lodge Creek, south of Clark Canyon Reservoir. There are lots of beaver ponds on the upper water, but the trout are spooky here. Keep low, use a long leader, and lay the line on the water delicately.

Dad Creek Lakes: Two small potholes up the Dad Creek drainage. The upper one is barren, but the 3½-acre lower pond is fun for for cutthroats to 16 inches.

Divide Creek: Brookies and cutthroats in this tumbling stream in the Ruby River drainage. Dance a size-16 Olive Stimulator or Lime Double-Wing on the miniature pools for lightning strikes from 6- to 10-inch trout.

East Fork Ruby River: Mediocre for brookies, cutthroats, and rainbows.

Estler Lake: In a cluster of lakes—Minneopa, Scott, Anchor, Boot, Twin, Tent, and Sawtooth—that are mostly tough hikes or rough four-wheel-drive and vary greatly in fishing quality. Estler, with cutthroats and rainbows to 10 inches, isn't one of the better ones, but is a good place for a base camp to reach the surrounding waters.

Eunice Creek: Too small.

French Creek: Brookies and cutthroats.

Gheny (Geinnie) Pond: A flat-bottomed depression right next to Montana 41 where the state dumps in planter rainbows throughout the summer. No scenery, no challenge—but if you're having lunch there and the rod is strung up anyway, why not?

Granite Creek: Too small.

Greenhorn Creek: Too small.

Indian Creek: Too small.

Johnson Lake: Closed to fishing.

Lake Canyon Lake: Cutthroats.

Ledford Creek: Brookies, cutthroats, and rainbows.

Lotts Slough: Poor fishing for occasional stockings of rainbows.

McHessor Creek: Too small.

Middle Fork Ruby River: A creek at best and a poor-fishing one at that for cutthroats and rainbows.

Mill Creek: Brookies and rainbows. This is a tributary of the Ruby and it flows right through Sheridan. The fishing is spotty at best, but the canyon section above town receives the least pressure.

Minneopa Lake: Cutthroats.

North Frying Pan Creek: Cutthroats to 6-inches that will fit in a "small" frying pan. Take a kid and drive up the Lemhi Pass road — take me, too.

Painter Creek: Too small.

Peppercoff Pond: Planted rainbows. A put-and-take borrow pit along Montana 41 just like Gheny and Silver Bow.

Rattlesnake Creek: Brookies, cutthroats, and rainbows. It is the outlet of Estler, Minneopa, and Tent lakes, but no one bothers to fish it much for 4- to 8-inch trout.

Robb Creek: Brookies, cutthroats, and rainbows.

Rock Creek: Too small.

Romy Lake: Fair for cutthroats to 12 inches. Privately owned and restricted access for this Ruby drainage water.

Sage Creek: Too small.

Selway Creek: Small brookies on this tributary of Bloody Dick Creek.

Shoestring Creek: A fun little meadow creek for small cutthroats. It feeds into Grasshopper Creek.

Silver Bow Pond: See Gheny, Peppercoff, and Smith ponds—same story.

Smith Pond: See above—even fake fishing is better than no fishing.

South Fork Warm Springs Creek: Too small.

Stone Creek: Too small.

Sunrise Lake: Way up there at 9,300 feet in the Ruby drainage in the Tobacco Root Mountains. You can get within spitting distance on the Wisconsin Creek four-wheel road. You'll find cutthroats to 12 inches in this 4-acre pond.

Sweetwater Creek: Too small.

Taylor Creek: Brookies and cutthroats.

Tent Lake: Cutthroats to 12 inches. This is one of those hike-in lakes (right above Minneopa Lake) where you need a float tube to get out for the best fishing.

Todd Spring Creek: Fee fishery. This tributary of the Ruby, just outside Sheridan, has cookie-cutter, 12-inch browns.

Trail Creek: Poor access.

Twin Lakes (Rattlesnake Creek): Cutthroats.

Twin Lakes (Tobacco Roots): Cutthroats.

Warm Springs Creek: Browns, rainbows, and whitefish.

West Fork Blacktail Creek: Brookies, cutthroats, and rainbows.

West Fork Ruby River: A little better than the East Fork or the Middle Fork of the main river, but still not great fishing for cutthroats, rainbows, and whitefish.

Ziegler Reservoir: Barren.

■ *Special thanks to Tom Heinsinger, Dick Oswald, Ryan Sandborne, Dick Sharon, Tim Tollett for their help on the Beaverhead drainage.*

Big Hole River
Photo by Don Roberts

BIG HOLE RIVER

For most of the year the Big Hole is not all that crowded. The exception is during the Salmon Fly hatch in June. Commercial outfitters from outside the area converge on the river. Why? There are three reasons. The hatch on the Big Hole occurs from early to late June, when there are no fishable Salmon Fly hatches on other rivers. The Big Hole runs high, and even gets tea colored with heavy runoff, but it seldom turns into a mud bath, and it's a fine dry fly river most years. And finally, there's always the chance to catch a trophy brown or rainbow.

Blaine Summers, who has fished the hatch for the past twenty-two years, says, "It's not a wading river during Salmon Fly time. The water pushes right up into the willows and the currents are just too strong and deep to stand up in. Some good anglers fish from the banks, walking along and looking for places to slap a fly out between the trees. But the best way to fish during high water is from a boat. The sharp caster can slap drys or drift nymphs along the edges. It's a fast game, bang that fly in there, but just about every trout, even ones up to ten pounds, is looking for the insects and will rush up and smash a fly."

The hatch usually begins around June 10th in the Twin Bridges area and is pretty much over four weeks later. Cold or hot weather can shorten or eliminate the hatch some years, but usually it progresses upriver 4 to 6 miles a day on the Big Hole.

There's a common strategy for Salmon Flies—fish the head of the hatch, where the insects are just starting to emerge and lay eggs. On some rivers it is almost a waste of time to fish in the middle of the hatch, where the large Salmon Flies are so abundant that the trout get satiated and stop feeding.

The Madison River is like that; so is the Henry's Fork in Idaho. But the Big Hole isn't. The angler can work nymphs in areas where the hatch hasn't started, and work active dry flies at the head of the hatch. Even in the middle of the hatch there always seems to be some cooperative trout, but the trick is to fish the dry fly in a dead drift over the best holding spots against the banks.

What does seem to put the trout off their feed is the heavy fishing pressure (Go figure . . .). In most areas there will be plenty of other boats and rafts, crowds walking the shore, and the usual madness associated with the Salmon Fly hatch. A few days of this intense

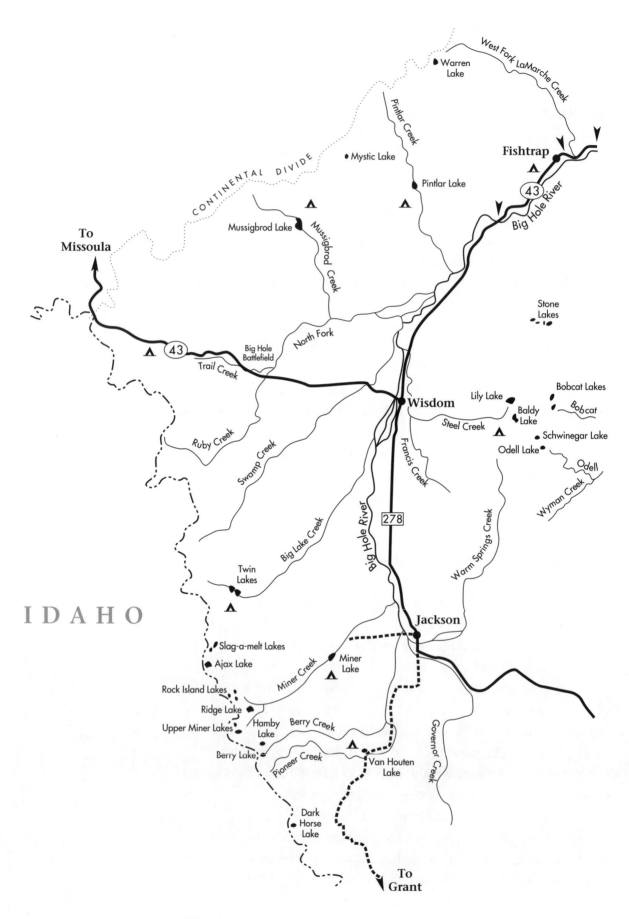

West Fork LaMarche Creek

Warren
Lake

Pintlar Creek

CONTINENTAL DIVIDE

Mystic Lake

Fishtrap

Pintlar Lake

Big Hole River

**To
Missoula**

Mussigbrod Lake

Mussigbrod Creek

Stone
Lakes

North Fork

Big Hole
Battlefield

43

Trail Creek

Lily Lake

Bobcat Lakes

Bobcat

Wisdom

Baldy
Lake

Steel Creek

Schwinegar Lake

Odell Lake

Odell

Ruby Creek

Swamp Creek

Francis Creek

Wyman Creek

Big Lake Creek

278

Big Hole River

Warm Springs Creek

Twin
Lakes

I D A H O

Jackson

Slag-a-melt Lakes

Miner Creek

Miner
Lake

Ajax Lake

Rock Island Lakes

Governor Creek

Ridge Lake

Berry Creek

Upper Miner Lakes

Hamby
Lake

Berry Lake

Pioneer Creek

Van Houten
Lake

Dark
Horse
Lake

**To
Grant**

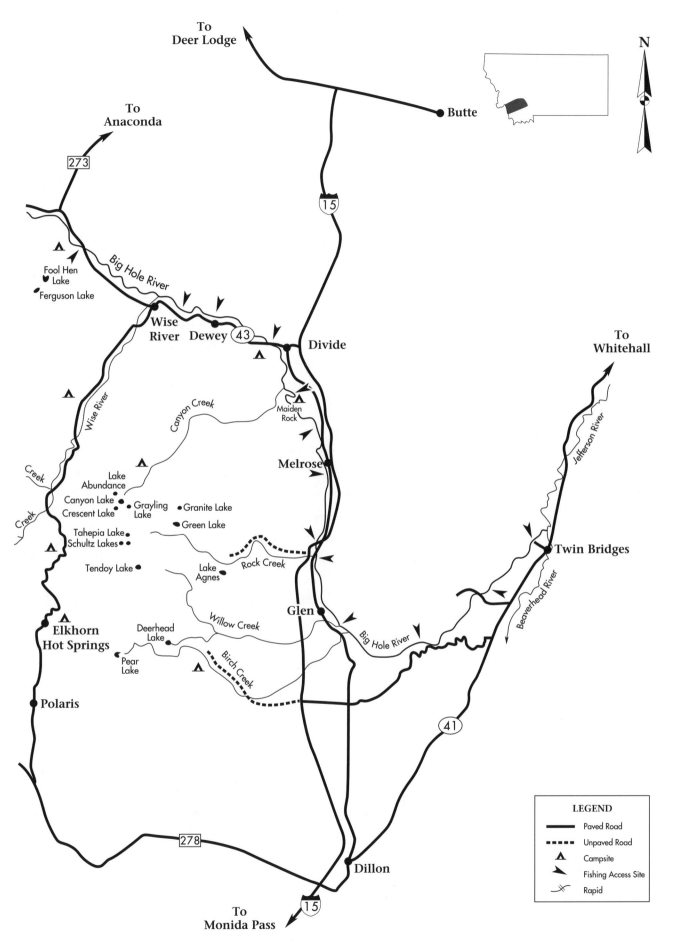

To
Deer Lodge

Butte

N

To
Anaconda

273

Big Hole River

Fool Hen
Lake

Ferguson Lake

Wise
River

Dewey

43

Divide

To
Whitehall

Wise River

Canyon Creek

Maiden
Rock

Jefferson River

Melrose

Creek

Lake
Abundance

Canyon Lake

Grayling
Lake

Granite Lake

Crescent Lake

Green Lake

Creek

Tahepia Lake

Schultz Lakes

Rock Creek

Twin Bridges

Tendoy Lake

Lake
Agnes

Glen

Big Hole River

Elkhorn
Hot Springs

Deerhead
Lake

Willow Creek

Beaverhead River

Pear
Lake

Birch Creek

Polaris

41

278

Dillon

To
Monida Pass

15

LEGEND

———— Paved Road

▪▪▪▪ Unpaved Road

⛺ Campsite

➤ Fishing Access Site

Rapid

activity turns the trout wary and seems to make them less willing to come to the surface.

Blaine Summers's favorite trick? "I'll still fish an adult imitation rather than a nymph, but I'll fish it wet. The drowned fly, even a few inches under the surface, gets a lot more trout when the boats are as thick as ticks."

Another trick of the locals is to let all of the out-of-area guides start floating early. The locals put their own boats in later in the day and cover rested water. Often, they'll still be floating during the early evening hours and the female Salmon Flies won't be flying in the chillier air, but for the last few miles of the trip they'll match the big, size-8 Great Gray Spotted Sedges instead with a gray and green Emergent Sparkle Pupa and catch a lot of trout.

Most people concentrate their efforts during the Salmon Fly hatch on the 30-mile stretch between Wise River and Glen. The river is the perfect size for floating and there are large trout in this water. Dry flies such as the Bird's Stone, Sofa Pillow, and Fluttering Stone (this last pattern developed by Big Hole guide Nevin Stephenson), or nymphs such as a Montana Stone, Kaufmann's Stone, or Natural Drift Stone bounced on the bottom, take trout consistently.

There are populations of Salmon Flies above Wise River, and they'll still be hatching into July some years. The key is knowing the river—one section will have insects and another one won't. The best populations of Salmon Flies are in rougher, steeper areas.

After mid-July the water level stabilizes and a good portion of the crowd has moved on to other western rivers. There are still plenty of anglers fishing the Big Hole, but it's possible to find some solitude.

The Big Hole's reputation as world-class trout water is deserved, but on some days the river shuts down and no one can take decent fish with any consistency. Return a few days later and the surface will be alive with feeding trout of all sizes. Then, a few more days down the calendar and the trout will seem to have vanished from the face of the earth.

This fickleness may be due to stresses from irrigation, especially on the lower river. The return flows off the fields are warmer and saturated with nutrients. With any stretch of warm, still days the river seems to get tough during the summer months. If there's some rain, or just a few cold nights, it can suddenly get generous.

Headwaters to Wise River—The river begins in the Beaverhead Range of the Bitterroot Mountains south of Jackson, running by Wisdom at 6,058 feet, and then on to Wise River about 30 miles downstream. From the headwaters to Wisdom there are brook, cutthroat, and rainbow trout. There is also a remnant population of the nearly extinct fluvial (stream-dwelling) grayling. Around Jackson there are about 300 brookies per mile, with a few reaching 18 inches. The Montana Department of Fish, Wildlife, and Parks (FWP) biologists have supported an aggressive harvest of the brook trout in the upper reaches to make room for the grayling, but as a result, the remaining brook trout, on average, are getting larger. Rainbow numbers increase steadily as the river winds towards Wise River; both brook and cutthroat numbers decrease; and the grayling get really scarce.

Really just a creek, this is the home of the last significant population of fluvial grayling in the lower forty-eight states. Water depletion and warming from irrigation, overgrazing, and destruction of the spawning tributaries; competition from non-native fish; and proposed logging in the drainage threaten to eliminate even these few wild fish. To protect the species, FWP has instituted catch-and-release regulations along the entire river to protect the grayling.

During the hot, low-water summer of 1994, the department shut down a major portion of the river to all fishing to save the fishery. This act (with the support of many shops and guides on the Big Hole) demonstrates how serious the state is about preserving the grayling. Population numbers have climbed in recent years.

The trout are smaller in the upper water, but this is a great area to wade. In many sections this is a meadow stream. The river stays cool enough through the summer months for good terrestrial fishing. A good grasshopper imitation usually takes trout. The fish aren't extremely critical during the hatches, and general dry flies and nymphs work consistently.

POPULAR FLIES

Bird's Stone

Black Creeper

Brooks' Stone

Crowe Beetle

Crystal Bugger

Dark Spruce Streamer

Double Wing

Egg Sucking Leech

Elk Hair Caddis

Emergent Sparkle Pupa

EZ Caddis

Fluttering Stone

Foam Ant

Goddard Caddis

Humpy

Kaufmann's Stone

Matuka Sculpin

Montana Stone

Natural Drift Stone

Pheasant Tail

Prince Nymph

Rusty CDC Spinner

Sofa Pillow

Sparkle Dun

Spider

Stimulator

Ted's Stone

Woolly Bugger

Wulff

Yellow Marabou Muddler

Yellow Yummy

Fly Pattern for the Big Hole

It seems like every outfitter from every river drainage in the state converges on the Big Hole during Salmon Fly time. It's natural for them to not only adopt the locally effective patterns, but to take them back with them to their own waters. That is how the Fluttering Stone became a widely popular imitation for the adult Salmon Fly.

FLUTTERING STONE

Hook: 2X long dry fly (4–8)

Body: orange polypro yarn (twisted and extended)

Wing: natural light elk hair

Overwing: dark elk hair (short)

Hackle: brown saddle

Antennae: stripped brown hackle stems or flat brown monofilament

Nevin Stephenson, guiding out of the Complete Fly Fisher on the river, developed the Fluttering Stone as a "high-riding" adult pattern. What he discovered during his years on the Big Hole was that trout often refused a flush-floating imitation. On warm days, when the females would crash on the water to lay their eggs and then beat frantically with their wings to swim to the bank, the trout wanted an active fly. The Fluttering Stone is so heavily hackled that it can be skittered over the surface.

The pattern was an immediate favorite with both guides and clients. It caught fish; and just as important it brought the kind of thumping, heart-stopping strikes that fishermen remembered long after the trout was released. The Fluttering Stone became the most popular Salmon Fly imitation on the Big Hole in its first season.

Wise River to Maiden Rock—During the winter it's easy to see where the river changes character. Just above Wise River, where Montana 43 crosses the river, springs enter the Big Hole. The upper river will be frozen until it reaches those springs, and then suddenly it will be ice-free. The springs signal not only more constant temperatures but also richer water for both insects and trout.

From Wise River to Maiden Rock, the Big Hole holds 2,000 rainbows and 300 browns per mile, some approaching five pounds (or, rarely, larger). The hatches are heavier in this section and the trout can get fairly selective at times. The early Grannom appears in May,

and triggers heavy feeding. The Salmon Fly dominates most of June, but there are good hatches of the Great Gray Spotted Sedge and the Golden Stone, too. In early July, two large mayflies, the Brown Drake and the Green Drake, emerge in good numbers. The Pale Morning Dun and the Trico are the main midsummer mayflies. The Little Sister Sedge (with massive flights every evening) and the Spotted Sedge are important summer caddisflies. In the fall the Blue-Winged Olive and the Tiny Blue-Winged Olive are dependable hatches. There are enough of the Giant Orange Sedge in the fall to attract trout, too.

This is a stretch where it's important to match the hatch closely, if not exactly. Stuart Decker says, "The trout are getting fussier all the time. There's still a great 'Royal Wulff hatch,' when the fish are looking up and a general attractor works, but when the hatches are happening, the size and outline of the fly becomes critical."

Stuart recommends specific parachute patterns for the river. Most guides stress the visibility of the fly, but on the Big Hole, with the glare bouncing off the riffles, a flat, drab dry fly can be impossible to see. The Parachute Caddis is tied with matching wing and body colors, but there's a white post of hair sticking up. The Parachute mayfly has the post, but the favorite variation also has a trailing shuck.

The Big Hole is a great terrestrial river. The Spruce Moth goes through its cycles—in 1996, the populations were low, but they'll build to a new peak. This is one river where you don't want to be caught without a flying ant imitation. During August and September, flights of black ants spatter the water and the trout go berserk. It's a grasshopper stream all summer, with the combination of grassy meadows and regular warm winds that push insects out onto the water. "The key," says Stuart Decker, "is to use a size-8 or -10 fly, not a huge one."

Maiden Rock to Melrose Bridge—From Maiden Rock to the Melrose Bridge, the river has 3,500 trout per mile, equally divided between browns and rainbows. There are also lots of Mountain Whitefish (just try drifting a nymph through certain runs). This is bigger water, and for many anglers it is more challenging. The simple act of wading on slick, round boulders in a fast current can be tough for less agile fishermen.

Early or late in the season, this section fishes fine all day, but by midsummer it can slump. In the bright hours in the middle of the day, the fish, especially the browns, go into hiding. If the day isn't too hot, there may be a good evening rise. There are fine caddis flights, and standard patterns, such as the Elk Hair Caddis and the Emergent Sparkle Pupa, are effective. On really hot days, or after a stretch of warm ones, the only good surface fishing may be in the morning. There always seem to be straggling mayfly spinners, left over from the nighttime egg laying, and a size-14 Rusty CDC Spinner is an especially consistent searching pattern.

When trout aren't looking to the surface, you can work nymphs effectively through the runs and riffles, but the catch will be predominantly rainbows. A standard selection of nymphs—Hare's Ear, Prince Nymph, Pheasant Tail—will work in the moderately broken water, but the big stonefly patterns take larger fish in the heavy runs. Good patterns include weighted versions of the Brooks' Stone,

Kaufmann's Stonefly, and Ted's Stone, but the traditionalist might consider George Grant's woven-bodied stonefly nymphs, such as the Black Creeper, developed for this river. No flies sink faster than these patterns, the hard bodies cutting through the currents. No other flies have caught as many five-pound-plus trout on the Big Hole.

Melrose Bridge to Glen—In this stretch, the number of trout drops to 2,000 trout per mile, with about 1,700 of these being browns. Perhaps 150 per mile are in the 18- to 22-inch class. All of the standard techniques and flies will work at times in this water, but the preponderance of browns means that you will have to focus on cover. The fish hold especially tight to banks, sunken logs, and large rock shelves when they're not actively feeding.

Streamer tactics work throughout the drainage, but they are especially important in this section. The main fly is the Woolly Bugger, in all of its variations, from a Crystal Bugger to an Egg Sucking Leech. One favorite is called the Yellow Yummy (green chenille body, yellow hackle, and yellow marabou tail).

Bugger experts don't just cast and strip-retrieve the heavy fly. They fish it below a big indicator, a cork or foam ball large enough to qualify as a bobber, and put extra wire or lead weight on the leader. Cast an up-and-across-stream lob, and lift the rod high to keep as much line off the water as possible. Follow the fly downstream until it can't drift dead anymore and then, as it swings below you, start a pumping retrieve.

Glen to the Confluence with the Beaverhead—This final section is primarily big brown trout water. Don't bother with this stretch until autumn unless you really know the water, or are a fan of futility. The trout are hiding in cool water away from the warm flows of the main river. But come autumn, work this water hard with a Matuka Sculpin, Yellow Marabou Muddler, Dark Spruce Streamer, or Woolly Bugger. Fishing this stuff is not glamorous but it is productive. Size 4 up to 2/0 is not out of line.

While the Big Hole (and the Bighorn and the Madison and the Missouri) have taken some heat from fly fishers and writers about the number of angler-use days it receives each season, this is still a river that every fly-fishing addict should spend some time discovering.

Fishing Waters in the Big Hole Drainage

Ajax Lake: You reach Ajax by rough road (when open) west of Bannack. It is 20 acres and 100 feet deep in places. Ajax is fun fishing for the cutthroats, rainbows, and hybrids that swim around the downed timber and along the drop-offs. The biggest fish top out at 15 inches or so, but the numbers are good. It's a good place for spotting and casting to individual trout.

Baldy Lake: You have to hike several miles from the end of the Lacy Creek Road, starting at the point where it's closed, up and into this one at over 8,000 feet. Baldy is deep and over 30 acres with Yellowstone cutthroats, rainbows, and hybrids over a foot.

It's surprisingly popular for a hike-in lake. Brian Esterman, who fishes it several times a season, says, "Baldy is high enough that there's no summer slump. The fish hang near the edges and they're always within reach of a well-presented fly. I use drys, patterns like the EZ Caddis and Sparkle Dun, on 12-foot leaders with 6X tippets mostly, but that's personal preference. My friends use general nymphs or Woolly Worms and do well here."

Berry Lake: Berry is up in the Pioneer Creek country and way back away from the crowds. This lake is 11 acres, deep, and full of fat cutthroats to several

Be careful with your back cast. Hooking one of these gives catch and release a whole new meaning.
Photo by Dan Abrams

pounds. A serious effort is required to reach this place and the fishing can be tough. It's the kind of lake where you go in and camp for three or four days, hoping to be there when the fish go on a feeding spree. Take small (size 16 or smaller) terrestrials, such as a Foam Ant or Crowe Beetle, for the evening rise.

Start at the Pioneer Creek trail and trek from Pioneer Lake (may be barren) to Highup Lake (certainly barren) to Skytop Lake (also barren). From there it is 1½ miles along the Divide to Berry. Watch out for weather up here. Lightning in the exposed rocks is nasty and sudden storms with cold rain or snow sweep over the crest in the fall.

Bobcat Lakes (North, South, West): Up the Wise River drainage at over 8,000 feet, the chief attraction in these small lakes are the grayling that on extreme occasions may top a foot.

Canyon Creek: A typical pretty mountain stream with brushy, downed-timber banks and lots of pocket water and rapid riffles before running into the Big Hole not far from Maidenrock. There is a campground on the upper reaches, which have a few small trout. The lower stretch has cutts, rainbows, and brookies to maybe 12 inches. Most of the tributaries of the lower Big Hole also have good runs of brown trout in the fall, usually beginning in mid-September and running through the end of the season, November 30. These trout will strike streamers and larger nymphs drifted in front of them. At this time of year, walk the stream banks quietly until you find the fish under the banks or other cover. Many fly fishers do not like to fish for trout when they are on their redds. A number of fisheries biologists now believe that trout are stressed less here (if played fairly, quickly, and properly released) than when taken well below their spawning gravels downstream, when they still have several miles to travel. The choice is yours, but always put the welfare of the trout first.

Canyon Lake: Canyon is reached by 4 miles of good trail above the campground and at the base of 9,810-foot Maurice Mountain. Marshy, shallow, and around 20 acres, Canyon has good numbers of cutthroats in the 10-inch class and a few up to several pounds. Plenty of flies and lures and Day-Glo-orange, garlic-flavored marshmallows are flung into the water here, so the fish are wary and not easily fooled—why eat feathers when you can dine on a marshmallow Caesar Salad? But a weighted, olive gold-ribbed Hare's Ear on a long, fine leader worked slowly towards shore takes fish.

Crescent Lake: About a half mile above Canyon Lake, Crescent is over 20 acres in scree and scrub timber with plenty of cutthroats that reach 16 inches. Crescent isn't all that deep (22 feet maximum) and that makes it a good place to use sinking line techniques. One favorite method here is the YoYo retrieve—the angler fishes a floating fly, such as a Floating Damsel, with a fast sinking, 30-foot shooting head. The line drags the bottom and the fly rides over weeds and obstructions.

Dark Horse Lake: Dark Horse is reached by too many trucks, cars, mountain bikes, nomadic camel caravans, etc., for obvious reasons— it is a beautiful cirque lake with decent fishing for healthy cutthroats that are fools for dry flies and flashy streamers. Fish the lower end, with its shallow bench, morning and evening. The road from Skinner Meadows is poor but usable all summer.

Deerhead Lake: Deerhead is on the trail from the Dinner Station Campground northwest of Dillon. Used as irrigation storage, it is still good action for some sizeable cutthroats. It's small (15 acres), shallow (15 feet), and weedy. It doesn't take a genius to figure out that damsels are important here.

Ferguson Lake: In the Alder Creek drainage, less than 20 acres, it has cutthroats, rainbows, and hybrids. Ferguson has extensive shallows surrounding a middle basin that's nearly 50 feet deep. The fish, up to 15 inches, are real cruisers and will rush a long way for a fly. Why? It's the competition created by good numbers of trout. A flashy wet pattern, like a Silver Invicta or a Diving Caddis, worked quickly to cover a lot of water, is deadly on Ferguson.

Fool Hen Lake: You reach this small lake from the Alder Creek trail along Fool Hen Creek to fish for cutthroats that may reach 15 inches.

Francis Creek: Southeast of Wisdom, running through National Forest, then sage flats to Steel Creek, this is still a pretty much un-spoiled stream that has brookies, whitefish, and a few small (but eager) grayling. Easy and enjoyable dry fly water with light rods at ten paces.

Governor Creek: Governor is in the Headwaters of the Big Hole. It has brookies, grayling, and rainbows. You need permission for most of its length as it flows through hay fields and open meadow country. Irrigation doesn't help the situation here.

Granite Lake: Reached from Melrose way up the Cherry Creek Road, this is not exactly stupendous fishing, but there are a few large cut-throats that occasionally deign to snag a small nymph. Dry flies apparently are considered declassé by these educated trout of breeding and panache.

Grayling Lake: Grayling is several miles above Canyon Creek Camp-ground. The grayling are few and far between, but there are some cutthroats to a foot or so. Stomach samples of the trout showed a diet of mostly midges in this lake and, not surprisingly, a size-18 to -20 dark pattern is the best fish-catcher.

Green Lake: This one is above 8,300 feet on the east side of Granite Mountain several miles above the Rock Creek Guard Station. It holds some cutthroats, a few rainbows, and hybrids to a couple of pounds.

Hamby Lake: Hamby is about a half-dozen miles southwest of Jack-son with fair numbers of grayling that reach 15 inches or a bit larger along with some cutts and brookies and even rainbows. It's over 35 acres in timber-and-rock high country above 8,000 feet.

Ken Mira concentrates on high lakes in the spring: "Hitting a lake at ice-out often means going through snow drifts. I carry snow shoes and push into Hamby as early as possible. From 1990 to 1995 the ice has gone off the lake anywhere from May 29th to June 21st. I fish the same lakes every year and can pretty much guess, depending on the spring weather, when they'll open up. I'll start on low elevation waters and work my way higher and higher.

"I specialize in lakes like Hamby that have good, strong inlet streams. Sometimes there's only a small circle of open water around the creek mouth, but that's enough area for good fishing. There are a lot of trout stacked up getting ready to spawn, but for me the attraction is that this is the time to get the biggest fish in the lake. What's the usual size of the cutthroats and rainbows in Hamby? 12 to 15 inches. I've gotten trout there up to 21 inches in the spring. I use a small streamer, a size-8 Green and Yellow Stub Wing Bucktail or a Yellow Marabou Muddler, to catch the bigger fish."

Lake Agnes: Agnes is full of grayling of around 10 inches. It's almost 100 acres, located above the Brownes Lake Campground up the Rock Creek Road. It's a short hike from the campground—less than a mile—and that makes it a popular spot. Fishing pressure doesn't seem to educate the grayling, however.

Lily Lake: Lily is about 10 miles east of Wisdom and has some cutthroats, rainbows, and hybrids. There seems to be a real split in the trout population—most of the fish are in the 8- to 12-inch range, but there are some real trophies here. There doesn't seem to be any trout in the in-between sizes. The big boys, generally the hybrids, probably switch over to a diet of their smaller cousins. The last couple of miles into 14-acre Lily are by good trail.

Miner Lake: You can reach Miner by road west of Jackson, so it's quite popular with area residents and visitors alike. It's good for brook trout and grayling, especially along the channel near evening. There are some cutthroats, too. Canoes or float tubes help reach the fish.

Mussigbrod Lake: You can drive to this one in the Rolls to fish for grayling to 12 inches and brook trout to 14 inches. There is a Forest Service campground and lots of trash fish (no proven correlation between the two). The reservoir is drawn down a good deal for irrigation in the summer, leaving a rim of mud along the shallows. A boat is a big help on this 100-acre lake.

Mystic Lake: Mystic has lots of rainbows that are hit by the horseback crowd. A float tube would play well here, especially along the edges of aquatic growth. Try slowly working a small nymph, like a Pheasant Tail or a Pearl Serendipity, parallel to the weeds. Mystic is in the Anaconda-Pintlar Wilderness north and west of Wisdom.

North Fork Big Hole River: The North Fork wanders through grass and willow country to the Big Hole north of Wisdom. It's mainly brook trout water, with some of the fish growing fat and over 15 inches. There are also whitefish, and maybe a stray grayling. Z-Wings and Elk Hairs for the caddis and Sparkle Duns and Parachutes for mayflies will usually fool the brookies, though some nymphs are not a bad idea either.

O'Dell Creek: A small stream followed by road and trail, it receives quite a bit of pressure for its size, but still manages to produce good numbers of small brookies, grayling, and some rainbows.

O'Dell Lake: Lots of people reach this one by trail from the end of the Lacy Creek Road. They come here mainly for the 10- to 14-inch grayling and they stay at the campsite at the south end. It's a pretty busy spot in the summer, but after Labor Day the hordes diminish and it's fun to use a float tube to fish the shallows on the north end, where the fish seem to concentrate. Pattern type isn't critical, but grayling have small mouths and any fly larger than size 14 is not as effective as tinier offerings.

Pear Lake: Pear Lake is above 8,500 feet, beyond the end of the Birch Creek Road, over 35 acres (when not drawn down for irrigation), with good numbers of 12-inch cutthroats.

Pintlar Lake: It's about 30 minutes north of Wisdom. Less than 40 acres and only 20 feet deep, Pintlar has mainly cutthroats along with some rainbow and brook trout. You reach it by road and it has a campground. There is some draw-down. Float tubes or canoes make the fishing a little easier. Strip a dragon fly or a damsel fly nymph slowly along the bottom.

Ridge Lake: Ridge Lake is west of Jackson, off the Rock Island Lakes Road, in high country. It's a short hike up to the lake. Ridge is good action for cutthroats of 10 to 15 inches. Try skating a Dancing Caddis when the water goes flat in the evening.

Rock Island Lakes: These four lakes are up 4 miles of trail heading off from the Miner Creek Road west of Jackson. There is some decent fishing for cutthroats and a few rainbows.

Ruby Creek: Ruby heads in the mountains below Big Hole Pass and flows for a dozen miles to the North Fork not too far from the Big Hole battlefield. This small stream is pounded by anglers for little brookies and other trout. There's better water in the area.

Schultz Lakes: These two lakes are located about 20 miles up the Wise River Road at 9,000 feet. Both are less than 10 acres but have fair numbers of cutthroats and rainbows over a pound and up to several, though they are receiving a lot of attention these days and their numbers are suffering a bit as a result.

Schwinegar Lake: Schwinegar is 5 acres and good fishing for small grayling. It's up the Lacy Creek Road.

Slag-A-Melt Lakes: These two are up the Big Swamp Creek Road in the Beaverheads. North Slag-A-Melt has brookies and South has some chunky cutthroats plus a few brook trout. The lakes provide marginal fishing in glacial cirque country.

South Fork Big Hole River: This stream forms the Big Hole when it joins forces with Governor Creek above Jackson. It's good fishing for brook and rainbow trout, but most of the water is on private land, making access sporting. Irrigation takes its toll on this stream.

Steel Creek: Steel hits the Big Hole south of Jackson. It's good autumn fishing for brook trout to 15 inches and a few grayling. Something like a Royal Trude or an Orange Double Wing make good attractor drys in the fall.

Stone Creek Lakes: In the mountains on the west side of the Wise River, these two small lakes provide decent fishing for cutthroats running from 8 to 15 inches.

Tahepia Lake: Tahepia is a rainbow trout lake at almost 9,000 feet in glacial cirque country in the Wise River drainage above the Mono Creek Campground. It's a little over 15 acres and only 20 feet deep, but something keeps it from freezing out and it grows healthy fish to 15 inches.

Tendoy Lake: This one is high in the Pioneers. It is ice-free only a few months of the year, but offers average fishing for average cutthroats after ice-out. It's only 30 acres, but it's 100 feet deep (which is what saves it from freezing out).

Ten Mile Lakes: These are a half-dozen small lakes above 8,800 feet in the Anaconda-Pintlar Wilderness. They were originally managed for rainbows but are now being taken over by cutthroats that do well in the clear water. You can reach them by a lengthy hike from the end of the Grassy Mountain Road.

Twin Lakes: You'll find these 25 miles south of Wisdom. They're fished by just about everyone owning fishing gear in the area. The two lakes are joined by a small channel and combine for 75 acres of water. They hold large lake trout to twenty pounds, plus brook trout, grayling, and rainbows. You can catch those lake trout in the fall on streamer flies when they cruise the gravel shallows. The nastiest weather is the best fishing time.

Upper Miner Lakes: Both Upper Miner and Upper, Upper Miner receive occasional plants of Yellowstone cutthroats that sometimes survive the winter and sometimes do not. Upper Miner also has brookies and the other lake has some rainbows.

Warm Springs Creek: A headwaters stream of the Big Hole, Warm Springs passes just south of Jackson and provides nice dry fly action with Wulffs, Humpies, and other delicate patterns for 10-inch brook trout and some whitefish.

Warren Lake: Warren Lake is in the Anaconda-Pintlar Wilderness far back up the West Fork of LaMarche Creek. It's a 9-mile hike (enough to discourage the backpacking wannabees), but this 18-acre lake is good fishing for cutthroats to a couple of pounds.

Willow Creek: This 20-mile long stream flows north behind Twin Adams and Sugarloaf mountains in the Pioneers. There are lots of cutthroats and rainbows to a foot or a little more, plus some nice browns in autumn in the lower reaches (as is true of most of the Big Hole tributaries between Twin Bridges and Wise River). Streamers will take these fish when they are on the run as winter approaches. You can get away with floating lines in the smaller streams, making casting much easier and safer. A 20-inch trout in a 20-foot-wide stream is an engaging proposition.

Wise River: Wise River flows for about 30 miles through the Pioneer Mountains and enters the Big Hole at the town of Wise River. It's beautiful water that offers some good fishing in spots, but pollution from mining, scouring from floods decades ago, and heavy dewatering from irrigation do a number on the populations of catchable brookies and rainbows. The low, clear water of midsummer also makes the fish very spooky; as a result, most anglers do poorly here.

It's amazing how good this stream becomes once you start creeping and crawling among the boulders. The trout concentrate in the pools and when they're not frightened out of their holding areas, they'll take any reasonable dry fly. Goddard Caddis, Stimulators, Wulffs, Humpies, and Renegades all work well, but for special excitement try Spiders skittered across the river's surface on hot, windy summer afternoons. This pattern drives trout crazy throughout the state when the caddis and the wind play together.

Other Waters

Albino Lakes: Frozen out.

Albino Creek: Barren.

Alder Creek: Brookies, grayling, and rainbows.

Anchor Lake: Cutthroats.

Andrus Creek: Brookies, cutthroats, and grayling.

Bear Creek: Too small.

Bear Lake: Brookies.

Bear Wallow Creek: Too small.

Bender Creek: Too small.

Berry Creek: Brookies and cutthroats, including some to 16 inches. If you're bushwacking your way up to Berry Lake, you might as well stop and pop dry flies (try a size-16 Foam Beetle) on this outflow stream. It's dewatered on the lower end.

Big American Creek: Brookies and cutthroats.

Big California Creek: Poor for brookies and rainbows, but the Big Hole–Anaconda Road crosses it at the mouth, so many people hit it.

Big Lake Creek: Brookies, cutthroats, and rainbows.

Big Moosehorn Creek: Brookies.

Big Swamp Creek: Brookies and cutthroats.

Birch Creek: Brookies and cutthroats.

Blacktail Creek: Too small.

Bobcat Creek: Cutthroats and rainbows.

Bond Creek: Too small.

Bond Lake: Cutthroats, grayling, and rainbows up to a foot. This weedy, 20-acre lake, a mile hike up from the Willow Creek Road isn't good in midsummer due to irrigation draw downs, but it's worth fishing after ice-out.

Boot Lake: Cutthroats, grayling, and rainbows.

Brownes Lake: Brookies and rainbows.

Bryant Creek: Brookies.

Buckhorn Creek: Too small.

Bull Creek: Brookies, cutthroats, grayling, and rainbows.

Camp Creek: Brookies and rainbows.

Cherry Creek: Poor fishing.

Cherry Lake: Cutthroats.

Corral Creek: Too small.

Cow Bone Lake: Cutthroats and rainbows.

Cow Creek: Too small.

Cox Creek: Brookies, cutthroats, and rainbows.

Crystal Lake: Rainbows.

Dark Horse Creek: Brookies and cutthroats. This outflow from Dark Horse Lake is followed by a good dirt road, and as a result, gets fished a lot, but it's an easy place to catch small trout.

David Creek: Cutthroats and rainbows.

Deep Creek: Brookies, grayling, rainbows, and whitefish.

Delano Creek: Too small.

Divide Creek: Brookies and rainbows.

Doolittle Creek: Brookies.

Dubois Creek: Too small.

East Fork LaMarche Creek: Cutthroats.

Elbow Lake: Cutthroats.

Englejard Creek: Brookies and cutthroats.

Englejard Lake: Cutthroats.

Fish (Hicks) Lake: Cutthroats and rainbows.

Fish Trap Creek: Brookies and rainbows.

Fool Hen Creek: Brookies and rainbows.

Fox Creek: Brookies, cutthroats, and rainbows. This tributary of Governor Creek has easy access and good fishing for trout up to 12 inches. It's worth a Sunday drive up the road.

French Gulch: Brookies, rainbows, and whitefish.

Gold Creek: Too small.

Grouse Creek: Too small.

Grouse Creek Lakes: Rainbows. Good numbers of them to 12 inches in these three small lakes. Go up the Wise River Road to the Grouse Creek trail and hike 4 miles to the first pond.

Hall Lake: Cutthroats.

Hamby Creek: Too small.

Harriet Lou Creek: Too small.

Hidden Gem Lake: Brookies.

Highup Lake: Barren.

Hopkins Lake: Cutthroats.

Howell Creek: Brookies and rainbows.

Indian Creek: Too small.

Jahnke Lake: Cutthroats.

Jerry Creek: Brookies, cutthroats, grayling, and rainbows. A bouncing mountain stream full of little holes and those holes are full of trout to 10 inches. The stream enters the Big Hole at the Jerry Creek Bridge just below the town of Wise River.

Johanna (Secret) Lake: Cutthroats.

Johnson Creek: Brookies, rainbows, and whitefish.

Joseph Creek: Brookies and rainbows.

Lacy Creek: Brookies, cutthroats, grayling, and rainbows.

Lake Abundance: Some cutthroats to a foot or so.

Lake Geneva: Cutthroats.

Lake of the Woods: Cutthroats and rainbows.

LaMarche Creek: Brookies and rainbows. Limited access.

LaMarche Lake: Cutthroats.

Lena Lake: Cutthroats and rainbows.

Libby Creek: Too small.

Lion Lake: Cutthroats and rainbows. It's fertile with extensive weed beds. Trout grows quickly to the 12- to 14-inch range. Hike 5 miles up the Forest Service trail at the Canyon Creek Ranger Station.

Little Camp Creek: Too small.

Little Joe Creek: Brookies and cutthroats.

Little Lake: Cutthroats.

Little Lake Creek: Brookies and cutthroats.

Little Moosehorn Creek: Brookies.

Lost Horse Creek: Too small.

May Creek: Too small.

May Lake: Cutthroats.

Meadow Creek: Brookies.

Middle Fork Fishtrap Creek: Brookies and rainbows.

Middle Fork LaMarche Creek: Too small.

Middle Fork Lake: Brookies and rainbows.

Mifflin Creek: Too small.

Miner Creek: Brookies and grayling.

Mono Creek: Brookies.

Moose Creek (Wise River): Brookies, cutthroats, and rainbows.

Moose Creek (French Gulch): Brookies, cutthroats, and rainbows.

Morgan Jones Lake: Brookies and rainbows.

Mudd Creek: Too small.

Mussigbrod Creek: Brookies and grayling. Easy to drive to from Wisdom and popular with campers, but it still produces some surprisingly nice brookies to 15 inches.

North Fork Divide Creek: Brookies, cutthroats, and rainbows.

Old Tim Creek: Brookies.

Oreamnos (Goat) Lake: Rainbows.

Pattengail Creek: Brookies and rainbows.

Peterson Lake: Cutthroats and rainbows.

Pine Creek: Too small.

Pintlar Creek: Brookies, cutthroats, and rainbows.

Pioneer Creek: Brookies and cutthroats.

Pioneer Lake: There may or may not be cutthroats here on any given year. It freezes out periodically.

Plimpton Creek: Brookies.

Rainbow (Land) Lake (Anaconda-Pintlar Wilderness): Rainbows.

Rainbow Lake (Rock Creek): Cutthroats.

Reservoir Creek: Brookies and rainbows.

Rochester Creek: Too small.

Rock Creek (Dillon): Brookies and rainbows.

Rock Creek (Wisdom): Brookies, cutthroats, and rainbows.

Sand Creek: Brookies and cutthroats. Fish the outlet just below Sand Lake for an occasional surprise cutthroat/rainbow hybrid that runs bigger than average here.

Sand Lake: Cutthroats.

Sawlog Creek: Too small.

Seven Mile Creek: Too small.

Seymour Creek: Brookies.

Seymour Lakes: Brookies, cutthroats, and rainbows.

Sheep Creek (Wise River): Too small.

Sheep Creek (Trail Creek): Brookies.

Six Mile Creek: Brookies, cutthroats, and rainbows.

Skinner Meadow Creek: Brookies.

Skytop Lake: Barren.

Slag-A-Melt Creek: Brookies.

Slaughterhouse Creek: Brookies and extraneous body parts.

Squaw Creek: Brookies.

Stewart Lake: Brookies.

Sullivan Creek: Brookies.

Sumrun Creek: Brookies and grayling.

Swamp Creek (Wise River): Too small.

Swamp Creek (Wisdom): Brookies and grayling.

Ten Mile Creek: Brookies and rainbows.

Thief Creek: Too small.

Thompson Creek: Brookies, cutthroats, and grayling. A tributary of Plimpton Creek that's easily reached by road and trail. It's fun to find the occasional grayling hiding out from civilization.

Tie Creek: Poor access.

Timberline Lake: Cutthroats.

Tom (Long Tom) Lake: Brookies and cutthroats.

Toomey Creek: Brookies.

Torrey Lake: Cutthroats.

Trail Creek: Brookies and whitefish.

Trapper Creek: Brookies, cutthroats, and rainbows. Hurt by old mining activity in the area and still not fully recovered. Take the road near Melrose up to the ghost town of Hecla.

Trout Creek: Too small.

Tub Lake: Cutthroats.

Twelve Mile Creek: Brookies and cutthroats.

Van Houten Lake: This one has a campground and is reachable by road, so a lot of people fish here for rainbows and brook trout. It's located south of Jackson.

Vera Lake: Cutthroats.

Waukena Lake: Cutthroats. There are plenty of nice fish up to 15 inches in this 30-acre lake. Go to the Rock Creek Ranger Station to find the trail for the relatively easy 3-mile hike.

West Fork Deep Creek: Too small. Poor access.

West Fork LaMarche Creek: Brookies and rainbows.

West Fork Ruby Creek: Too small.

Wyman Creek: Brookies and rainbows.

■ *Special thanks to Danielle Cuite, Stuart Decker, Brian Esterman, Norman Johnson, Ken Mira, and Blaine Summers for their help on the Big Hole drainage.*

*Duck Lake with Chief Mountain
in the background*
Photo by John Holt

THE BLACKFEET RESERVATION

"Wind-blasted, wide-open country dotted with glacier-scoured depressions that are now spring-filled with nutrient water that grows very large trout" conveys a superficial sense of the fishing opportunities lying out on the wild grass prairie of the Blackfeet Indian Reservation.

Rainbow, brook, and cutthroat trout regularly grow past the five-pound mark by feeding on the abundant populations of damsel and dragon flies, midges, leeches, caddis, mayflies, terrestrials, scuds, and smaller fish. In mild years, growth rates of an inch per month have been documented.

With all of these big fish cruising around like out-of-control Trident submarines in search of a vanished communist threat, why isn't the reservation overrun with fly fishers?

The reasons are simple. The wind often blows for weeks straight at over 30 miles per hour making fishing, especially from a float tube, difficult, if not impossible. There are also times when the trout head for deep water and sulk, especially during the heat of summer.

And, finally, quality food, lodging, and equipment outlets are in short supply. Browning, the largest town on the reservation, does offer a couple of motels, restaurants, and cafés, and there's some fishing gear available. But that's about it, if you plan on staying on the Blackfeet Reservation. Except for private campsites, there is no camping allowed on the reservation. Most people that fish here are from west of the mountains—towns like Whitefish and Kalispell—or from Great Falls and Helena to the south.

One other frustrating fact is that non-tribal members cannot fish after sunset, a time when some huge fish begin to suck down insects with loud slurps, making large rise forms out there in the gloom of dusk. Nor can you cast a line before sunrise.

So why bother coming to the reservation at all?

Well, there is the sight of the Rocky Mountain Front rising snowcapped into the sky across the entire western horizon. There are elk, sharp-tailed grouse, grizzlies, Hungarian partridge, deer, eagles, and other animals roaming the million-plus acres. The prairie grasses light up in emerald green in the spring, with bunches of wild flowers glowing all over the place.

And there are the trout. Sure, there's a good chance that the wind will blow you off the water or that the fish may do a vanishing act, but if you are willing to fish hard all day for a week, you will catch a large trout. Perhaps one over ten pounds if you are fortunate.

Lakes like Mission, Mitten, Duck, Kipp's, and Four Horns hold plenty of sizable trout (and those are just a few of the waters). A set of current regulations are a must. They contain a map that will help you navigate out here. Roads not marked with brilliant neon signs often degenerate into two-lane ruts that really do lead to fine lakes. Other waters have frozen out or are temporarily closed. The situation is in a constant state of flux. A little inquiry is often needed to find out what is what. This is all part of the adventure, so relax, keep your eyes open and go with the flow.

There is big water here and a float tube or kick boat are helpful. So are neoprene waders, even in summer, because springs keep most of the lakes cool all season. You'll need 7-weight rods, or larger, to punch casts into the winds and to shoot long casts out to cruising fish. Shooting heads are also gaining in popularity. Other than sunscreen, sunglasses, raingear, warm clothing, a cooler full of chilled beverages, tribal permits (never forget these), a stout vehicle for the rough "roads" that quickly turn impassable with rain or melting snow, and a tape or two of Be'la Fleck to fill the drive time between lakes, you really don't need anything special.

Pattern selection is not elaborate. Hare's Ear Nymphs in tan, gray, and olive, sizes 12 to 18, cover a lot of insects. Some damsel patterns, especially Bigg's Specials in 8 and 10, are necessities, as are brown, black, and purple marabou leech patterns in sizes 2 through 6. A good choice for a scud imitation should include an Olive-Gray Bead Head Scud and an Olive Rollover Scud in sizes 8 through 14—the size 8 is there for shocking the spoiled, overfed trout into striking sometimes. Prince Nymphs also take fish, especially when worked in the wind over exposed points (cast perpendicular to the direction the waves are running and strip the fly quickly back to shore). An Olive Halo Emerger for the escaping nymph, a Speckled-Wing Paradun for the resting dun, and a Gray Clear Wing Spinner for the

Tribal permits are required and a set of current regulations are a must. Call the Blackfeet Nation at 406-338-7207 or if no answer, 406-338-6326.

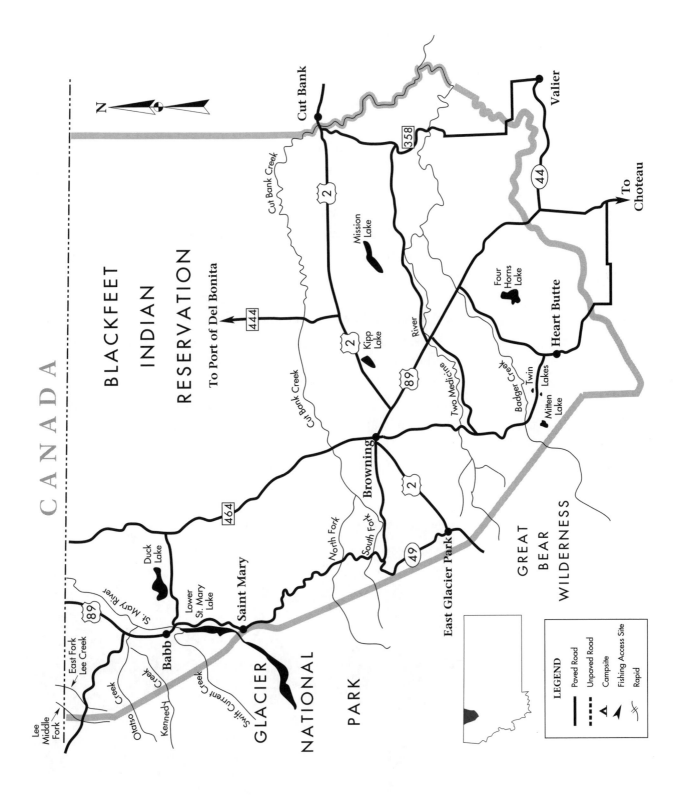

CANADA

N

BLACKFEET

INDIAN

RESERVATION

To Port of Del Bonita

Cut Bank

Cut Bank Creek

Valier

358

2

44

To
Choteau

Mission
Lake

Four
Horns
Lake

Heart Butte

444

2

Kipp
Lake

89

River

Two Medicine

Badger Creek

Twin
Lakes

Mitten
Lake

Cut Bank Creek

464

North Fork

South Fork

Browning

2

49

GREAT
BEAR
WILDERNESS

Duck
Lake

St. Mary River

Lower
St. Mary Lake

Saint Mary

East Glacier Park

89

East Fork
Lee Creek

Lee
Middle
Fork

Otatso   Creek

Kennedy   Creek

Swift Current   Creek

Babb

GLACIER

NATIONAL

PARK

LEGEND
Paved Road
Unpaved Road
Campsite
Fishing Access Site
Rapid

spent egg-layer, all in sizes 14 to 18, handle the *Callibaetis* mayflies, which seem to hang around most of the warmer months, but peak in August and early September. An Adams will approximate the clumps of midges that sometimes appear. Hoppers, ants, and beetles are good in July, August, and the first part part of September.

In March and April, big rainbows move up to the gravel shorelines of the wave-swept southeastern shores of the larger lakes and go through a daisy-chain, false-spawning ritual. Large, gaudy streamers cast over and in front of the fish provoke severe responses. Many of the best rainbows of the year are taken at this time. This is also a time of wind, sleet, snow, and rain, so you've got to want this type of action to enjoy it. Finding the fish is a matter of walking the banks and looking for the dark, swirling shapes. The trout move back and forth between deep water and the shallows. Often they will circle madly for only a few minutes before vanishing for an hour or a day. And there are times, when the ice is pulling back from the shoreline, that a small nymph cast onto the frozen floes and then jerked into the water will trigger a strike from trout hiding just below the shelf. They can hear the fly scratching across the ice. This is big-fish, capricious angling at its elaborate best. The rainbows are firm and full of fight at this time of year, running and jumping at the first tug of the fly when it interrupts their wild, futile procreational ritual.

You may see elk on your travels through the Blackfeet Reservation.
Photo by Dan Abrams

Fishing Waters of the Blackfeet Reservation

Duck Lake: Duck is justly famous for large rainbows during the spring season, but the setting is trailer-court decor wall-to-wall. The drill is to stand half-frozen as deep as you can wade and make long casts with Woolly Buggers out into the lake. The earthly reward for this is a ripping strike just often enough to keep you out there.

East Fork Lee Creek: Heads below Chief Mountain and flows for 6 miles before crossing over into Alberta. Not bad fishing with drys for brook trout and cutthroats to 12 inches.

Four Horns Lake: Four Horns sits in a valley that just funnels the wind. This lake is often too covered in white caps for safe fishing, but when it is calm it can be especially good at the top end where an inlet stream enters. This little stream winds across a high plateau and picks up drowned terrestrials. There are few fish in the stream to intercept this food line and all of the insects are dumped into the lake. The trout (and some walleyes) stack up in this area.

Kipp's Lake: Kipp's is ugly and great fishing. It is a featureless bowl that sits out on the prairie. The bottom is thick with both weeds and food forms for the rainbows. The secret on Kipp's is to move the fly very slowly because these trout don't have to rush to feed.

Middle Fork Lee Creek: This beaver-dammed stream begins on the northern slopes of Chief Mountain and flows for 5 miles across open, windy country before crossing over into Canada. Brookies and cut-throats are taken here.

Mission Lake: Mission is richly carpeted in weeds, and so full of bottom food forms that it's hard to get the fish to strike at times. It sits in a beautiful, high valley and is sheltered a bit by the winds. The most reliable summer action comes with the damsel emergence every morning. If you get there at sunrise you will find rainbow trout snatching some of the millions of hatching insects that are swimming into the shore. Get there later in the morning and you might find the water covered with *Callibaetis* duns, the wings so thick that they create a silver shimmer, but often there's not a single fish rising anywhere on the lake because they've glutted themselves on those early damsels.

A typical Blackfeet Reservation rainbow.
Photo by John Holt

Mitten Lake: This is another scenic, high valley lake. It's the place to go for sinking-line, slow-retrieve tactics during the middle of the day. Here's where the scud patterns work well. Some areas of the lake are better than others, and the regulars seem to know where the good weed beds are located—it seems to be a matter of depth. The trout on Mitten might be concentrating at certain levels at different times of the day.

Otatso Creek: Comes out of Otatso Lake in Glacier National Park and flows for 6 miles to Kennedy Creek. There's fishing for cutthroats and some nice bull trout. Access is either from the park or across Blackfeet Tribal land (with permission).

St. Mary River: Running very swiftly and sapphire clear out on the high plains east of the Rocky Mountain Front, the St. Mary River is a wild, little-fished stream with decent numbers of cutthroats, rainbows, and a few brook trout. The river flows onto the Blackfeet Indian Reservation before disappearing into Canada with its load of snow and ice melt from the distant peaks of Glacier National Park. Access is not the greatest and the fishing is not world class and you do need a tribal permit to cast a line here, but the St. Mary is still a wonderful little river to spend an afternoon on.

Almost no one fishes here, but large cutthroats can be taken at brief and rare windows of opportunity that open just a crack. The formula includes periods of consistent and diminished release from Swiftcurrent Dam, periods of warm, high overcast when hoppers are leaping blithely to their deaths on the river; or when large, dark stoneflies are crawling out from the water to dry on warm rocks and then take flight in the pure sky above. Then the trout can be fooled. The big cutthroats in the river are spooky and hard to catch, and discharges from Swiftcurrent Dam screw up the fishing more than occasionally, but there are those moments when everything is right on the St. Mary.

The best patterns are likely to be things like Joe's Hoppers and Dave's Hoppers in sizes 6 to 10 from early July into the summer, but some anglers do well with large attractors like Goofus Bugs, Wulffs, Double Wings, and Humpies. Big stonefly nymphs, such as the Kaufmann's Stone or Brooks' Stone, sometimes fished in tandem with a smaller fly, such as a Prince Nymph, Hare's Ear, or Bead Head Twist Nymph, drifted along the bottom (with a few twist-ons to offset the current) will often take the trout and always entice the greedy white-fish. The stream does not open until the first of June and the runoff from the Rockies is often in full swing at this time. By July the levels have stabilized and fishing can be quite good for the smaller trout, especially toward evening (no fishing after sunset is allowed).

Streamers like the Zonker, Gray Ghost, Black-Nosed Dace, and similar flashy patterns, cast across stream and allowed to swing with the current, will pull up reluctant fish. So will large wet flies fished the same manner. Using two or even three wets can simulate a hatch of artificial food that fools the cutthroats into feeding.

This river is not exceptionally fertile despite its verdant surroundings (from late spring into midsummer). Any fly that reflects the light and acts lifelike will probably attract a strike. Catching fish in the St. Mary is not all that important. Just being alive in this wind-blasted, wild country is what matters.

POPULAR FLIES

Adams

Bigg's Special

Black-Nosed Dace

Brooks' Stone

Dave's Hopper

Double Wing

Goofus Bug

Gray Clear Wing Spinner

Gray Ghost

Hare's Ear Nymph

Humpy

Joe's Hopper

Kaufmann's Stone

Marabou Leech

Olive-Gray Bead Head Scud

Olive Halo Emerger

Olive Rollover Scud

Prince Nymph

Speckled-Wing Parachute

Wulff

Zonker

Twin Lakes: This is not one of the "big-fish" lakes and there are two of them. They are separated by the road between Heart Butte and Browning, about 4 miles northwest of Heart Butte. Fishermen who tire of the slower trophy hunting should know about these waters. They can come here and fish for trout that rise all morning to the *Callibaetis* hatch. The rainbows here are mostly under 14 inches, but there is the occasional bigger one in these lakes.

By midsummer, the waters have warmed to the extent that most of the lakes are in the doldrums, though fish will be taken working down deep, along weed beds, around springs and on the surface during cooler, overcast days.

From September into winter (lakes are open all year), the trout key at first on various autumn caddisflies, the late stragglers of the *Callibaetis* hatch, and then on small fish as the thick growth of aquatic plants dies back. The withering of the vegetation allows fly fishers to work the bulky patterns more effectively. Trout will often be seen prowling near shore. A cautious approach and well-timed cast ahead of a cruiser consistently takes such a fish.

All in all, the Blackfeet Indian Reservation is a land where serious fly fishers (read: those willing to put up with austere conditions and willing to work at their fishing) can reasonably expect to take one or more trout over five pounds in a week's fishing. This time frame includes at least one-third of the daylight hours rendered unfishable because of high winds.

If you can handle arm-numbing casting, rough weather, hot sun and perhaps a large trout, this is not a bad spot to spend some time. The Blackfeet Reservation and its permit fees should be considered a bargain and a privilege for non-tribal members. The place is a hell of a lot cheaper (and often better fishing) and just as scenic in its own way as New Zealand.

Other Waters

Beaver Lakes: Private.

Boulder Creek: Bull trout and cutthroats.

Goose Lake: Brookies.

Kennedy Creek: Bull trout, cutthroats, and rainbows.

Lee Creek: Brookies and cutthroats.

Lower St. Mary Lake: Bull trout, cutthroats, lake trout, rainbows, whitefish, northern pike, and ling.

Pike Lake: Sporadic access. Northern pike.

Pine Coulee Creek: Brookies, cutthroats, and whitefish.

Roberts Creek: Brookies.

Swiftcurrent Creek: Cutthroats, rainbows, and northerns.

Willow Creek: Brookies and cutthroats.

■ *Special thanks to Guy Tucker for his help on the St. Mary River.*

Clarks Fork of the Yellowstone
Photo by Stan Bradshaw

CLARKS FORK OF THE YELLOWSTONE

At its beginning, the Clarks Fork of the Yellowstone is a true mountain stream. Formed by snow and glacier melt in the barren reaches of the Beartooth Plateau just a few miles east of Cooke City on the northern border of Yellowstone National Park, the Clarks Fork is a fast-flowing, riffle-and-pocket-water stream. It runs south into Wyoming for a crooked piece before crossing back into Montana about 10 miles south of Belfry.

Near the headwaters, a dry fly attractor, as subtle as a Deer Hair Woolly or as garish as a Royal Humpy, from size 12 to size 18, will turn Yellowstone cutthroats and an occasional brook trout up to 10 inches on a good day. You can easily reach much of this alpine water by short hikes from the Beartooth Highway. In spring and summer wildflowers brighten the landscape and hoary marmots whistle back and forth among themselves in the jumbled, shattered rock. The country is spectacular, with ragged peaks over 12,000 feet, remnant glaciers, snowfields, and sapphire blue lakes clouded with glacial flour of ground and pulverized rock. Storms roll by swiftly overhead, filled with thunder and lightning. The air is often charged with static electricity and the scent of ozone drifts by. These disturbances disappear as quickly as they come, rumbling out onto the flatlands.

The river is born in Montana but after a quick 3 miles passes into Wyoming (where it is also good fishing). When it reenters Montana, Montana Highway 72 parallels the Clarks Fork. The river from the Wyoming line downstream to Bridger is also rapid, pocket-and-riffle water with mainly mountain whitefish and some large browns. There are also a few brookies, cutthroats, and rainbows. This water would be truly classy stuff if it were not so heavily dewatered for irrigation. Low flows, the flush of returning water, and overgrazing by cattle cause severe sedimentaion that chokes both insect life and spawning gravels. Clean up this problem and you immediately create another excellent trout stream.

Past Bridger the same problems exist, exacerbated by natural sedimentation and alkalinity from surrounding unstable soils. There are a few impressive browns up from the Yellowstone, plus some rainbows, ling (ugly, ugly fish), sauger (a lethargic version of the walleye), and some muscle-bound catfish. Big streamers imitating forage fish will take the browns in the fall in this often turbid situation.

In the Beartooths the river drains less than 120 square miles, but there are hundreds of named and unnamed lakes in this small area. Many freeze out on a regular basis and are subsequently barren. Most of the water is between 9,000 and 10,000 feet and one lake is at 11,200 feet, the highest in the state. Crazy Lake, Daisy Lake, Goose Lake, and Lulu Pass jeep trails lead into the backcountry, but these conduits are often narrow, rocky, and hazardous to travel, especially during and after the frequent snow and rain storms. Grizzlies also make this country home, but are little trouble if you keep a clean campsite. The lakes around Cooke City are usually free of ice by late May or early June, but the higher elevation waters often do not clear until August.

From a great beginning in pristine country, the Clarks Fork dies a quick death from a fly fishing perspective almost as soon as the river wanders back into Montana. Perhaps someday the river will have an opportunity to show us what kind of trout stream it was in the past.

Fishing Waters in the Clarks Fork Drainage

Albino Lake: Albino is way up in the clouds—over 10,000 feet—on the Beartooth Plateau (no trees here), and 40 acres with well-defined dropoffs. The 5-mile hike into Albino starts at Island Lake on the Beartooth Highway. This lake has good numbers of Yellowstone Cutthroats (the species of choice in this area) that grow to 15 inches. They occasionally feed on the surface, especially at dusk, as with all mountain-lake trout, but nymphs work better, especially if they have just a hint of flash. A Flashback Callibaetis, Twist Nymph, or Gold Ribbed Hare's Ear are all good patterns. These flies reflect the available light, drawing the curious but finicky fish. Greasing the nymph so it rides in the meniscus is also a productive ploy. For deeper presentations, don't forget the Olive Woolly Worm with a tuft of red at the tail. The cutts here love to hit these as they slowly sink to the bottom or are pulled back to the surface with the smallest of lifts.

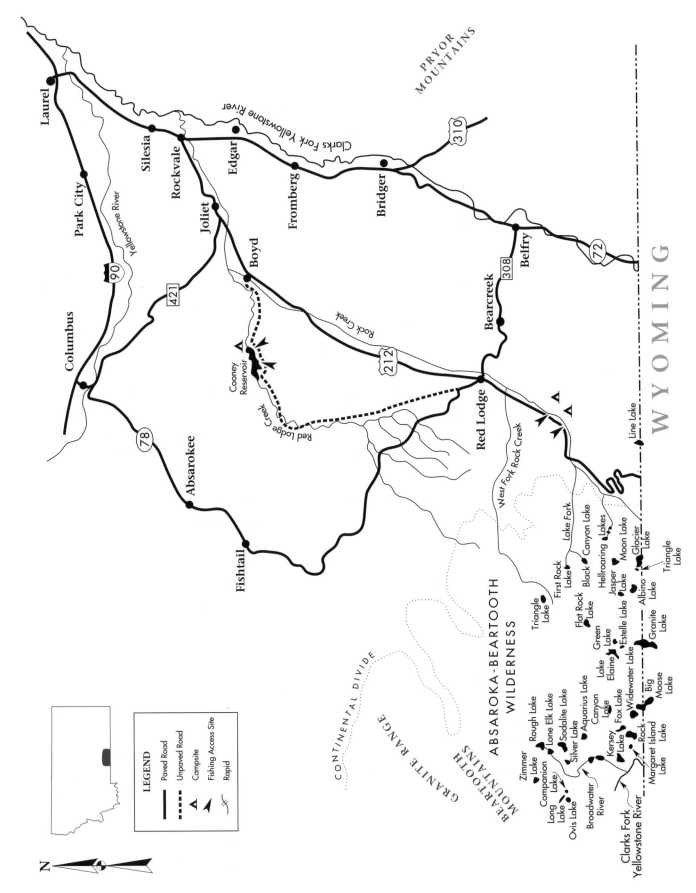

CLARKS FORK OF THE YELLOWSTONE

WYOMING

PRYOR MOUNTAINS

Clarks Fork Yellowstone River

310

72

Belfry

Bearcreek

308

212

Rock Creek

Boyd

Fromberg

Bridger

Edgar

Rockvale

Silesia

Joliet

421

Laurel

Park City

Yellowstone River

90

Columbus

78

Absarokee

Fishtail

Cooney Reservoir

Red Lodge Creek

Red Lodge

West Fork Rock Creek

Lake Fork

ABSAROKA-BEARTOOTH
WILDERNESS

CONTINENTAL DIVIDE

GRANITE RANGE

BEARTOOTH MOUNTAINS

Line Lake

Triangle Lake

Glacier Lake

Albino Lake

Moon Lake

Jasper Lake

Hellroaring Lakes

Canyon Lake

Black Lake

First Rock Lake

Flat Rock Lake

Triangle Lake

Green Lake

Estelle Lake

Granite Lake

Elaine Lake

Widewater Lake

Big Moose Lake

Lake Elaine

Canyon Lake

Aquarius Lake

Fox Lake

Rock Lake

Kersey Lake

Sodalite Lake

Silver Lake

Lone Elk Lake

Rough Lake

Margaret Island Lake

Broadwater River

Zimmer Lake

Companion Lake

Long Lake

Ovis Lake

Clarks Fork
Yellowstone River

LEGEND

Paved Road
Unpaved Road
Campsite
Fishing Access Site
Rapid

N

61

Big Moose Lake: This one's an 84-acre lake on the Montana-Wyoming line. Take the Crazy Lakes Trail out of the Cooke City area. Big Moose has a few large brook trout, some rainbows, and plenty of gregarious grayling that love tiny drys—size 20 and smaller. It's fun to grease up a Griffith's Gnat or a Black Halo Midge Pupa and wait to see what will hit it.

Black Canyon Lake: Every six years or so, over 8,000 Yellowstone Cutthroats of 2 inches are air-dropped into this 60-acre lake lying at the foot of Grasshopper Glacier. The fish average less than a foot but sometimes reach a couple of pounds in this 185-foot-deep, cream-and-jade-colored lake. You'll climb high enough to look the mountain goats in the eye at 9,400 feet. Start at U.S. 12 and hike 2½ miles up the Broadwater Creek Trail to Curl Lake. Circle past Broadwater Lake (connected to Curl) and climb 3 miles up the Lake Fork Rock Creek Trail to Black Canyon.

Bluewater Creek: This is a little gem for spring creek lovers. There's 13 miles of it, flowing from Bluewater Springs to the Clarks Fork of the Yellowstone. The lower reaches are hammered by irrigation and only poor fishing. Drive up a good county road (across the river from Fromberg) 5 miles and start there. It is rattlesnake infested all along (crowd control). The stream has good numbers of fat, one-to-two-pound browns that rise well to terrestrial imitations. The best fish hold in creases under the brush and a daring caster who hammers a fly deep into the thickets takes trout all day.

Canyon (Crazy) Lake: Canyon Lake is long, narrow, and deep (like most lakes formed in a steep canyon). Hit the trail at the north end of Fox Lake, which isn't far from Cooke City, and hump the 1½ miles up to Canyon. There are very big cutthroats and rainbows here, along with the regular foot-long variety, but they hold so deep that unless they're feeding they are hard to take with a floating line. A few people fish it with fast sinking lines and weighted nymphs.

Bailey Smith lists his favorite flies, "A Muskrat and a Light Bead Head Possie are my standards. The important part is the retrieve. It has to be as slow as possible so that the sinking line doesn't slant up

POPULAR FLIES

Black Halo Midge Pupa

Dave's Hopper

Deer Hair Woolly

Flashback Callibaetis

Gold Ribbed Hare's Ear

Griffith's Gnat

Henry's Fork Hopper

Humpy

Krystal Egg

Light Bead Head Possie

Mohawk

Muskrat

Olive Woolly Worm

Pink Trude

Red Serendipity

Royal Humpy

Timberline Emerger

Twist Nymph

off the bottom. The idea is to crawl the flies up the 'slope' in steep lakes. It should take at least 5 minutes to bring in a fifty foot cast."

Companion Lake: This is a good place to go for fast catches of 10-inch brookies. It's a few hundred yards east of Long Lake (which, in turn, is accessible by jeep road). There are usually enough people here to make fishing a social event.

Cooney Reservoir: Fifteen minutes west of Boyd. It's about 640 acres, perhaps 20 feet deep, and planted each season with a couple of strains of rainbows and lots of "ferocious" walleyes that all do fairly well together in this open-country reservoir. This is a place where a setup of a nightcrawler, a garlic marshmallow, and a kernel of corn, squeezed onto a single hook, is the hot item. But it's still a fun place for kicking around in a float tube and casting a fly.

Early in the season, usually by May, the fly fishing gets poor because of the muddy runoff from Willow Creek and Red Lodge Creek. The best time on Cooney is in late June and early July, but there are so many little fish, both trout and walleyes, that it's often necessary to ignore strikes to let the fly sink into deeper water. The reward for this patience and perseverance are the occasional rainbows to three or four pounds.

Elaine Lake: Hit the trail off the Beartooth Highway 20 miles east of Cooke City. It's 8 miles up to Granite Lake and then another 2½ miles up to Elaine. Is there any doubt why this is known as a good place for horsepackers? The lake is packed with small brook trout that thrive in the 100-plus acres.

Cooney Reservoir can get pretty zoo-like in the summer.
Photo by Stan Bradshaw

Estelle Lake: This is another good spot for small brookies. It's on the same trail as Elaine, sitting about a mile east of that lake. It's only

18 acres, but it seems like every foot of it has a willing trout. If you put two or three wet flies on a leader, you will hook more than one trout often enough.

First Rock Lake: Take U.S. 212 20 miles south from Red Lodge and hit the Lake Fork Rock Creek Trail. Hike 6½ miles to Keyser Brown Lake and then another mile to First Rock. It's still another brook trout lake, with a few cutthroats thrown in for good measure, but the fish are small (read: overpopulated) and could use some pressure.

Flat Rock Lake: At almost 10,000 feet, the site of the annual Flat Earth Society Convention, this is a wind-swept, 35-acre lake on the desolate Beartooth Plateau. Hop from Long Lake to Star Lake to Green Lake to Summerville Lake to Flat Rock Lake. It's a wicked, high-elevation jeep ride and 2-mile climb. All this work is for cutthroats up to a foot or so. Don't worry about the crowds.

Fox Lake: Fox is about 10 miles east from Cooke City off U.S. 212. It has good populations of 10- to 12-inch grayling, brookies, and rainbows. It's long, narrow, and fairly deep, covering 120 acres in all. It's only the length of a football field from the highway.

Glacier Lake: You can get to within a mile of Glacier by the Rock Creek Road. It sits near the Wyoming line. Glacier is heavily planted with cutthroats every three years, which grow to two or three pounds if they live long enough. Glacier is a popular place, heavily fished for both the cutthroats and resident brookies. It's about 180 feet deep and nearly 180 acres.

Granite Lake: Twenty miles east of Cooke City, it lies in both Montana and Wyoming. It's reached by an 8-mile hike up Muddy Creek to 8,625 feet, where you will find 8- to 14-inch brookies and rainbows in this deep, 250-acre lake.

Green Lake: Green is about a mile southeast of Elaine Lake and filled with 10-inch brook trout (whose ancestors must have been glad to leave the blighted streams of the East to the hardier brown trout and come West where they could overrun so many waters perfectly suited for them). Anyway, they thrive in this 36-acre, 130-foot deep lake.

Hellroaring Lakes: These are dozen miles south of Red Lodge off U.S. 212. There are twelve lakes in all and about half of them are barren (the secret is knowing which ones). Anyone lacking local and current information can play safe and fish Hellroaring Lake #2. It's planted with cutthroats every eight years and in peak years it's good fishing for trout up to three pounds. This is serious thunderstorm country.

Jasper Lake: It sits at over 10,000 feet. Go to Albino Lake and then hike a half mile north to 55-acre Jasper. It's planted periodically with cutthroats that will reach four or five pounds before the cycle begins to decline and populations dwindle toward it's next eight-year stocking.

Matt Quinn actually tries to hit Jasper (and Albino) near the end of the stocking cycle. "There won't be much left except big fish. There's a little natural reproduction here, but not enough to crowd the lake. I'll hike up and stay for a week, not fishing much unless the trout begin rising. Even then it'll be slow, but nearly every cutt will range from three to six pounds. My favorite method is a two-fly rig, with a dry fly like a size-18 Pink Trude for an indicator and a nymph like a size-20 Red Serendipity for a dropper."

The most consistent fishing in these lakes is in the third, fourth, and fifth years after stocking. Information on plantings is available from regional headquarters of the Montana Department of Fish, Wildlife, and Parks. It's worth checking on specific waters before wandering into this hard-to-reach country. Often a lake that was hot last year, is dead this year, while a water

One of the Hellroaring Lakes.
Photo by Don Pilotte

just next door is prime this season. A quick visit or phone call can eliminate a lot of frustration (and useless hiking if trout are the major goal of the expedition).

Kersey Lake: Kersey is easy to reach by 4-wheel drive up Sedge Creek just 3 miles out of Cooke City. Kersey is nearly 120 acres by 70 feet deep with good-sized brookies, some cutthroats, and maybe a stray lake trout or two.

Lake Creek: Lake Creek begins as ice-melt from Castle Rock Glacier. It flows through lakes such as Long View and Green before emptying into Granite. The water between the various lakes is worth fishing. This is good pocket water for brook and cutthroat trout. Nothing fancy is required here in the way of patterns, but pick something buoyant and visible, such as a Humpy or a Mohawk, in sizes 14 through 18.

Lake of the Winds. Good cutthroat water at almost 10,000 feet.
Photo by Don Pilotte

Lake of the Winds: This one is planted every eight years with cutthroats and is good fishing for fat trout. It was once planted with goldens, but they're long gone. It's 40 acres at almost 10,000 feet in barren, windy country. Hike about 3 miles from Fox Lake to Russell Lake to Marianne Lake and north to Lake of the Winds.

Line Lake: Line is very good for cutthroat that average a pound or more, but it's tough fishing because of the steady and hard winds. It's small, only 5 acres, and there's no place on it to escape the gales. You can reach it by going up Line Creek from the Beartooth Highway.

Little Falls Lake: Below Green Lake, it's 11 acres and over-populated with stunted brook trout that need to have their ranks thinned a bit.

Lone Elk Lake: Climb above Broadwater Lake, up beyond 10,000 feet. The lake is green from glacial flour and dark, high-contrast flies are consistently better than lighter ones in Lone Elk. A Timberline Emerger is one of the best patterns. Brookies to 16 inches and grayling over a pound do very well here.

Long Lake: This one is easy to drive to with a 4-wheel vehicle off U.S. 212. Wind 5 miles up the Goose Creek jeep trail to reach Long (and go another half mile to reach Ovis). It's filled with smallish brook trout and a few cutthroats that have washed down from Ovis Lake. Long is well named, stretching over a third of a mile, but covering only 12 surface acres.

Margaret Lake: Less than 4 acres, it's only a short jump from Vernon Lake. It's tough to fish from a brushy and soggy shoreline, but there are some large cutthroats swimming in here. This is a good spot to pack in a kick boat.

Moon Lake: Moon is well above 10,000 feet in barren rock and wind country in that Glacier Lake cluster. Ever try breathing at 10,000 feet? This is not the place for aerobics. Altitude sickness (with a throbbing headache being one of the first symptoms) is a possibility. Moon, at roughly 80 acres, is planted periodically with cutthroats that might reach 20 inches on rare occasions.

Ovis Lake: It's below Sheep Mountain, not far by jeep trail from Long Lake. It's the better of the two lakes, with bigger fish that average maybe 12 inches. It's a popular drive-to spot throughout the summer, but crowds disappear after Labor Day.

Red Lodge Creek: Followed by road all the way from Joliet to the confluence of the East and West Forks, Red Lodge has two distinct sections. The 15-mile stretch above Cooney Reservoir has undercut, brushy banks that hold plenty of brown trout. The fish run mostly between 10 and 15 inches, but there are bigger ones to 24 inches. The broad valley is good grasshopper country, and by late July patterns such as the Dave's Hopper and Henry's Fork Hopper are the most consistent midday producers. The lower stretch, below Cooney

Reservoir, is marginal fishing. It runs through open, grass and cottonwood country, too, but there are mainly trash fish, whitefish, and a few large brown trout here.

Rock Creek: It headwaters on the Beartooth Plateau in Wyoming and flows for 27 miles to the Clarks Fork near Joliet. There are five public access sites and it's fished quite a bit for browns, brookies, rainbows, and whitefish. Willows and cottonwoods line the banks, providing excellent cover that protects the fish and also eats a fly every now and then.

Rock Island Lake: Rock Island is planted from the air every three years with lots of cutthroats that grow to a couple of pounds. There are also some naturally sustaining (it's almost impossible to eradicate the vermin) brook trout. Reached from Cooke Pass, 7½ miles up the Crazy Lake Trail, the lake is 137 acres by 110 feet deep. It's known locally for big trout that are sometimes easy to catch and sometimes impossible to even find when they disappear into the deep.

Rough Lake: Rough Lake is over 100 acres, deep, high (over 10,000 feet), and not far from Lone Elk Lake. It is filled with nice brookies and pitifully small grayling that spawn in the clear gravels at the base of a waterfall.

Matt Quinn goes up there after the first snowfall of the autumn. "By late August, or September for sure, there'll be a squall that'll put new snow in the mountains, but after that we'll usually have a piece of nice weather. That's the time to go after the spawning brookies. The fish stack up thick at that waterfall at Rough, and I'll cast an egg pattern, usually an orange or yellow Krystal Egg, up into the spill and let it drift naturally back to me and my float tube. I'll get a lot of 10- to 13-inchers, but I'll also catch the occasional three-pounder."

Sliver Lake: Accessible from the Sky Top Creek Trail, in the Rough Lake area, it's only 7 acres and shallow; but Sliver Lake holds some big brook trout that wander down from Hunger Lake just upstream.

Sodalite Lake: Start at the Broadwater Creek Trail off U.S. 212, hike up past Curl Lake and Broadwater Lake, and after about 5 miles you'll reach Sodalite. This lake is in the Broadwater drainage at 9,840 feet, measures 26 acres by 90 feet deep, and is loaded with skinny, "starvin' Marvin" brook trout that grow to a big-headed 14 inches.

Triangle Lake: Triangle is managed for cutthroat trout on an eight-year cycle. These fish do well in this 6-acre pond (small but surprisingly deep at 35 feet). This is another of those "can't get there from here" waters—start at the West Fork Rock Creek Trail and with the aid of a compass and good topo maps head west to find Triangle.

Widewater Lake: Reached from the popular Crazy Lakes Trail off U.S. 212, it sits a half mile below Fox Lake. Widewater is about a 6½ mile hike. It holds good numbers of grayling, brookies, and cutthroats to a couple of pounds.

Zimmer Lake: Go to Broadwater Lake and hike 5 miles up the Broadwater River–Zimmer Creek Trail. It is 26 acres by 55 feet deep and sits not far from Grasshopper Glacier. It's planted every eight years with cutthroats that grow nicely from 2 inches to a couple of pounds even at this 10,000-plus-foot altitude.

Other Waters

Abandoned Lake: Brookies.

Alp Lake: Brookies and cutthroats.

Aquarius Lake: In out-of-the-way country about a half-dozen miles from Cooke City at over 9,000 feet. Drive east 3 miles from Cooke City and take the Sedge Creek Road to Kersey Lake. Hike up the inlet stream 2½ miles to Sedge Lake. With a compass, hike cross country northeast for a half mile to Aquarius. Your reward? Pretty scenery, solitude, and 12-inch cutthroats.

Arctic Lake: Barren.

Astral Lake: Brookies and New Age music.

Bald Knob Lake: Brookies.

Basin Creek Lakes: Small brookies.

Bear Creek: Too small.

Big Butte Lake: Barren.

Bob and Dick Lakes: A half mile upstream from Long Lake and moderately popular for brookies to 10 inches.

Bowback Lake: So many waters; so little time. It reputedly has cutthroats to three pounds. It's right near Triangle, just a quarter mile to the north, but since none of my friends sent out on scouting expeditions have found it yet, it looks like the fish in Bowback are safe for a little bit.

Broadwater Lake: Brookies and cutthroats.

Burnt Fork Creek: Too small.

Cliff Lake (Moccasin Lake): Brookies.

Cliff Lake (Farley Creek): Grayling.

Cloverleaf Lakes: Cutthroats.

Cole Creek: Too small.

Cottonwood Creek: Poor fishing.

Copeland Lake: Brookies really are a mixed blessing in this section of the state. They stunt out at 6 inches in Copeland (which is 8½ miles up the Elk Park-Big Basin Trail from U.S. 212).

Corner Lake: Cutthroats.

Crescent Lake: Brookies.

Curl Lake: Brookies and cutthroats.

Daly Lake: Brookies.

Derchemaker Pond: Private.

Dollar Lake: Cutthroats and grayling.

Dude Lake: Cutthroats and folks in garish cowboy shirts.

Elbow: Too small.

Farley Lake: Packed with 10- to 12-inch brook trout. It's 1 mile above Elaine Lake. Matt Quinn and his pack goat, Rufus, go up to this one to throw "as long of casts as possible, and then to bet if a small fly like a wet Renegade can make it all the way back." Both Matt and Rufus eat fish for breakfast up here.

Five Mile Creek: Poor fishing.

Gallery Lake: Rainbows.

Gertrude Lake: Brookies.

Golden Lake: Cutthroats.

Green Lake: Brookies.

Greenough Lake: Rainbows. It's easy to get to this shallow, 1 acre pond up the Rock Creek Road 15 miles out of Red Lodge; and the rainbows make a nice change for this region.

Grove Creek: Too small.

Harney Creek: Too small.

Hileman Pond: Posted.

Hogan Creek: Too small.

Hunt Creek: Too small.

Hunter Lake: Brookies and rainbows.

Jack Creek: Poor fishing.

Jordan Lake: Cuttroats.

Keyser Brown Lake: Brookies and cutthroats.

Lady of the Lake: Brookies and cutthroats.

Lady of the Lake Creek: Brookies.

Lake Fork Rock Creek: Drains Second Rock, First Rock, and Keyser Brown Lake. The section between First Rock and Keyser Brown is excellent fishing for brookies to 16 inches.

Leaky Raft Lake: Cutthroats. The raft is gone.

Lillis Lake: Brookies in this 4-acre, lily pad-choked pond just below Kersey Lake. It's good fishing early in the season, while there's still open water, for 10- to 12-inch trout.

Little (Washtub) Lake: Brookies.

Long View Lake: Cutthroats.

Lost Lake: Cutthroats.

Lower Aero Lake: Brookies and cutthroats.

Mariane (Morqaine) Lake: Brookies.

Marker Lake: Cutthroats.

Marsh Lake: Rainbows.

Martin Lake: Brookies.

Mary Lake: Brookies.

Moccasin Lake: Brookies.

Otter Lake: Brookies.

Production Lake: Brookies.

Queer Lake: Brookies.

Question Mark (Kidney) Lake: Brookies.

Recruitment Lake: Brookies.

Round Lake: Brookies.

Russell Creek: Brookies. The stretch between Russell Lake and Fox Lake is worth fishing for 8- to 10-inch fish.

Russell Lake: Brookies.

Second Hidden Lake: Brookies.

Second Rock Lake: It's just above First Rock Lake. The mix of brookies and cutthroats to one and a half pounds make this 26-acre lake a worthwhile destination.

Sedge Creek: Cutthroats.

Sedge Lake: Cutthroats and grayling.

September Morn Lake: Brookies.

Shelf Lake: Brookies.

Ship Lake: Brookies.

Silvertip Creek: Too small.

Skull Lake: Brookies.

Skytop Creek: Grayling.

Skytop Lakes: Grayling—marginal at best. These six lakes, a half mile up from Rough Lake, sit at 10,500 feet in elevation.

Sliderock Lake: Brookies.

Smethhurst Lake: Barren (this is actually one of the Hellroaring Lake chain).

Sodalite Creek: Brookies and cutthroats.

Star Creek: Brookies.

Star Lake: Cutthroats.

Stash Lake: Cutthroats.

Summerville Lake: Brookies.

Thiel (Tiel) Creek: Too small.

Thiel (Tiel) Lake: Brookies.

Timberline Lake: Brookies.

Upper Aero Lake: Cutthroats.

Vernon Lake: A quarter mile south of Lillis Lake. Just like Lillis it gets choked with lily pads and fishes best for 10- to 14-inch brook trout early or late in the season.

Wall Creek: Too small.

Wall Lake: Brookies.

Wapiti Lake: Brookies (another one of the Hellroaring Lake chain).

West Fork Broadwater River: Brookies.

West Fork Rock Creek: Brookies, browns, and rainbows.

West Red Lodge Creek: Brookies and browns.

Willow Creek: Brookies.

Wright Lake: Brookies.

■ *Special thanks to Matt Quinn, Ron Romanello, and Bailey Smith for their help on the Clarks Fork of the Yellowstone drainage.*

Gallatin River
Photo by Glenda Bradshaw

The Gallatin River is a nice place to spend a summer afternoon casting Wulffs of one color or another along the bankside runs, around midstream boulders or along bouncing riffles. The trout will be mostly rainbows and they will not often exceed 12 inches, but you'll catch plenty of them, and wading along the river as it dances over a colorful streambed on a warm July day is a simple pleasure.

This doesn't mean that there aren't good-size rainbows and browns in the 115 miles of river between Yellowstone National Park and the headwaters of the Missouri. Browns of over five pounds are taken each year, especially in autumn. Rainbows of similar size are also taken, usually by anglers working large nymphs along the bottoms of deep, fast runs.

Big fish are always a top attraction on Montana's rivers, but a day making short casts with an easy-to-see dry and taking fish without constant mending and reaching is a pleasing change of pace from the intense techniques often required to connect with the big boys. To escape the increasingly annoying levels of entomological Latin dogma that pervade some of the corners of fly fishing is a relief, too. The upper stretches of the Gallatin are the spots to view mountain vistas and striking cliff formations. And, since most of this river is within yards of U.S. 191, you just pull over to one side of the road, rig up, and start casting.

Boundary of Yellowstone Park to the Taylor's Fork—Upstream from the Taylor's Fork, the river is narrow, shallow, and often braided as it flows over a gravel streambed along willow-lined banks. The Madison and Gallatin ranges dominate the skyline. There are mainly rainbows with some browns in this water. The populations aren't high—just 350 trout per mile over 8 inches—but there are bigger fish in the scattered, deep holes. Find those holes and their concentrations of trout and this part of the river suddenly becomes a fine little fishery.

The wild part of the upper river that breaks away from the highway, and runs north and east, does have a good trail running up into the alpine headwaters and the mountains of Yellowstone. You will see moose, elk, deer, and perhaps a grizzly along the way through beautiful country.

Special fishing permits are required in Yellowstone National Park.

73

For some reason, I seem to take the most trout in this small water on soft-hackled patterns cast quartering upstream and then pulsed lightly just below the surface, especially in the bankside runs and through the sapphire pools. A 10-incher is a trophy, but the casting is rewarding if only for the fact that you are alive in pristine mountain terrain.

Taylor's Fork to Gallatin Gateway—Mark well the location of the Taylor's Fork (actually called Taylor Creek on the topographical maps). It is a major tributary and it, more than anything else on the river, controls the fishing downstream from its mouth.

The problem is the exposed banks and cliffs on the Taylor's Fork. These natural formations dump gray soup into the water with any high runoff or even a good rain. The silt stays suspended and washes far down into the main Gallatin. Fly fishing suddenly turns nearly impossible for days at a time. During the high-water months of May through early July the river is entirely "mudded out."

From the Taylor's Fork down to Gallatin Gateway, there are populations of rainbows up to 5,000 fish per mile in some sections. Fish average about 12 inches with some of several pounds holding in the deeper water or under banks. The salmon fly hatch comes off in June. After this, terrestrials play well in the summer, and there are also caddisflies from June into fall. Hoppers, beetles, and ants cover the warm weather action, but these "occasional" terrestrials are over-shadowed (as is every other food item) by one of the best spruce moth populations in the state.

The spruce moths flop down on the water by the millions in this forested, canyon stretch of the river during a good year from July through August. This is mass suicide—this is not the occasional, accidental blow-in. The insects don't belong on the water, and once their powdery, scaled wings get wet they are trapped on the surface. These chunky, size-10 bugs are too much to ignore for even the best trout. Suddenly the river is producing 14- to 20-inch rainbows and browns on dry flies instead of the 10-inchers.

The trout feed on the spruce moths for weeks at a stretch and then suddenly do become selective. It's time to put away the Wulffs and the Humpies and tie on a matching, size-10 or -12 Spruce Moth.

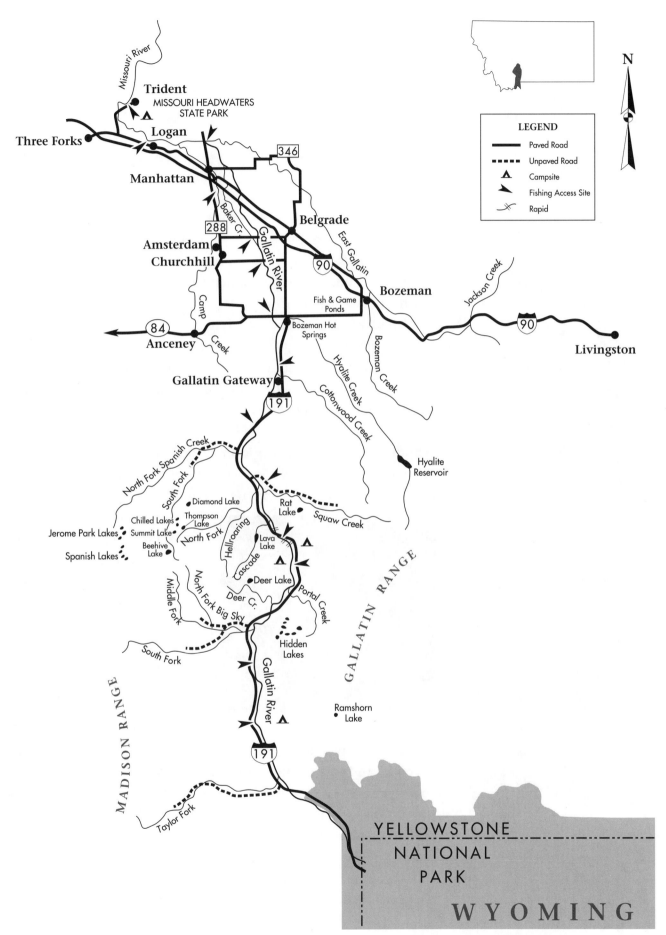

N

LEGEND
Paved Road
Unpaved Road
Campsite
Fishing Access Site
Rapid

Missouri River

Trident
MISSOURI HEADWATERS
STATE PARK

Three Forks

Logan

346

Manhattan

288

Baker Cr.

Belgrade

East Gallatin

90

Amsterdam

Churchhill

Gallatin River

Bozeman

Jackson Creek

Fish & Game
Ponds

84

Camp Creek

Bozeman Hot
Springs

Bozeman Creek

90

Livingston

Anceney

Gallatin Gateway

Hyalite Creek

Cottonwood Creek

191

Hyalite
Reservoir

North Fork Spanish Creek

South Fork

Diamond Lake

Rat
Lake

Squaw Creek

Chilled Lakes

Thompson
Lake

Jerome Park Lakes

Summit Lake

North Fork

Hellroaring

Lava
Lake

Beehive
Lake

Spanish Lakes

Cascade

GALLATIN RANGE

Middle Fork

North Fork Big Sky

Deer Cr.

Deer Lake

Portal Creek

South Fork

Hidden
Lakes

Gallatin River

MADISON RANGE

Ramshorn
Lake

191

Taylor Fork

YELLOWSTONE
NATIONAL
PARK

WYOMING

A Special Fly for the Gallatin River

Most anglers realize how important terrestrials are throughout Montana during the summer and fall months. Look in any fly box and there are probably grasshopper imitations (the most popular in the state, in order, are Joe's Hopper, Dave's Hopper, Schroeder Hopper, and Henry's Fork Hopper). In a really well-stocked box there are usually some ant imitations (McMurray Ant, Foam Ant, Deer Hair Ant), and beetle imitations (Crowe Beetle, Foam Beetle, Mohawk). What's usually missing is a specific Spruce Moth imitation.

SPRUCE MOTH

Hook: standard dry fly

Body: cream or ginger mink fur (dubbed thick and rough)

Wing: light elk hair (flared)

Head: the flared tips of the elk hair (trimmed to shape)

You will find the occasional spruce moth on most Montana waters, but heavy concentrations occur along stream banks lined with pine trees. The canyon stretch of the Gallatin has some of the "best" infestations (other fine spruce moth streams include Rock Creek and the Thompson River west of the Divide and the Sun and the Smith east of the Divide). When you find these moths flopping on the water, you will need this imitation very badly.

And it's time to stop the blind casting and start stalking the trout making the biggest, slurping rise forms.

Gary LaFontaine, in *Trout Flies*, wrote, "Chuck Xue told me about catching a 20-inch brown during a spruce moth fall on the Gallatin. The fish was bleeding badly from an injured gill and couldn't be revived. Chuck kept it. He examined the stomach contents, the entire digestive track gorged and distended, and counted over 150 spruce moths in this one trout. The fish, from the time the hatch started until he was caught, couldn't have been feeding more than two hours."

Throughout the summer, if the fish aren't up on dry flies, try a weighted stonefly nymph. Just about any pattern will do, as long as it's black and has rubber legs.

Gallatin Gateway to Gallatin Forks—There are good and bad stretches on this part of the Gallatin. Sections of it are sucked dry every year for irrigation. Anyone crossing over the river on Interstate

90 in August must wonder about the bed of rocks. The dewatered areas never recover insect and fish populations from season to season.

The valley portion of the river in general is much slower and warmer than the upper river, which stays in the 60-degree range even in July and August, and the lower river offers much richer habitat wherever there's continual flow. Over 1,000 rainbows in the 12- to 14-inch range and an equal number of browns running to 18 inches were discovered in one survey. There are also very large browns that will come to large streamers in the fall. Try twitching sculpin patterns of 1/0 and 2/0 along the bottom and over the rocks to goad the browns into taking.

If you are in an aggressive mood and feel up to some challenging work, put on a short, stout leader at the end of a quick-sinking line and a large nymph, like Charles Brooks' Assam Dragon, and probe the depths of some racy, deep run. To fish water like this properly you must cross well above the run so that you cast from just short of midstream. You will be in fast water well over your knees right next to even faster water over your shoulders. Fall here and you'll likely wind up rolling all the way to the dried out, lower river.

With a 6- or 7-weight sinking line, a 4- or 5-foot leader tapering to a delicate tippet in 1X or 0X, a size-4 Assam Dragon or a size-2 Girdle Bug, a lead twist-on or two (far-and-fine fishing at its delicate best), and a 9-foot rod, you begin your exploration of this deep, rough-water environment. Actually, this is not as awkward or as difficult as it may seem and the technique works very well on all similar waters throughout Montana.

Starting at the head of the run, cast the contraption about twenty feet upstream, allowing it to sink to the bottom, and work right through the run. Keep the slightest bit of slack in the line, but not so much that you can't feel, see, and sense (this comes on rapidly with experience) the nymph bouncing along the gravel and rounded rocks of the streambed. When a good trout hits here it will be a vicious strike as the fish zips up after the food and then powers straight back to cover. You'll know when this happens.

At the end of the drift, allow the fly to swing in the current for a few seconds, enough time to take out the belly that accumulated in the line as it fought the many conflicting currents in the water column. On occasion a big boy will hammer the fly at the last moment. A half-dozen casts or more are needed to work a stretch thoroughly before lengthening the cast a few feet and repeating the procedure.

The Gallatin's exceptional whitewater makes it a popular destination for serious whitewater enthusiasts.
Photo by Stan Bradshaw

POPULAR FLIES

Adams Parachute

Baetis Wulff

Bitch Creek

Olive Comparadun

Disco Midge

George's Brown Stone

Girdle Bug

Goddard Caddis

Griffith's Gnat

Matuka Spruce

Muddler Minnow

Olive Gold Ribbed Hare's Ear

Pheasant Tail

Prince Nymph

Serendipity

Shroud

Spent Partridge Caddis

Timberline Emerger

Twist Nymph

Woolly Bugger

Yuk Bug

Zonker

Gallatin Forks downstream to the Missouri River—From the Gallatin Forks, where the East Gallatin empties in, down to Three Forks the river runs through mostly private land. Floating is allowed in this section and it is the best way to cast to a nice balance of rainbows and browns. For wading anglers the bridges are the main public access in this section. There are soft, limestone walls where the water digs out deep, swirling holes. Trout hang in these pools and feed on good hatches of Pale Morning Duns, Tricos, and Blue-Winged Olives—in this spring-creek-like environment the Gallatin suddenly becomes a more technical river.

The best times of the year to fish the Gallatin are before the runoff in late spring and just after the runoff subsides and the water begins to compress. During the earlier period, in March and April, the river is in superb condition. It might muddy up on warm days, but it stays clear and fishes well on nymphs on cool days. Patterns such as the Prince Nymph and George's Brown Stone produce well anywhere on the river.

During the later period, after runoff, a dark-colored streamer, like a Woolly Bugger, snaked through the rocks and along the bottom near shore or through the heart of strong runs, can turn some very big fish in the middle to lower sections of the Gallatin.

Autumn means big browns on the spawning move. This translates into streamer and nymphs, like Zonkers, Muddler Minnows, Matuka Spruces, Bitch Creeks, Girdle and Yuk Bugs, and of course, Buggers. If you're floating below the confluence with the East Gallatin, cast one of these bank-tight and let it drift with a little action, or cast it to shore and quickly strip it back to the raft. When wading, cast upstream or work your way out into the river and cast to shore. Felt-soled waders help on the slippery rocks, as does a wading staff at times.

Blue-Winged Olives also provide some action, especially during the hatches on overcast or rainy autumn afternoons. A greased olive Hare's Ear covers some emerging activity. Baetis Wulffs are nice, easy-to-see selections, as are light and dark olive Comparaduns, for the adult insects.

Wherever and whenever you decide to fish on the upper river, the choices you make will not be disappointing. Because this water is closed to fishing from boats, it's perfect wading water. If you have the means to float, the lower river gives an added bonus of some truly large trout. The Gallatin is a fine trout stream in all aspects—scenery, water quality, and numbers of catchable fish.

Fishing Waters in the Gallatin Drainage

Baker Creek: This is an agrarian, small stream out in the open not far from Manhattan that has a decent run of brown trout in the fall, plus fair numbers of resident rainbows and browns. It is touched at various spots by a county road.

Beehive Lake: Beehive is a 3-acre hole that is an amazing 70 feet deep in places. Obviously, there are real steep drop-offs in this pond. It lies at over 9,000 feet, a mile hike up from the Spanish Lakes (a 9-mile hike from the end of Spanish Creek Road). It's fairly popular even though there's only average fishing for average-sized Yellowstone cutthroats.

Benhart Creek: This fine, spring-fed water has brookies, browns, and rainbows in good numbers with some size, but the surrounding land around Belgrade is being cut up, subdivided, posted, and made more or less off-limits for most fly fishers.

Benhart is well known for its difficult trout. This is spring creek fishing at its most technical; it will make you start babbling Latin or discoursing on the qualities of 8X versus 7X, or wondering what you would ever do with a fly larger than size 20. The Pale Morning Duns, the Tricos, and the Blue-Winged Olives are all important on this stream, but for really fussy fishing try matching the Tiny Blue-Winged Olives, the size-24 *Pseudocloeon* mayflies that start blanketing the water in September.

Camp Creek: This heavily-posted stream is in the Gallatin Valley. It enters the main river near Manhattan. In the last 7 miles there is a lot of irrigation seepage draining into it, turning Camp into a spring creek of sorts. There is good brown and rainbow trout fishing if you can get on it from county roads. Landowners sometimes grant permission to fish.

Chilled Lakes: Hike up the North Fork Hellroaring Creek trail to Thompson Lake and then to 3-acre, lower Chilled Lake a quarter mile away. It's in the Spanish Peaks at more than 9,000 feet, and there's good fishing, augmented by periodic plants, for cutthroats that might average 12 inches in a good year.

Deer Lake: Deer Lake is in a glacial cirque above 9,000 feet. The Deer Creek trail starts right off Montana 191 on the west side of the road about 20 miles south of Gallatin Gateway. It's a 5-mile hike to 7-acre Deer Lake, which has good numbers of grayling that reach a foot or so. They have moments when they display suicidal tendencies towards small dry flies—size 20 and down. Effective patterns include tiny versions of the Griffith's Gnat, Shroud, Adams Parachute, and Spent Partridge Caddis.

Diamond Lake: Everyone has to walk the last leg into this lake—the trail is too rough for horses. Go up the South Fork Spanish Creek trail for 5 miles, then cross country for about 2 miles to a small, deep lake that has some very big rainbows that are tough to catch but have been known to hit a slowly sinking fly.

Guy Kline has caught trout to six-and-a-half pounds by "hanging a small, unweighted nymph, a pattern like a Disco Midge, Twist Nymph, or Serendipity, under an indicator and letting it bob up and down on the wind chop. Sometimes I've fished one 'cast' an hour before I got a strike on Diamond."

East Gallatin River: The East Gallatin drains both the Gallatin and Bridger mountains and flows for almost 40 miles to the main river near Manhattan. Most of the stream runs through private hay fields but there is public access here and there, so once you're on the water, if you stay below the high water marks, you can fish to your heart's content. The river has good populations of aquatic insects because of the nutrients that enter the spring-fed water from the fields. Hoppers and other terrestrials are also present in significant quantities. The upper dozen miles are mainly rainbow water. The lower stretches are brushy with undercut banks, providing excellent habitat for both resident and spawning brown trout that average 13 inches and run into several pounds. Streamers take the fish in autumn, and hoppers are productive from midsummer until the first succession of killing frosts. The hoppers will still work for a week or so after this period. The fish don't know any better. *Baetis* sometimes draw the trout to the surface in the afternoons in the spring and fall.

Fish and Game Headquarters Ponds: These three ponds are located just north of the old headquarters in Bozeman and planted with some huge, extraneous brood stock of rainbows and some brookies. Not wilderness fishing to be sure, but a curiosity that can turn up a trophy trout. Try a Purina Fish Chow, size 12.

East Gallatin River
Photo by A. Schlechten
Courtesy of the Montana Historical Society, Helena

Hidden Lakes: Reached from the Portal Creek Road, there are eight lakes in all, lying at close to 9,000 feet. Several of the lakes have goldens ranging from a few inches to several pounds. The big ones are hard to catch unless they have moved into the connecting streams. When they're in the streams, a large, weighted Muddler or other streamer pattern worked across their noses will provoke strikes. The little goldens will take nymphs and dries worked near shore or along outlets. Goddard Caddis works well in the outlets.

Hyalite Creek: Hyalite flows from Hyalite Reservoir for 23 miles across an alluvial fan to the main river near Belgrade. The upper reaches, also known as Middle Creek, are good pocket water with Wulffs and Humpies and such for rainbows, cutthroats, brookies, and even grayling and a very few browns. The lower reaches are not all that great, except for an occasional fat brown in the fall. Sculpin patterns lobbed to the banks and bounced along the rubble and muck will do the trick.

Hyalite Reservoir: South of Bozeman in a timbered canyon it's about 200 acres when not drawn down 30 feet or more. You can reach it by road. There is a boat ramp. Yellowstone cutthroats grow big here and there are grayling that approach a couple of pounds. Thirty thousand cutthroats are planted each year to keep the numbers of fish up in the face of extreme angling pressure of all disciplines. Summer often sees a good hatch of Panther Martins.

"Environmental Forestry" in the
West Fork drainage
Photo by Stan Bradshaw

Jackson (Rocky) Creek: Jackson forms the East Gallatin River when it joins Kelley Creek. Good fishing for small brookies, cutthroats, and rainbows, plus a few decent browns in the lower reaches in the fall.

Jerome Lakes: These three lakes are at nearly 9,000 feet in the Madison Range up Falls Creek. You reach them from either the South Fork Spanish Creek trail or up from the Jack Creek campground. None of the lakes is over 5 acres and they provide fair fishing for average cutthroats, with an occasional trout to a few pounds.

Lava Lake: Perhaps 20 acres, it's up Cascade Creek. It has rainbows of about 10 inches and a few to a couple of pounds that cruise the drop-offs in search of stray nymphs and small drys.

Mystic Lake: Mystic has lake trout, brookies, and cutthroats to a few pounds. This 8-square-mile lake used to be closed because it is the water supply for Bozeman. You can reach it on foot from the end of the road up Sourdough Creek.

Ramshorn Lake: You reach this one by trail from the end of the Buffalo Horn Creek road. It has good fishing for foot-long cutthroat trout that see a lot of flies, lures, and bait.

Rat Lake: Made famous (or infamous) in *A View from Rat Lake* by John Gierach. It's up Squaw Creek. Rat Lake is 18 acres and shallow. It's really popular because of rainbows that exceed five pounds. If you can lug a float tube in here, try working damsel or dragonfly nymphs tight to the aquatic plants. Let the nymphs sink and then crawl them back along the bottom. Slow, tedious work, but this will take the big trout. Other favorite nymph patterns for near-surface work include the Timberline Emerger, Pheasant Tail, and Twist Nymph.

South Fork Spanish Creek: This is a good mountain stream with plenty of pocket water holding brook trout to perhaps 12 inches but averaging smaller. Beaver ponds hold the best fish.

Spanish Lakes: These two lakes in Spanish Peaks country are less than 10 acres, but have some Yellowstone cutthroats to 15 inches or a bit larger.

Squaw Creek: Squaw Creek is followed by road and trail into timbered mountain country. It's good fast-water dry fly and nymph fishing for cutthroats, rainbows, and brookies. A wet fly worked through the pools near the main current seams will also take fish. Some browns head up the lower reaches in autumn.

Summit Lake: This one has some fat cutthroat trout in its 1.5 acres. To reach Summit, take a long walk up the North Fork Hellroaring Creek trail.

Taylor Fork Gallatin River: Taylor Fork is followed by a lousy gravel and dirt road that winds and lurches past the Nine Quarter Circle Guest Ranch, then on to Taylor Falls (the last couple of miles by trail). The stretches by the ranch and down to U.S. 191 are heavily fished by dudes, but some nice rainbows, cutthroats, and a stray brookie or two can be taken with stealth. Use wet flies or nymphs around the large rocks and boulders or along the brushy banks. The same holds true for very few browns

The upper Taylor Fork is home to fat cutthroats.
Photo by Stan Bradshaw

83

in the fall. A pretty, easy-to-wade, open, sage-brush country trout stream with some nice mosquitoes in June and July. Hoppers play well here in the heat. The upper reaches can be good for fat cutthroats to 10 inches.

Thompson Lake: Thompson is in the Spanish Peaks area and gets hit hard by pack strings and hikers. Can you say "Woodstock"? All in all, there is still some fair fishing for cutthroats that average less than a foot.

West Fork of the Gallatin River: This used to be one of the prettiest little trout streams in the West, but the Big Sky development killed that off. Gone now are the wide-open sage benches and brushy runs that were filled with cutthroats, rainbows, and brookies that loved any type of dry fly they could clamp their jaws on. Now there are condos and paved roads and hotels and ski runs and poor fishing. Can you say "trashed"?

Other Waters

Arden Lake: Cutthroats.

Asbestos Creek: Barren.

Asbestos Lake: Barren.

Bacon Rind Creek: Too small.

Bear Creek: Rainbows.

Bear Lakes: Cutthroats.

Beaver Creek: Rainbows.

Beaver Creek Lakes: Cutthroats.

Big Bear Creek: Cutthroats.

Big Bear Lake: Cutthroats.

Big Brother Lake: Cutthroats and rainbows.

Bluff Lake: Cutthroats.

Bozeman (Sourdough) Creek: Brookies and rainbows.

Bridger Creek: Brookies, browns, cutthroats, and rainbows.

Buck Creek: Cutthroats and rainbows.

Buffalo Horn Creek: Rainbows.

Buffalo Horn (Fish) Lakes: Cutthroats.

Cache Creek: Cutthroats.

Cascade Lakes: Rainbows.

Chiquita Lakes: Cutthroats.

Cottonwood Creek: Brookies.

Crystal Lake: Cutthroats.

Deer Creek: Too small.

Dry Creek: Brookies, browns, and rainbows.

Dudley Creek: Brookies.

East Fork Hyalite Creek: Not open until mid-July.

Emerald Lake: Cutthroats and grayling.

Falls Creek: Cutthroats.

Fall Creek Lake: Cutthroats.

Flanders Lake: Rainbows.

Godfrey Canyon Creek: Poor fishing.

Golden Trout Lakes: Goldens.

Grayling Lake: Grayling.

Heather Lake: Cutthroats and grayling.

Hellroaring Creek: Rainbows.

Hermit Lake: Cutthroats.

Hyalite Lake: Cutthroats and rainbows.

Kelly Canyon Creek: Too small.

Lake Solitude: Cutthroats.

Lightning Creek: Cutthroats and rainbows.

Little Hellroaring Creek: Too small.

Little Wapiti Creek: Rainbows.

Lizard Lakes: Cutthroats.

Lower Falls Creek: Cutthroats.

Marcheta Lake: Rainbows.

Meadow Creek: Poor access.

Mirror Lake: Cutthroats.

Moon Lake: Rainbows.

North Fork Spanish Creek: Brookies.

Pass Creek: Too small.

Pine Lake: Cuttroats and cutthroat/rainbow hybrids.

Pioneer Lakes: Cutthroats.

Porcupine Creek: Browns, rainbows, and whitefish.

Ray (Rey) Creek: Posted.

Reese Creek: Posted.

Sage Creek: Too small.

Slide Lake: Rainbows.

Smith Creek: Browns and rainbows.

South Cottonwood Creek: Posted.

South Fork of West Fork Gallatin River: Cutthroats.

Spanish Creek: Brookies, browns, and rainbows.

Specimen Creek: Too small.

Spring Branch of the South Fork Ross Creek: Posted.

Spring Creek: Brookies, cutthroats, and rainbows.

Swan Creek: Cutthroats and rainbows.

Teepee Creek: Too small.

Thompson Creek: Posted.

Timberline Creek: Too small.

Upper Falls Creek Lake: Cutthroats.

Wapiti Creek: Rainbows.

West Fork Hyalite Creek: Brookies, cutthroats, and grayling.

■ *Special thanks to Bob Blevins, David Howe, Guy Kline, and A. W. Slominski for their help on the Gallatin drainage.*

Jefferson River Canyon
Courtesy of the Montana Historical Society, Helena

T H E   J E F F E R S O N

Any fly fisher familiar with the Jefferson River immediately thinks of brown trout lying tight to brushy banks that line a meandering river of large holes connected by deep, dark runs that are fed by shallow riffles running swiftly over gravel bars and drop-offs.

Logjams, cottonwoods, undercut grassy shorelines, narrow canyon stretches, and wide-open country studded with the isolated Tobacco Root Mountains on the east and the Highland Range off in the west complete the picture.

Formed at the confluence of the Beaverhead and Big Hole rivers with a nice assist from the Ruby just upstream, the Jefferson runs 80 miles until it joins the Madison and Gallatin rivers to form the Missouri. Over 200 feet wide for much of its length, the Jefferson can be divided into three general sections—the upper river between Twin Bridges and Cardwell, the canyon stretch, and the final lower river pitch downstream from Sappington Bridge to Trident.

Most of those who float or wade the river concentrate their efforts on the upper river which has a faster flow, relatively speaking, than the rest of the river. This portion has the most catchable trout per mile and is considered the best water. Browns outnumber rainbows by about seven to one with an average size of just under 15 inches. This brown-to-rainbow ratio holds up pretty well for most of the water. There are also large numbers of mountain whitefish that are always on the lookout for a nymph bounced along the bottom. Current regulations allow anglers to keep five browns, but the action is strictly catch-and-release for rainbows, which are making slow inroads on the population dynamics of the Jefferson.

The river braids a good deal up here and the current scours gravel sufficiently to attract fair numbers of spawning browns in the fall.

Probably the best times to work the Jefferson are from April through mid-July, using large nymphs like the Prince or Montana. Allow time off to let the spring runoff to have its way. As soon as the water begins to lower and clear, pound the current seams and buckets (convergences of varying speeds of water) with Woolly Buggers, Girdle Bugs, Matukas, and similar large patterns. Some of the best action of the season takes place on the Jefferson and most other rivers in the western third of the state during this week-long-or-so period of compression.

From September through the cold of November, diehard anglers work the river for large spawning browns that will top five pounds. If you're willing to heave large (1/0 or 2/0) Matuka Sculpins, you'll turn some impressive trout with sink-tip lines cast quartering upstream along the banks, and then working the sculpin along the bottom rocks and gravel. Lobbing the heavy stuff slightly sidearm avoids potential mid-flight collisions between weighted streamer and skull. The casting can be tedious, but if you work the stretches of the river that are flushed clear of irrigation silt you will normally take several hefty browns. Dead sculpins, with mouth-shaped chunks missing from their sides, are not an uncommon sight in the still water near shore. Fishing Matukas is not the thrill-a-second angling in the caddis falls of evening, but the browns you connect with are worth the effort.

While weighted streamers and sink-tip lines are usually the most effective approach for browns, there are periods when the trout hold near the surface—under banks, just below foam eddies or beneath logjams. A pattern retrieved along the bottom may miss these trout entirely. A floating line with an unweighted Bugger or similar fly cast line-tight across stream, then dead drifted or twitched slightly, often spells the difference between few, if any, browns and steady action. Allow the streamer to swing out with the current and flutter at the end of the line for a few seconds. Big trout often snap at the fly as it hangs suspended in the river's current. When the usual, down-deep, quickly-stripped approach proves unproductive, thirty minutes playing around with this variation is often useful.

State fishing access sites and bridges on county roads provide access to the upper river.

For the floater, several large irrigation diversions present potential hazards that require caution and often a brief portage. From a mile above Ironrod Bridge to below Silver Star, irrigation diversions can lead to extremely low water levels in the summer. In the drought of 1988, the river was sucked almost bone dry with miles of stre-

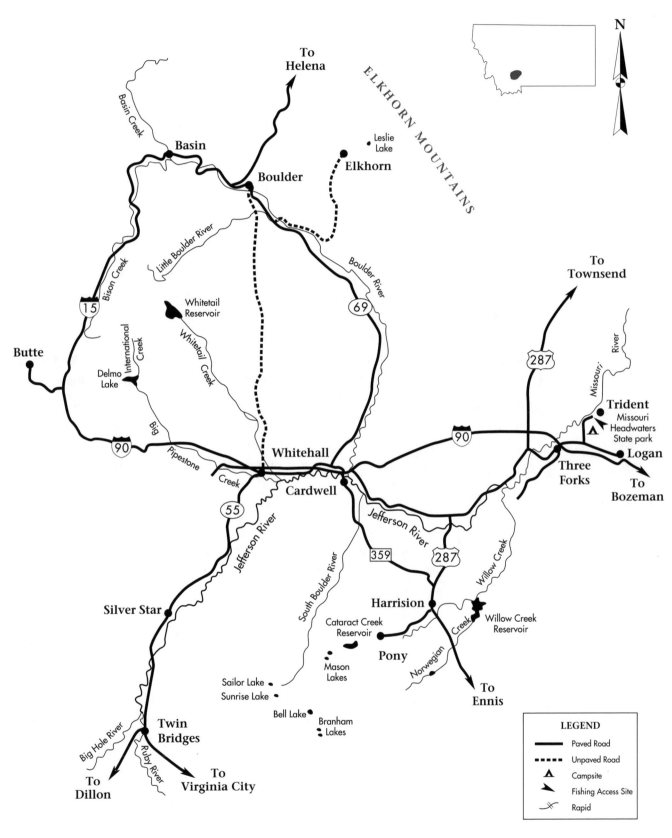

N

To Helena

ELKHORN MOUNTAINS

Leslie Lake

Basin Creek

Basin

Boulder

Elkhorn

Little Boulder River

Bison Creek

15

Whitetail Reservoir

Boulder River

69

Butte

International Creek

Whitetail Creek

Delmo Lake

To Townsend

287

Missouri River

Big

90

Pipestone

Whitehall

Creek

Cardwell

Trident
Missouri Headwaters State park

Logan

90

Three Forks

To Bozeman

55

Jefferson River

Jefferson River

South Boulder River

359

287

Willow Creek

Silver Star

Harrision

Cataract Creek Reservoir

Willow Creek Reservoir

Pony

Mason Lakes

Creek

Norwegian

To Ennis

Sailor Lake
Sunrise Lake

Bell Lake

Branham Lakes

Big Hole River

Twin Bridges

Ruby River

To Dillon

To Virginia City

LEGEND

Paved Road

Unpaved Road

Campsite

Fishing Access Site

Rapid

89

ambed exposed to the sun. How sufficient numbers of trout survived to repopulate the river is something of a mystery and a minor natural miracle. Irrigation damages much of the river, and in dry years, some potentially top-notch tributaries. When the water is returned to the riverbed, it is often choked with silt and chemicals and warmed to near lethal levels. Another diversion to watch for is at Guy George Bridge near Waterloo.

The canyon stretch of the river below (east of) Cardwell is quite deep and slow. Along here you can get to the river both from the road and from railroad tracks. The fishing is often good because cliffs shelter the river from the sun during the dog days of summer.

The trout run about an inch or so smaller in the lower section of the Jefferson. U.S. 10 and a couple of campgrounds provide access. An abandoned limestone quarry and the last, crumbling vestiges of an old wooden flume used to transport water to nearby mining operations in the early 1900s are visible on the limestone walls. Full-sinking lines with big nymphs and streamers dredging the bottom are the best play.

The lower Jefferson runs over a gravel and small-rock bottom through fields of hay. Towering cottonwoods line the banks. The first part of this section is mostly one channel, but the river braids wildly between Three Forks and the Missouri Headwaters State Park, creating some navigational problems for floaters. During low water, you can drag your boat as much as you row it along here. Aluminum canoes can be heard for miles as they bang along the rocky streambed. Trout tend to shy from this cacophony. Hopper and beetle patterns are prime selections during the summer days, especially along the hay fields.

Work the undercuts and clear gravel areas of this part of the river. Yuk Bugs, Girdle Bugs, and Bitch Creeks are local favorites, though many anglers prefer drys from size 10 to 16. This approach makes sense in low, clear water conditions because the drys are less likely to be spotted for fakes than are the submarine-sized streamers.

POPULAR FLIES

Adams

Bitch Creek

Clouser Deep Minnow

Elk Hair Caddis

Girdle Bug

Humpy

Matuka Sculpin

Montana Nymph

Pink Cahill

Prince Nymph

Renegade

Trude

Woolly Bugger

Wulff

Yuk Bug

Some obvious picks include Elk Hair Caddis in sizes 14 to 16, especially on overcast days and in the evenings in spring and fall, and, because of the slow current, some Callibaetis in the warm months. Adams, PMDs, Blue-Winged Olives, Callibaetis Thorax, and perhaps a Pink Cahill for the sake of impulse, work well in the early morning and along about dusk.

In the riffles, attractors like Wulffs, Trudes, Renegades, and the durable Humpy bring the trout up with some regularity. Most anglers use these patterns in size 12 and smaller. During bright light conditions on hot afternoons, try size 8 or 10. The big, bushy, imitation has a bit more appeal for the fish. On overcast days, try a Gray Wulff. Actually, large nymphs bounced along these riffles is the most productive technique, if you don't mind catching a crazed whitefish every now and then.

While floating the Jefferson is usually an all-day affair, wading presents problems that are borderline insurmountable on many sections. The river has steep banks and is too deep in many areas to wade comfortably or even safely. Choose your entrances and beats with care or you'll wind up totally soaked. With a little scouting and caution, there are runs that can be fished adequately on foot, even from the banks.

The Jefferson River doesn't have the reputation of many other streams in the state, in part because it doesn't have the classic fast-water riffles of the Madison or the pods of large feeding trout found on the Missouri or Bighorn. The action is often slower with fewer trout. In this open valley you can bake in the summer sun or freeze in an autumn snow squall that howls through your clothing.

Regardless of these conditions, the fact remains that the Jefferson is a pretty good river if you like to hunt brown trout with an occasional rainbow thrown in for good measure.

JEFFERSON RIVER

Fishing Waters
in the Jefferson Drainage

Bell Lake: This one is 18 acres at almost 9,000 feet. It's east of Thompson Peak and reached by trail for cutthroats of about a foot.

Big Pipestone Creek: Big Pipestone begins as the outlet of Delmo Lake and is followed by county road for 20 miles to the Jefferson near Whitehall. Good brown trout fishing in the lower reaches in autumn and there are some cutthroats in the upper section.

Bison Creek: Heading northeast of Butte not far from Elk Park Pass, Bison runs mainly north for over 15 miles to the Boulder River near Basin. The upper section flows through open fields with small rainbows and brook trout. The canyon stretch is tough to fish but has some trout. The final section is silted up and hard-hit by local anglers for mainly put-and-take rainbows.

Boulder River: This was once a quality trout stream, but heavy-metal pollution from mining has choked the streambed and killed off much streamside vegetation that used to offer shelter for the browns. Stream alteration and cattle stomping along the riparian areas add to the woes of this little river. The upper 17 miles above Bison Creek are the best water, with over 1,500 brook trout per mile averaging about 9 inches with a few to 15. Dry flies worked tight to bankside cover take the trout, as do wets fished through the same locations. Try dead drifts, then some action, and finally allow the pattern to hold in the current, undulating from side to side at the end of a drift.

The stretch below Bison Creek runs through a canyon that is poor habitat due to the steep gradient and pollution. The upper part of this water is fair for rainbows and brookies. Nymphs down deep work best. Below severely polluted High Ore Creek trout all but disappear.

The final 50 miles down to the Jefferson at Cardwell is mainly brown trout water with perhaps as many as 3,000 catchable fish per mile. Once again, metal contamination plus high water temperatures combine to slow growth rates and depress trout numbers. The last few miles of the river are flushed to some extent by springs and small creeks. Browns are found at well over 1,000 per mile. Unfortunately, most of the best water flows through private land and is posted. You need to wade a good piece to reach the best fishing. A run of large browns heads upstream in the fall, but the fish are blocked by an irrigation diversion, which has led to the closure of four "airline" miles of the river up from Cardwell after September 30.

The upper run is paralleled by I-15 and the lower part is followed by Montana 69. An interesting sidelight of dubious distinction lies just to the west as you look back from the river's mouth along I-90. A mining company has blasted and hauled away the entire eastern face of Dry Mountain. And we all thought ants were industrious.

Branham Lakes: These two lakes are less than 20 acres each in the Tobacco Roots at over 9,000 feet. They're managed now for Lake DeSmet rainbows that grow to a couple of pounds on occasion.

Cataract Creek Reservoir: Southwest of the ghost town of Pony, where you can score an ice cream cone on a hot summer's day, this one is about 30 feet deep by 160 acres in open foothill country with brookies and rainbows that may top a few pounds on good days.

Delmo Reservoir: Delmo is west of Whitehall up the Big Pipestone Creek Road. Deep, but drawn down a lot in summer for irrigation, it has a boat ramp. It's fair fishing for rainbows and bunches of Yellowstone cutthroats planted each year. A few reach several pounds and are sometimes taken on nymphs and streamers by the creek inlets.

International Creek: Some good rainbows are taken in the lower reaches above Delmo Lake on drys in this small stream.

Leslie Lake: Leslie is about nine acres and fairly deep in a glacial cirque below Crow Peak. A rough 6-mile jeep road from the ghost town of Elkhorn goes within three-quarters of a mile of the lake. It's fished a good deal but is still quite decent for cutthroats up to three pounds and averaging a bit less than a foot.

For the larger fish try a Clouser Deep Minnow, a butter yellow variation to match the coloration of the small cutthroats. Work the drop-offs around the edges by wading out and casting as parallel as possible to the depth line.

Little Boulder River: This one heads below Haystack Mountain and joins the main river southeast of Boulder. The lower willow-lined stretches have nice browns and brook trout. The upper section provides fishing for rainbows and cutthroats holding in the headwaters.

Mason Lakes: Not too far from Pony in the Tobacco Roots, both are less than 5 acres, dammed, and reached by trail for fair catches of rainbows. You'll do well if you are up to lugging a light-weight float tube into the ponds.

Norwegian Creek: It flows to Willow Creek reservoir 8 miles through open, hilly country, including some beaver ponds, for nice rainbows, some brookies, and a few good browns. You can get to it by county road. Make sure you check your regulations on this one—it's only open from the third Saturday in June to protect the spawning rainbows.

Sailor lake: Reached by rough road up the South Fork, Sailor is a dozen acres, fairly deep and periodically good fishing for brookies and rainbows.

South Boulder River: You'll find classic pocket water in the upper reaches of this 20-mile stream that heads above Mammoth. Brookies and rainbows nail Wulffs, Renegades, and Humpies in the fast water, and there are some nice browns in the lower, slower private reaches.

Sunrise Lake: In the Tobacco Root Mountains at 9,300 feet in a glacial cirque, this small lake has good numbers of eager cutthroats in the 12-inch range.

Whitetail Creek: Whitetail heads a dozen miles east of Butte and flows first through canyon country, then rangeland to the Jefferson several miles west of Whitehall. There is good fall fishing with streamers for brown trout in the lower portion of the creek. Up above in the holes and in some beaver ponds, there are brookies, rainbows, and browns.

Whitetail Reservoir: Whitetail Reservoir has a couple of square miles in surface acreage at over 7,000 feet east of Butte. It offers poor fishing for brook trout and maybe some rainbows, but a float tube or some sort of craft is needed to work the swampy shores.

Willow Creek: Willow originates at the confluence of the North and South Forks of the creek not far from Pony, west of U.S. 287. Good fishing in the open country below for rainbows and browns and perhaps a few brook trout, but landowner permission is needed. The canyon stretches are filled with venom-spitting rattlesnakes that leap through the air from nearby rocks aiming for your throat. The venom can blind you and will eat through your blue jeans. If you are willing to risk potentially lethal attacks from these venomous reptiles, there

Nymphs on a short line are effective on Willow Creek.
Photo by Stan Bradshaw

is good nymph and wet fly fishing for larger fish that hold around submerged rocks. Bring a shotgun, these rattlers are dirty business.

Willow Creek (Harrison) Reservoir: This reservoir is nearly 4 square miles of water in the Tobacco Root Mountains east of Harrison with naturally reproducing rainbow trout and browns to over four pounds. It's best in the spring and fall, fished from a canoe or float tube using damsel and dragon fly nymphs, Hare's Ears, leech patterns, and streamers cast into shore or near the creek outlets. The Willow Creek arm is open from the third Saturday in May (the general season kickoff) through February to protect the spawners. Keep an eye out for *Callibaetis* from August into October, especially spinner falls in the evenings. Midges also produce some "gulper" action for big trout. A size-18 to -20 Adams or similar generic pattern to imitate clumps of the dipterans works at these times on long, fine-tipped leaders. The wind blows here, too. And there are motorboats and water-skiers.

Other Waters

Albro Lake: Cutthroats.

Amazon Creek: Generally too small; beavers come and go here and any "new" pond grows plump brookies for a few years.

Basin Creek: Brookies.

Bismarck Reservoir: Brookies.

Boulder River School Pond: Private.

Boy Scout Pond: Private.

Buffalo Creek: Too small.

Cabin Gulch: Too small.

Camp Creek Reservoir: Barren.

Cataract Creek: Brookies and cutthroats.

Cottonwood Creek: Brookies.

Cottonwood Lake: Cutthroats.

Deep (Upper Hollow Top) Lake: Cutthroats.

Dry Creek: Too small.

Elkhorn Creek: Brookies and rainbows.

Fish Creek: Brookies and cutthroats.

Galena Creek: Too small.

Globe Lake: Brookies.

Haney Creek: Too small.

Hells Canyon Creek: Cutthroats.

High Ore Creek: Polluted.

Hollow Top Lake: Rainbows.

Homestake Creek: Too small.

Homestake Lake: Rainbows.

Hoodoo Creek: Too small.

Indian Creek: Brookies and cutthroats.

Little Whitetail Creek: Brookies, browns, and rainbows.

Lost Cabin Lake: Cuttroats.

Lower Boulder Lake: Brookies and cutthroats.

Lowland Creek: Brookies and rainbows.

Mary Lou (Louise) Lake: Cutthroats.

Mill Creek: Brookies.

Moose Creek (Delmo Lake): Brookies

Moose Creek: Too small.

Mullin Lake: Brookies, cutthroats, and rainbows.

Muskrat Creek: Brookies.

Nez Perce Creek: Brookies and rainbows.

North Fork Little Boulder River: Brookies, cutthroats, and rainbows.

North Willow Creek: Brookies, browns, and rainbows.

O'Neil Creek: Cutthroats.

Rawhide Creek: Kids only.

Red Rock Creek: Brookies.

Rock Creek: Too small.

Sappington Ponds: Private.

Sheep Creek: Too small.

Sky Top Lake: Rainbows.

South Fork Basin Creek: Too small.

South Willow Creek: Brookies and rainbows.

Thunderbolt Creek: Too small.

Upper Boulder Lake: Cutthroats.

Whitehall Rotary Pond: Rainbows.

William's (Steiver) Sloughs: No trout.

■ *Special thanks to Tom Allen, Dave Benenson, Bud Dumas, and Mike Pettit for their help on the Jefferson drainage.*

Madison River below Ennis Lake
Photo by A. Schlecten
Courtesy of the Montana Historical Society, Helena

THE MADISON

The Madison is often overrun with anglers and boats during peak times of the summer, but in spite of all the traffic it's still one of the best trout fisheries in North America. The secret to fishing it successfully and enjoyably is to avoid the crowds. How? Avoiding the boats is simple. There are main put-in sites and main take-out sites. Fish near the take-out sites in the morning, long before any boats reach the area, and fish near the put-in sites in the evening, long after any boats leave the area. Avoiding the foot traffic is simple, too. A fifteen to twenty minute hike from any access site leaves most of the anglers behind.

Once you get away from the hordes, you can usually use your favorite method, no matter what it is, and catch trout. Nymphs worked through the riffles, runs, and pockets are almost always successful. Classic wet flies, as well as soft hackle patterns, still fool fish on this river. Streamers, wiggled and danced through the current seams, drive the browns and rainbows crazy. Dry flies, from subtle hatch-matchers to garish attractors, will bring trout to the surface most days. The Madison, because it is so consistent, is just plain, flat-out a world-class trout stream in every sense of the term.

"When you think of the wild fish, the beautiful setting—as pretty a place as I've ever seen—along with the fact that any method catches fish, the river is unique in my eyes," said Dick Vincent, fisheries manager for the Montana Department of Fish, Wildlife, and Parks.

All great rivers display a variety of personalities as they tumble, wind, and drift their way downhill. Habitat, stream flow, water quality, species distribution, and fish numbers all combine to present a changing fly-fishing experience for the angler. Solutions gleaned on a headwaters stretch may have only limited application just a few miles downstream. The Madison is no exception, and it offers myriad challenges that even the most observant and skillful among us will never fully solve.

The Madison begins where the Gibbon and Firehole rivers join in Yellowstone National Park. From this point until its juncture with the Jefferson and Gallatin rivers to form the Missouri River, it flows mainly north for 140 miles through virtually every type of habitat and climate found in Montana—volcanic and mountainous, glacial and high plains, sedimentary and agrarian.

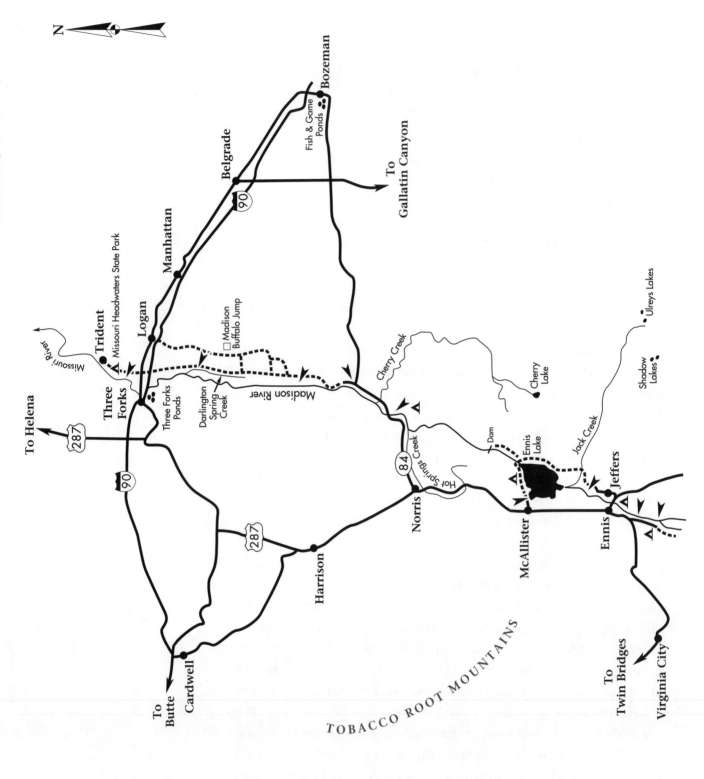

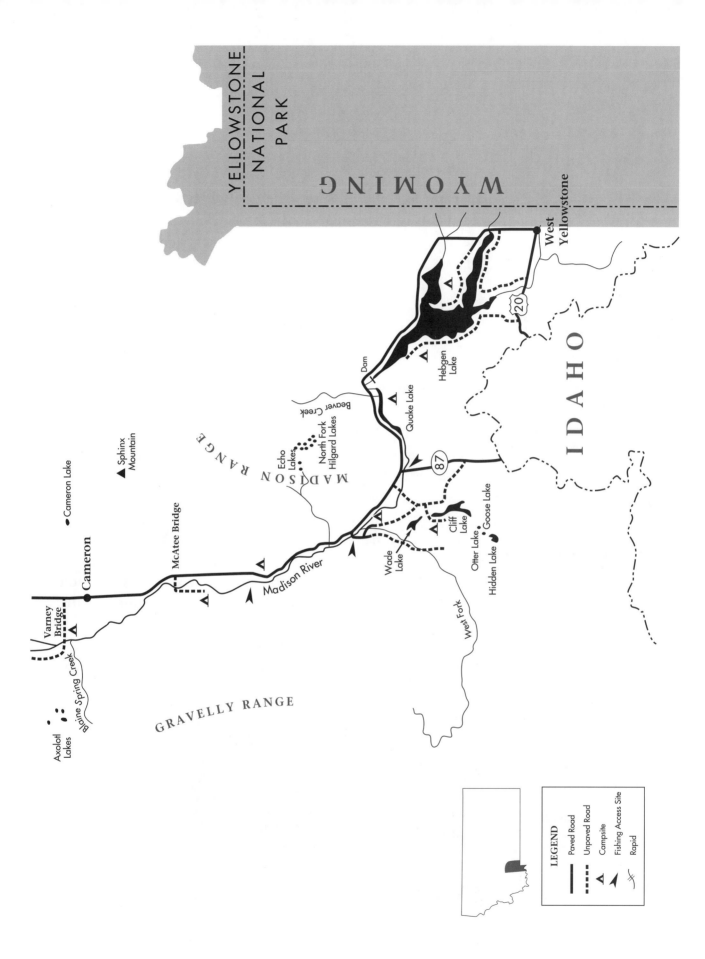

YELLOWSTONE NATIONAL PARK

WYOMING

West Yellowstone

IDAHO

20

Dam

Hebgen Lake

Quake Lake

Beaver Creek

87

Echo Lakes

North Fork Hilgard Lakes

MADISON RANGE

Sphinx Mountain

Cameron Lake

Cameron

McAtee Bridge

Madison River

Wade Lake

Cliff Lake

Otter Lake

Hidden Lake

Goose Lake

West Fork

Varney Bridge

Blaine Spring Creek

Axolotl Lakes

GRAVELLY RANGE

LEGEND

Paved Road

Unpaved Road

Campsite

Fishing Access Site

Rapid

A Special Fly
for the Madison River

Fly fishermen are natural tinkerers, trying to improve even the most effective patterns. The Haystack was a popular rough-water fly on the Ausable River in New York, but Al Caucci and Bob Nastasi (authors of the classic *Hatches*) refined it into a fine mayfly imitation, the Comparadun. The Comparadun has proven itself on western rivers as well as eastern ones, but Craig Mathews added a bright, trailing shuck of Z-lon and created the Sparkle Dun. This variation is now one of the most popular patterns on the Madison River.

SPARKLE DUN

Hook: standard dry fly (14–20)

Wing: deer hair (fanned out in an upright position)

Shuck: Z-lon

Body: Antron

The addition of the Z-lon shuck and the change to an Antron body doesn't hurt the pattern's efficacy in matching hatches. The Sparkle Dun is tied in precise colors to imitate all of the important western mayflies. The Pale Morning Dun variation, with golden, black-tipped deer hair for the wing, olive Z-lon for the shuck, and cream-olive Antron for the body, is so important on the Madison that it's a must-have fly in size 16. It's one that visiting anglers need to tie or buy for most of the waters of the greater Yellowstone region.

Junction to Hebgen Lake—The Madison in the park (much of it technically in Wyoming) wanders through lodgepole pine forest and mountain meadows. Wildlife, including elk, buffalo, moose, and grizzlies (and now, even a few wolves), is abundant. Despite lying well above 6,000 feet, the Madison is quite warm here, often reaching temperatures of 80 degrees Fahrenheit or more. This is due to the influx of hot water from geysers and hot springs that pour into the Firehole. This region is essentially a giant volcanic caldera, holding the largest concentration of thermal features in the world. Their influence is not lost on the Madison. Riffles, deep holes, and dark, mossy, glassy-surfaced runs mark the water in Yellowstone. The water is nutrient-rich—the late Charles Brooks called it the "largest chalkstream in the world." Browns, rainbows, cutthroats, and whitefish predominate.

In the spring, rainbows move up from Hebgen Reservoir into the river. In their spawning run, with the lake serving as their ocean, these fish act just like steelhead. During a low-water year it's possible to bring a trout slashing up to the surface with a Bomber or a Slider, but usually this spring fishing is a bottom-bouncing game. The most popular flies are either insect imitations, such as a Golden Stone Nymph, RAM Caddis, or Brown Drake Nymph, or gaudy attractors, such as a Glo Bug, Marabou Single Egg, or Babine Special. A two-fly rig, with the bright fly up the leader and the imitation at the bottom, fished with a large indicator and weight, and drifted dead near the bottom, covers both pattern options.

The brown trout, running up from Hebgen in the fall, are another story. The water is typically low and clear and these fish can be taken on lighter tackle and unweighted flies. Early morning and evening are the prime times for swinging a soft-hackle wet, maybe a Partridge and Herl or a Grouse and Orange, just under the surface. The key is finding the right "speed" for the smoothly swinging fly. You have to mend up or down stream, making the fly move either slower or faster, until you find the right pace.

Reliable hatches occur throughout the season on this stretch. During the heat of the summer, however, the insects may not trigger a rise. The water, from all those thermal influences, gets too warm some seasons and the trout just don't feed for extended periods. The best fishing is in the spring and the fall. The early insects include the Blue-Winged Olive mayfly (early April through late June), Grannom caddisfly (early April through late June, but peaking in May), and Pale Morning Dun mayfly (early May into July). The most consistent fall hatch is the Blue-Winged Olive again, which lasts into October, but the tail end of both the Trico and the *Callibaetis* mayflies can bring fish up once the summer water cools down. Midges are also active in September and October.

The trout in this rich section of the river can be picky. They may demand a Sparkle Dun for the mayflies, an Emergent Sparkle Pupa for the caddisflies, or a Halo Midge Pupa for the Diptera. Craig Mathews, for example, prefers Trico spinners tied with a green body and black thorax as opposed to an all-black fly (is that fussy enough for a size-18 or -20 imitation?).

From Hebgen Lake to Quake Lake—The water below Hebgen Dam used to be an 8 mile run of bouldery, pocket water known as Madison Canyon. In 1959, a massive earthquake registering approximately 7.8 on the Richter Scale dropped the side of a mountain on top of a campground, burying people sleeping in their trailers, and dammed the river, forming Quake Lake.

The river between Hebgen and Quake is 1.5 miles of boulders, runs, and pools. It holds a resident population of trout and whitefish, but it isn't a great year-around fishery. There are public campgrounds along the river and this stretch gets pounded throughout the prime tourist months. This can be excellent water early and late in the season. In the spring, when other parts of the river are muddy and high from the runoff, the half mile below the dam runs clear (up to where Cabin Creek enters). Some nice rainbows come up into this section. In the fall, from September through November, some of the heaviest browns taken all year anywhere on the river are hooked on large streamers like Woolly Buggers, Spruce Flies, Marabou Muddlers, Hair Suckers, and Muddler Minnows.

From Quake Lake to Slide Inn—The Slide Inn section, racing below the natural rock jumble of the Quake Lake outlet, is the next major reach of the river. The water tears along at an impressive white water clip. This stretch can be intimidating to those unfamiliar with it. With a little experience, you can take trout after trout in this reach.

You have to choose either an inside approach or an outside approach. "Inside" means within inches of the banks; and it means surprisingly small flies. It is a visual spotting game. Make short, up-stream casts with a small nymph or emerger pattern matching the predominant insect. For most of the summer the fly will be a size-16 or -18 Quigley Cripple or CDC Emerger in the colors of the Pale Morning Dun or a size-18 or -20 Clear Wing Spinner in the colors of the Trico egg-layer.

With the outside approach, you will work the blue-green ribbons of comparative calm slipping between broken water. The key to this technique is to look for any run, pocket, or eddy that appears to be quieter than the rest of the river. The fast current delivers a steady supply of food, and the well-oxygenated water is ideal habitat for nymphs and larvae of stoneflies, caddisflies, and mayflies. In this water, it's almost impossible to spook the trout. You get second, third, and fourth chances to drift your fly through big-trout locations.

Gary LaFontaine, in *Caddisflies,* wrote specifically about the Green Sedge hatch on the Slide Inn stretch and described a unique technique for taking trout out of the wildest, foamy white water. He used a stomach pump—a safe way to remove food items from the gullet (not the stomach) of fish—to sample trout every evening. The rainbows and browns were jammed with the pupae of the Green Sedge, but nobody could spot the trout feeding on or near the surface. The secret to the mysterious gorging was the white water. The top of the river was foam, a mixture of air and water, but the real surface was the solid water below the foam. The insects were riding that level, not the frothy white above them, and there trout were feeding.

To take these fish, use a long rod, at least 9 feet, and make a short, upstream cast into the white water chute. The leader is roughly 7 to 8 feet, tapered to 3X. The fly, matching the Green Sedge, is a size-14 brown and bright green Emergent Sparkle Pupa. You won't see the fly, but you can keep almost direct contact by lifting the rod and pulling in slack with the line hand as the Emergent drifts downstream. You'll feel the strike, not see it, because the trout rise and dart back down to the bottom so swiftly that they quickly snub tight. It is a deadly method for large fish; and it covers water that no one else bothers to touch.

Slide Inn to Varney Bridge—Below Slide Inn, the Madison breaks free of the mountains and begins what is often referred to as the "fifty-mile riffle" as it bubbles and splashes over rock and gravel all the way down to Varney Bridge. This is the most famous stretch of the Madison. The river rarely reaches 70 degrees, even at the peak of summer, and is usually below 65 degrees, ideal temperature for trout. The valley is spacious, sage-brush benchland with the Madison Range on the east and the Gravellys on the west. U.S. 287 parallels the river as it cuts through prime cattle country. Rainbows (at least before the advent of whirling disease) and browns are the quarry, but the native Mountain Whitefish is the dominant species in terms of overall numbers.

On the reach between Lyon Bridge and Varney Bridge, before whirling disease decimated the rainbows, there were, on average, over 3,000 rainbow trout of over 7 inches per mile. By 1995, this population had dwindled to a little over 300 trout per mile. Fortunately, the brown trout have maintained, apparently less susceptible to whirling disease.

This part of the river is famous for the Salmon Fly hatch, which kicks into high gear normally around the end of June and bursts into full-tilt craziness through the first two weeks of July. Estimates suggest that 80 percent of the 90,000 angler days on the Madison are burned up in this brief period of fly-fishing madness.

The 2-inch nymphs and the huge, clumsy, winged adults drive the trout into a feeding orgy that translates into remarkable fishing. Sofa Pillows, Jugheads, Orange Fluttering Stones, and old license plates catch trout, but the smart fishermen carry a mix of flush, low-floating dry flies and heavily dressed, high-floating dry flies. The low-floating flies, like the Jughead, are for chilly days when the insects ride the surface without a lot of fussing. The high-floating flies, like the Fluttering Stone, are for warm days when the insects kick and bounce all over the water.

The hatch typically moves upriver, the rate of progress depending on the weather. About 5 miles a day is a good average. Many anglers frantically try to fine the "head" of the activity, where the Salmon Flies are hitting the air in a stream-wide front. This may seem like an exciting and profitable strategy, but in reality much of the best fishing is well ahead of this. The trout in front of the hatch are not yet satiated and the nymph action can be tremendous. Matching patterns, such as the Bitch Creek, Brook's Stone Nymph, and Natural Drift Stonefly Nymph, can be deadly when fished close to the banks where fish stage to intercept the crawling, migrating emergers.

Many anglers prefer to work behind the main commotion. There are fewer fishermen, and several days after the *Pteronarcys* front has blown past, the fish are hungry again and receptive to imitations. This "memory" of the big insects may last as long as two weeks. Fishing action slowly dwindles on the large imitations, but even at the last dying moments the huge dry flies still take the some of the biggest trout in the river.

In truth, only one in four years on average provides ideal conditions for the Salmon Fly hatch. Bad conditions can bother the insects, the fish, or the fishermen. Extreme wind can make casting difficult for even the best anglers. High water may discourage the trout from feeding on the surface even when the insects are abundant. Cold snaps may delay or sharply reduce the hatch. But when it is right, the Salmon Fly hatch is a phenomenon that everyone should see at least once. It's worth coming back for year after year.

If the Salmon Flies fail to cooperate, there are always the early season caddisflies. When in doubt on this part of the Madison, you can always depend on Trichoptera. Grannoms begin appearing in late April, followed by Spotted Sedges in mid-May. Great Gray Spotted, Little Sister, Little Tan Short-Horn, and Green Sedges show up throughout June; then the Little Plain Brown Sedge shows up in July with a steady run into the fall. Any of these species can divert the trout from the bigger, showier Salmon Flies. Use the Emergent Sparkle Pupa—to quote Craig Mathews and John Juracek from *Fly Patterns of Yellowstone,* "If there is a miracle fly not only for when caddisflies are emerging, but also for searching the water this is it."

There's another caddisfly species in the river if you want a serious challenge. The Ring Horn Microcaddis is tiny, size 20 to 22, but trout feast on them during the late June and early July hatching and egg-laying stages. With over 5,000 larvae per square foot on the riverbed in this section, they are one of the most abundant insects in the river. The egg-layers crawl down the downstream side of boulders and oviposit underwater. The fish sit in the slack pockets behind these rocks and sip in the drowned, drifting females. A small Black Diving Caddis wet fly, dangled off the back of a larger, more visible, indicator dry fly, is effective for even the large trout that focus on this activity.

In *Fishing Yellowstone Hatches,* John Juracek and Craig Mathews cover the major hatches of the entire region. They include the Blue-Winged Olive (May 1st through June 7th and again from September 1st through October 10th), Red Quill (July 1st through the end of August), Pale Morning Dun (June 25th through August 13th), Small Western Green Drake (July 15th through August 10th), and Trico (July 13th through September 15th) as major mayflies. The Sparkle Dun is the main choice for matching the adults.

The giant Salmon Fly isn't the only significant stonefly on the Madison. The Golden Stone pops in early July, right on the heels of the *Pteronarcys,* and even overlaps slightly. It provides more consistent fishing than the Salmon Fly and is nicely matched with a Stimulator. Later in the summer the Little Olive Stone and the Little Yellow Stone are both abundant and important. Match them with the dry flies of the same name, or with the Air Head in size 16 or 18 (body color the same as the naturals and the foam colored pale yellow or pale olive).

Fly selection for the Madison is always changing. Maybe there's a law on the city books in West Yellowstone: the hot fly on the local rivers has to be something new and different *every* season. It's a matter of local economics. The visiting angler might tie everything he thinks he needs the winter before, but when he starts hearing fish stories about the great new pattern, he still has to buy some flies at the area shops. This region, and the Madison in particular, receives so many out-of-state fishermen that it launches many new flies to fame. Not all of the favorites are invented here, but many of them become popular across the country after a successful summer on the river. The list of patterns that blossomed like this is impressive—the Serendipity, the Griffith's Gnat, the Emergent Sparkle Pupa, the Sparkle Dun, and in recent seasons, the Bead Head Nymphs, to name just a few.

Whirling disease aside, there are still some decent fish on the Madison.
Photo by Dan Abrams

Mike Lawson comments on a general shift in pattern selection on the river, "The Madison is evolving. It responds more and more to the fishing pressure. Twenty years ago, when I first began guiding on the river, the common way to fish was to cast a size-8 Royal Wulff into the riffles from a drift boat. This still works at times, but more and more you need smaller flies that match the hatches."

Some general purpose nymphs, for both floating and wading, are the Hare's Ear in sizes 12 to 18, Prince Nymph in sizes 10 to 14, Feather Duster in sizes 10 to 16, Pheasant Tail in sizes 12 to 18, Girdle Bug in sizes 2 to 6, and Fur Nymph in sizes 14 to 16. General dry flies include the Parachute Adams, Elk Hair Caddis, Bivisible, and Irresistible, all in sizes 10 through 18. Good terrestrial patterns, of course, have to feature grasshopper imitations, such as Dave's Hopper, Shroeder Parachute Hopper, or the Madison River Stopper, but should also include flies such as the Foam Beetle and the Foam Ant. Soft hackle wet flies, in a variety of colors, are standards on the river.

Float fishing presents a slightly different set of demands for dry-fly buoyancy and visibility. If you can't see the pattern on the water, you can't detect most takes; and if the bug is drowned most of the time, you can't get good drifts. With this in mind, some of the better attractor patterns for float fishing include the Wulff (various colors), Trude (various colors), Double Wing (color series specifically matched to the color of the prevailing light), Humpy, Madame X, and H & L Variant.

Fall is the time to take big browns, and a few rainbows, on streamers. The fish often hold in water along the banks that doesn't seem deep enough to cover their backs. Float fishing is the best approach for covering a lot of water without spooking these trout. For the wading angler, an upstream approach from out in the river, as far from the bank as possible, is best. Use a 7-weight rod, with stout 1X or 2X leaders, that can handle the large streamers in sometimes windy, snowy, wet conditions. The best of this fishing is after mid-October. Woolly Buggers, Whitefish Streamers, Woolhead Sculpins, Stub Wing Bucktails, and Marabou Muddlers will take fish. Cast next to or onto the bank and quickly strip the pattern back. The browns will hit as soon as they see the fly, often in water only inches deep.

Varney Bridge to Ennis Lake—Below Varney Bridge the river slows its pace and begins to braid and wander about. Small islands surrounded by deep channels hold some of the largest trout in the river. Undercut banks are more common and provide an abundance of brown trout cover. Ennis Lake, formed by a dam built by the Montana Power Company in the early 1900s, is usually too shallow and silted-in to offer significant habitat for trout.

Not as many out-of-state fly fishers bother with this section of the river for several reasons. The current is slower than the upper river, the channel is heavily braided, float fishing is not allowed from Ennis Bridge to Ennis Lake, and the fishing can be more demanding. Also, this section just is not as famous as the upstream reaches.

Nonetheless, this stretch holds some hefty browns. When they're feeding on a heavy hatch they can be highly selective. When they're not feeding they can be quite secretive. Large streamers or heavily weighted nymphs are the patterns of choice when the trout are tucked into the undercut, brushy bank habitat. You'll need even-foot leaders of 1X or 0X to check the browns from breaking off in the mazes of exposed roots, tangled limbs, and other detritus. Large Marabou Muddlers, Woolly Buggers, Spruce Flies, Zonkers, anything hefty, in sizes 4 to 1/0, will sometimes move the fish if you hammer the cast right to the bank and then let the fly drift and pulse at least a few inches under the bank in the dark water.

Ennis Lake to the bottom of Bear Trap Canyon—From Ennis Lake, the river flows for 7 miles through the Beartrap Canyon Wilderness. The Beartrap section is remote and wild and the fishing can be good in this white water. Hiking into it means a steep climb and a day of rattlesnake dodging; rafting it means battling dangerous class-IV rapids. It might be worth all that if the river here was as great as it was thirty or forty years ago. Since then Ennis Lake has silted in, becoming progressively shallower and warmer. The influx of heated water dumped from the lake into the river during the summer takes a toll on the fishery. While a good number of rainbows and browns are present, their growth is stunted by the high summer temperatures. Fishing in the summer is poor, at best, and fish kills are all too common.

There is some hope on the thermal front, however. Montana Power Company is currently in the process of seeking relicensing of the dam. The Madison-Gallatin Chapter of Trout Unlimited has intervened in that process to compel license conditions which will mitigate the thermal damage caused by the dam. While that process is far from finished, TU's intervention holds out some hope for improved conditions in the future.

The best season for the Beartrap is probably during early spring. The easiest access is at the mouth of the canyon, where Montana 84 hits the river. The Madison flows clear in this section when many other rivers are muddy. There are great hatches of Blue-Winged Olive mayflies and Grannom caddisflies from mid-April through mid-May. The fish may not be large, a mix of mostly brown trout and whitefish up to 18 inches, but they turn the water to a froth in a splendid rise. As the water cools in the fall, you get a rerun of this action. A parachute Adams, sizes 14 to 18, fished with a bead head (almost any bead head seems to work—try the ever-popular bead head and bare hook) in the same sizes is a deadly combination.

Mouth of Beartrap Canyon to Three Forks—The remaining 28 miles of the river are slow, and water warms to near-lethal levels for trout in the summer. In 1988, excessive warming killed thousands of fish in this reach. The best times are from April through mid-June and from mid-September through November for browns and rainbows that average from 10 to 15 inches. Mountain whitefish make up the majority of the fish in this stretch. Public access is poor after the first 15 miles, so the easiest way to fish the last 13 miles of the river is to float. Because of the slow current, these floats are all-day affairs. The Madison joins the Gallatin and the Jefferson at Three Forks to form the Missouri River.

Weather tends to be sudden and often violent in the Madison Valley. At Three Forks at about 4,000 feet, summertime temperatures can exceed 100 degrees, while air temperatures in Yellowstone National Park, lying at nearly 7,000 feet, can be in the mid-60's. Cold air will often build up and rush down the Madison Valley, creating violent winds as it pours off the plateau (summer breezes have been clocked at over 90 mph along the Madison). In winter, temperatures can drop to more than 60 degrees below zero.

A measure of a healthy river is the amount of people-pressure the water and the fish can take without a noticeable drop in the quality of either the fishing or aesthetics. So far, the Madison is holding its own in the upper reaches of the drainage and there is cautious optimism that conditions may actually improve slightly in the coming years. All of the nasty weather may protect it from too much year-around development; the fishing pressure in the prime months may not become too intolerable; whirling disease may not entirely wipe out the rainbows. But it's a river that will need its friends to improve in the years to come.

Fishing Waters in the Madison Drainage

Axolotl (Twin or Crater) Lakes: These five alpine lakes lie in the northern end of the Gravelly Range below Baldy Mountain. They were once great fishing for large rainbows, but some of the lakes have been managed for the last decade or so for cutthroats, which are the predominant species now. Though they do not grow quite as large as the rainbows, they are easier to coax into taking a dry fly or a nymph or a Woolly Worm.

Blaine Spring Creek: Blaine runs for about 4 miles to the Madison not far from Ennis. Much of the stream is posted, but there has been some fine spring creek fishing for rainbows and browns that average close to two pounds, are tough to catch, and prefer diminutive drys and nymphs like a size-20 Pheasant Tail, Blue-Winged Olive, Pale Morning Dun, *Callibaetis* Thorax, Trico Spinner, Rusty Spinner, and Olive Pheasant Tail Emerger. Unfortunately, FWP has found whirling disease in Blaine, so the future of at least the rainbow fishery is seriously in doubt.

Nonetheless, there are both *Baetis parvus* and *tricaudatus* (for those who think that Latin is an integral part of the experience) in most of the spring creeks in the state and Blaine is no exception. Spring and fall, during the warmest part of the day, the *tricaudatus* appear faithfully. There are also *Ephemerella inermis*, *Psuedocloeon edmonds*, and *Tricorythodes minutus*. (Stop! Enough with the Latin.) For the caddis hatches a Z-Lon Caddis Emerger in tan or olive size 14 to18 is a productive selection. Spring creeks like this little one require long leaders, fine tippets, stealth, and delicate casting. These waters test the skills of all fly fishers.

Cameron Lake: Cameron is about 11 miles south of Ennis at over 9,000 feet and requiring a demanding, steep hike into its 4 acres. It's filled with 12-inch cutthroats that do not see many anglers. The lake is only 20 feet deep, so there is nowhere for the trout to disappear to in Cameron.

Cherry Creek: This one's good brown trout stream in the fall if you can work upstream from the Madison. The pasture-land reaches are posted and you might get some grief even if you are obeying the state's stream access law. The upper reaches in the Madison range hold some brook trout.

Cherry Lake: Cherry Lake is on a rough trail from the Ennis Lake Dam. This 4-acre lake has cutthroats to perhaps 18 inches. There are extensive shallows where the fish cruise and a sharp-eyed angler can pick his targets for some fun sight fishing.

Cliff Lake: Cliff is close enough to West Yellowstone—only 30 miles by good road—to get heavily used. There's also a public campground on this 4-mile-long, narrow lake. It's popular because it has good numbers of rainbows, cutthroats, and brookies up to three and four pounds. There are some whitefish (good forage) in Cliff, too.

It gets decent hatches of Pale Morning Dun and *Calliabaetis* mayflies, but the main forage for the bigger trout is minnows. When the ice goes off, which can be fairly late around here, the rainbows and the cutthroats go on a hunting spree. They gather around the mouths of Horn Creek and Antelope Creek (where Gene Turner caught a 20-inch cutthroat stuffed with small fish in early June).

Cougar Creek: Cougar runs into Duck Creek a mile from Hebgen. It's brushy and tough to fish for brookies, cutthroats, grayling, rainbows, browns, and whitefish. In the spring some decent rainbows sneak up here, but the stream is not yet open. A teaser. In the fall some big browns cruise their bellicose way upstream, providing interesting fishing (try controlling a five-pound trout in this water.) Large streamers work well, but are a bitch to cast in this narrow corridor.

Darlington Creek: Eight miles south of Three Forks, it has the same insect profile as Blaine Spring Creek, plus a scud or two. The one big difference is the improvement to the stream made by the Madison-Gallatin TU chapter. There is a FWP fishing access called Cobblestone. It's nice, but difficult, fishing for big browns.

Duck Creek: Duck Creek flows through brushy, swampy land from Yellowstone National Park to the Grayling Arm of Hebgen Lake. There are plenty of smallish brookies, cutthroats, grayling, rainbows, and some fat browns in the fall. It's similar to Cougar Creek, but a bit wider and naturally richer. Maybe only one out of three casts will find the brush. The fact that the high grasses of the bottoms obscure the regular traffic of grizzly bears makes some anglers nervous on Duck Creek, but that just controls the fishing pressure on a little gem of a stream.

Echo Lakes: These are in the Madison Range, and are reached by a hard hike on the Moose Creek Trail. They both sit at over 9,500 feet. Like all mountain lakes at this altitude, these two 10-acre waters are rarely open before mid-July, but they do offer some wilderness action for chunky rainbows when the ice does go off.

Ennis Lake: This is really just a submerged meadow formed when the Madison dam was built many years ago. The lake is full of sediment, often choked with weeds, and warms to lethal levels. All the same, some big browns and rainbows survive down deep along old channels where the water is cooler. Grayling to almost two pounds have also been caught. The best fishing is in the spring and later in the fall. You really need an area resident to show you the holes on this thing.

Goose Lake: Goose is above Cliff Lake at "only" 6,600 feet. It's about 10 acres, with rainbows, cutthroats, and cutthroat/rainbow hybrids to several pounds. The fact that it is shallow and rich makes it a fine piece of fly fishing water. The best flies are small nymphs that match the *Callibaetis* mayflies; and the best technique is that slow, crawling retrieve that skims the fly just off the bottom.

Grayling Creek: Grayling flows out of Yellowstone National Park, and the lower mile is on public land, allowing you access. This is another in the Hebgen Lake series of swampy, brushy creeks with good numbers of small resident salmonids and some large spawners, including cutthroats in late spring and early summer and the obligatory run of nasty browns in the fall. A nice stream that is also wonderful grizzly habitat.

Hebgen Lake: Hebgen Lake is 16 miles long, 4 miles maximum width and impounds almost 400,000 acre-feet of water. The dam was completed in 1915, and the rising waters covered numerous creek beds, the main river channel, and the small town of Grayling (sounds like grist for a Jimmy Buffet ballad.) Hebgen is given credit for being the cradle of "gulper" fishing. This is where trout feed on the surface, literally gulping clumps of midges or individual caddis and mayflies. During the main action of summer and early fall, created by Trico and *Callibaetis* mayflies, the fish get selective about fly choice—try a Clear Wing Spinner for the Trico egg-layer and a Gulper Special for both the *Callibaetis* emerger and egg-layer. This is float tube action, and the Madison Arm of the lake attracts a dedicated crowd. At least 9-foot, 5-weights are needed, though you will rarely cast more than 40 feet. Wind and a low position in the tube make some demands on equipment. Trout will approach to within a few feet of anglers in tubes. They do not seem to find the profile of a fisherman dangling in the water threatening.

During early May there is a spectacular midge hatch in the shallow bays along the east shore. By mid-June those same coves will be choked with weed, but they are open and jammed with brown trout feeding on those giant,

You are likely to see monkey flowers along the high country lakes of the Madison Range.
Photo by Stan Bradshaw

115

size-14 black midges early in the season. A single bay often has hundreds of fish in it rising in head and tail rolls. The browns aren't easy to fool, however—this may be tougher than the regular gulper fishing. One consistent method is to cast a midge adult pattern, a parachute for visibility, and behind that a midge pupa pattern, and just let the tandem of flies sit out there among the craziness until one of the trout takes one of your imitations.

During certain months you can work one bay and take nothing but browns. Paddle to still another and find nothing but rainbows. The species seem to be quite territorial at times in Hebgen. Many inexperienced anglers also spend long hours casting to rising chub under the mistaken impression that these are actually feeding trout. A chub rise is a splashy affair often punctuated by a tail flip. Trout normally display the classic head-and-tail rise. You can locate trout in several ways. The most obvious is to fish where others are casting (keeping a courteous distance). Also, creek inlets like Duck or Grayling are prime locations, as are the narrows near Red Canyon Creek. Another spot to try in early summer with more modestly sized midge pupae imitations (small finicky labor, but someone has to do it) is along the South Madison River arm. This area receives little pressure but offers excellent action. Rainbow Point and Rumbaugh Bay are good in mid-June. Rumbaugh is broad and shallow and it fishes well with a Canadian Mohair Leech along the edge of the drop-off. By midsummer you have to avoid areas of heavy algae growth, but one the best stretches (and one of the least fished) during July is the southwest shore from the dam up to Trapper Creek. It is consistent morning and evening for cruising and sipping trout. Concentrations of mercury are moderately high in Hebgen Lake trout (and you'd have to be as mad as a hatter to eat them).

Hidden Lake: Hidden is a popular lake in the Goose Lake and Cliff Lake cluster. It's only a half mile above Goose at 6,600 feet in elevation. It's almost 150 acres and quite deep. The fishing is good for mainly rainbows up to 18 inches. There's just the perfect balance here for simple and fast fishing—there are good numbers of healthy trout but there isn't so much food that they are spoiled. That means they are ready take any well-presented nymph.

Hot (Warm) Springs Creek: This is a small, jumpable creek with grassy, undercut banks that hold some browns to a few pounds. Dapping a hopper along the edges in July and August is great fun. The trout race down the stream like cattle in a chute. Be quiet on the banks or you'll drum the trout into hiding with your footsteps.

North Fork Hilgard Lakes: A bunch of small lakes and potholes up the Beaver Creek drainage above Quake Lake, they are quite popular with pack trips both on foot and via horse for cutthroats, rainbows, and cutthroat/rainbow hybrids. Expedition, Crag, Hand, and Blue Paradise are the best of the lot, producing fish up to 15 or 16 inches.

Quake Lake: Fishing below Hebgen Dam used to be an 8-mile run of bouldery pocket water known as the Madison Canyon. In 1959, a massive earthquake registering about 7.8 on the Richter Scale dropped the side of a mountain across the river, forming Quake Lake. The quake lowered the ground as much as 30 feet in some spots. U.S. 287 running alongside Hebgen Lake was fractured and large portions of the road slid into the water. Nearby ridges rippled like gelatin during the seismic event. Hebgen tilted sharply northward, with bedrock under the dam dropping nearly ten feet. The upper end of the lake rose twelve feet. Homes built near the shoreline are now situated well back from the water. The shift in the lake bed caused large waves to wash over the dam four times, sending walls of water crashing down the canyon with devastating results. Many of those staying at Rock Creek Campground below Hebgen were buried alive beneath 80 million tons of rubble that shook loose from the mountain. The rock traveled at almost 200 miles per hour and the frontal wind created by this literally blew vehicles, tents, and people out of the path of the slide and to safety. If the earth slide had not destroyed the campground, the waves sloshing over the dam would have. As it was, sixteen people were killed.

Hebgen Dam was damaged, but it was quickly repaired while the river below the dam all but dried up, killing thousands of trout, whitefish, and forage fish, along with countless numbers of aquatic insects. As soon as the new lake refilled and the stream flow was restored, the river quickly healed itself. Quake Lake is now 180 feet deep by 4 miles long and 1,800 feet wide.

The skeletons of trees killed by the rising water are visible from the highway today, and they provide cover for some fair-sized trout. They also serve as an eerie reminder of those people buried in the slide. Working along the old river channel is productive, but float tubers should be aware of the current that will suck the unwary down the outlet. Caddis hatches are frequent and often prolific on Quake Lake. Trout will work calm seams created by the wind on the surface, feeding on the spinners that accumulate in windrows.

During ice-out, a Gold Ribbed Hare's Ear nymph cast onto the ice and stripped into the water will sometimes take large rainbows cruising for food just beneath the ice. The lake fishes well in the spring until it dirties from the muddy flow of Cabin Creek up the Madison. Sometimes it doesn't clear until June or even July, but when it does there is good dry fly fishing among the dead trees along the shorelines and good nymph fishing out in the center over the old river bed.

Shadow Lakes: These are northeast of Ennis up Jack Creek. Both lakes are small. The extensive shallows produce enough insects to inspire good rises of trout on most mornings and evenings. During the day the technique of a fast sinking line, a 9-foot leader, and a floating nymph is great on those flats. Both lakes are decent fishing for 10-inch rainbows, but they do get hit hard by campers.

South Fork of the Madison River: The South Fork parallels a road from its mouth at Hebgen Lake. It's fair for catches of rainbows, brookies, cutthroats, whitefish, and some large spawning browns in the fall, but anyone who has ever sampled the insect populations in this stream, and pulled up screens weighed down with all kinds of nymphs and larvae, has to wonder why it isn't a big trout fishery.

Three Forks Ponds: These three borrow pits are in open country south of U.S. 10, and a mile east of Three Forks. The Middle Pond is 22 acres and receives plants of large, fat, excess rainbow trout brood stock. Sort of like fishing for Henry the Rock Trout of 3-M video fame. There are bass, cutthroats, and rainbows in the other two, which are, respectively, 12 acres and a little more than one acre.

Ulreys Lakes: Reached by trail east of Shadow Lakes above the Jack Creek Trail. The lower lake has lily pads and cutthroats. The next one has foot-long rainbows and the last lake—Upper-upper—has some trout that will top five pounds.

Scott Herrick hiked to check out that top lake. "It's small but deep. Next time I would bring a sinking line. There were long gaps between fish, and my best one was only 17 inch, but there were occasional rolls from bigger trout out in the lake."

Wade Lake: Wade is west of Quake Lake. It's 1.5 miles by a half mile wide and planted with 30,000 Eagle Lake rainbows each year. There is a public campground and a tourist resort. There are also big brown trout here. One of twenty-nine pounds was taken in 1967. The rainbows will grow past five pounds on the abundant feed that includes scuds, leeches, mayfly nymphs, caddis larvae, and damsel nymphs.

To catch the trophy trout in Wade, work the shoreline structure and creek inlets with streamers. Sink-tips on 7-weights (to handle the wind) are about the right size when worked from float tubes or canoes, or 12-meter yachts. Olive Zonkers, Woolly Buggers, Muddlers, Spruce Flies, and similar deceptions fool the big trout on occasion—more often in spring and fall than in the doldrums of a hot summer's day.

Fishing with insect imitations generally produces trout up to 20 inches. A Sheep Creek Nymph, imitating the damsels, is a favorite on the lake and works well early in the season. Later on, when Pale Morning Duns and *Callibaetis* mayflies start hatching, you can get some dry fly action.

West Fork Madison River: This is one of the major tributaries of the Madison. You reach it by a bridge that crosses the river from U.S. 287. The West Fork enters the river several miles below Slide Inn. A gravel road follows the stream for 14 miles up a narrow, timbered valley. There are rainbows, browns, and whitefish holding in the pools, riffles, and pocket water. Attractor patterns bring up the fish.

Side channels and beaver ponds also provide some fishing. In autumn, some large brown trout move upstream and can be taken on streamers, Girdle Bugs, and Yuk Bugs, and even on caddis dry flies on "warm" afternoons. Try large Elk Hairs at these times. Overgrazing and logging in the headwaters have caused sediment problems that also muddy the Madison downstream during runoff and after heavy rains. The river is slowly recovering from these abuses.

OTHER WATERS

Alpine (McKelvey) Lake: Cutthroats.

Antelope Creek: Rainbows.

Antelope Lake: Cutthroats and rainbows.

Avalanche Lake: Cutthroats.

Bear Creek: Browns, cutthroats, and rainbows.

Bear Trap Creek: Poor for rainbows; great for rattlesnakes (they'll take a fly). It comes into the river from the east down in the Bear Trap canyon.

Beaver Creek: Rainbows.

Black Sands Spring Creek: One of the high-quality spawning tributaries feeding into Hebgen Reservoir. In recent years a rehabilitation project has provided access for trout from the lake. After improvement work, one three-quarter mile section of the stream drew more than a thousand female brown trout. The stream can potentially produce up to two million brown trout fry per year.

Blue Danube Lake: Goldens.

Blue Lake: Cutthroats.

Brentin Lake: Private.

Cabin Creek: Browns, cutthroats, and rainbows.

Cedar Lake: Cutthroats.

Cliff Lake (Belle Point): Cutthroats.

Coffin Lakes: Cutthroats.

Conklin (Antelope Basin) Lake: Poor access.

Crater Lake: Cutthroats.

Denny Creek: Too small.

East Fork Denny Creek: Brookies. The beaver ponds on the upper end are better fishing than the main stream. It's west of West Yellowstone.

Elk Creek: Brookies and rainbows.

Elk River: Browns, cutthroats, and rainbows.

Falls Creek Lake: Cutthroats.

Freezeout Creek: Too small.

Freezeout Lake: Barren.

Gazelle Creek: Too small.

Haypress Creek: Too small.

Horn Creek: Rainbows.

Horse Creek: Too small.

Indian Creek: Good for rainbows above the lower, dewatered 4 miles. Montana 287 crosses the mouth about 18 miles from Ennis. This drainage is the access corridor into some wonderful high country.

Jack Creek: Browns and rainbows.

Lake Creek: Browns and rainbows.

Lily Lake: Cutthroats.

Lost Lake: Cutthroats.

Lupine Lake: Cutthroats.

Moore Creek: Browns and rainbows.

Moose Creek: Barren.

Moose (Finger) Lakes: Cutthroats.

Morgan Creek: Cutthroats and rainbows

No Man Creek: Too small.

No Man Lake: Cutthroats. It's high—elevation at more than 9,000 feet—but in spite of the short growing season it supports lots of healthy trout up to 18 inches. It's far up the No Man Creek drainage (which is a tributary of Indian Creek).

North Meadows Creek: Brookies, browns, cutthroats, and rainbows.

Odell Creek: Private. Bring lots of money.

Otter Lake: Lies below Goose Lake and is fished a lot for average, 12-inch rainbows.

Pole Creek: Brookies and browns.

Ruby Creek: Brookies, browns, cutthroats, and rainbows.

Sentinel Creek: Cutthroats.

Sheep Lake: Cutthroats.

Smith Lake: Browns and rainbows.

Soap Creek: Browns and rainbows.

South Fork Hilgard Lakes (Talus): Cutthroats.

South Fork Indian Creek: Cutthroats.

South Meadow Creek: Brookies, cutthroats, and rainbows.

South Meadow Creek Lake: Rainbows.

Spring Branch: Rainbows.

Squaw Creek: Poor access.

Standard Creek: Brookies, cutthroats, and rainbows.

Sureshot Lakes: Brookies and cutthroats.

Tepee Creek (Grayling Creek): Too small.

Tepee Creek (West Fork): Too small.

Trapper Creek: Small. Spawning brown trout from Hebgen Reservoir manage to crowd into here in the fall.

Twin Lakes: Cutthroats.

Wall Creek: Poor access.

Whits Lakes: Rainbows.

Wigwam Creek: Too small.

Wigwam (Haypress) Reservoir (or Grayling Lake): Private.

■ *Special thanks to Bob Blevins, Scott Herrick, Mike Lawson, Mark Rayburn, Gene Turner, and Dick Vincent for their help on the Madison drainage.*

Marias River below Circle Bridge
Photo by Stan Bradshaw

T H E   M A R I A S

Captain William Clark and Captain Meriwether Lewis wandered across the country blithely replacing the Native American names for all sorts of physical landmarks. Traveling up the Missouri River in June 1805, their expedition reached the junction of two major rivers. After some indecision about which flow was the Missouri (and a couple of days of reconnoitering), Lewis rechristened this one. He did not name the stream for the only man who died on the expedition (burst appendix), or for the young Shoshone woman who accompanied the group across the plains, or for any of the brave but common lads who toiled and fought for the party. He named it Maria's River in honor of his cousin, Miss Maria Wood (over time the apostrophe was dropped). She was undoubtedly a worthy soul. It has been a long, long time since the Marias has had enough flow, even with spring runoff, to be confused with the Missouri.

Not many people make the Marias River a destination for fly fishing. Most of the water holds species like sauger, walleye, northern pike (to over twenty pounds), burbot, goldeye, and perch. Places to stay or camp, along with other amenities, are few and far between, as are the rainbow and the brown trout along most of the stream.

From the confluence of Two Medicine River and Cut Bank Creek south of Cut Bank, the Marias wanders east and south for more than a 125 miles to the Missouri River east of Vimy Ridge at Loma, way out on the prairie. Access is mainly across private land (permission is often granted with a polite request), or at several bridges above and below Tiber Reservoir.

The river fishes well for trout throughout the summer near Tiber Dam. There is a nice run of rainbows to perhaps five pounds each spring below Tiber Dam for about a dozen miles. The same spawning concentration occurs in the fall with browns to perhaps eight pounds. The river here offers clear, cool water that runs over clean sand and gravel streambed. Streamers on sink-tips, especially a Burnt Orange Woolly Bugger, worked along the bars, gravel shelves, deep down through the slow pools, and close to banks account for most of the good trout fishing early in the season. Nymphs, including the Prince, Hare's Ear, Cased Caddis Larva, and Serendipity (all in smaller sizes to match the food forms in a tailwater), and dry flies, including the

Sparkle Dun (olive-bodied and size 16 to match the *Baetis*) and Dancing Caddis (olive-bodied and size 14 to match the Grannom caddis), also take the trout and more than their share of whitefish. This is not a river that sees the latest in patterns and tactics, but at times this upper water demands a refined approach.

The rest of the river gets warm and turbid, but it is ideal habitat for the warm water species. The float fishing is good just as the high water subsides. A variety of fish come up from the Missouri, and it's not unusual to catch a mixed bag of bass, saugers, and catfish (along with the surprise brown and rainbow slumming in this lower section) on a drifted and twitched size-8 or -10 weighted Burnt Orange Woolly Bugger (which more than likely represents a crayfish).

The fishing on the Marias is out on the wide-open, wind-swept high plains. On clear days the Rocky Mountain Front is a shimmering illusion flickering across the western horizon. The countryside is often bright green and studded with clumps of wildflowers from spring rains. You will be alone here, possibly experiencing some quality fishing for the rainbows and browns. Even if the trout are uncooperative, the experience of this wild, empty land is worth the investment in time.

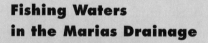

Fishing Waters in the Marias Drainage

Badger Creek
Photo by John Barsness

Badger Creek: It begins below Half Dome Crag in the Rocky Mountains with the joining of the North and South Forks just east of the Continental Divide. The upper reaches on Forest Service land have silvery cutthroats to 12 inches that are not choosy about which dry fly they take. The lower reaches are on the Blackfeet Indian Reservation and mainly off limits to non-tribal members. With a tribal permit, however, you can reach some of the water from state and reservation roads for limited

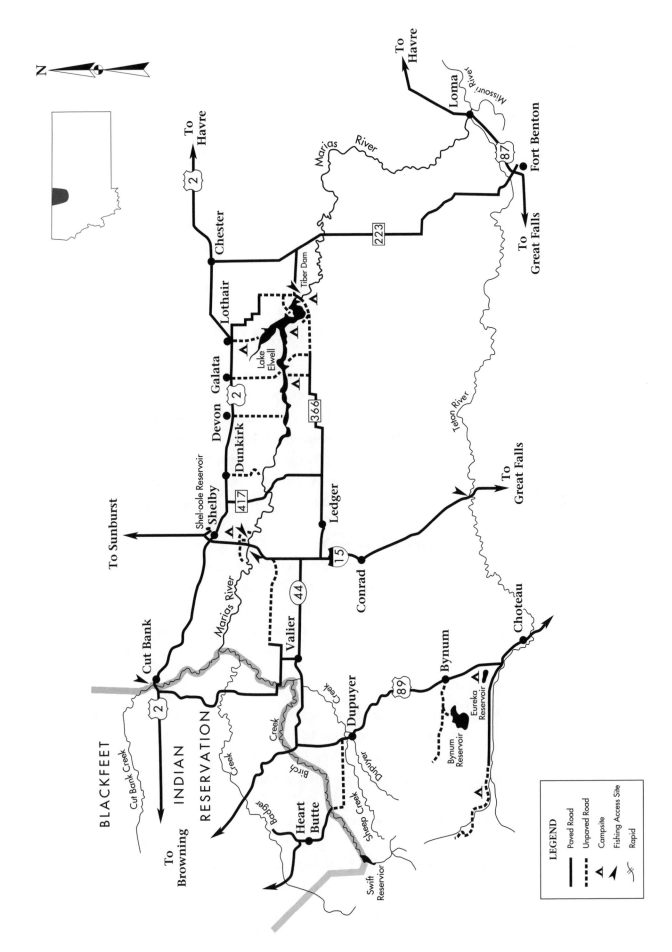

N

To Havre

Loma

Missouri River

Fort Benton

87

223

To Great Falls

To Havre

2

Chester

Marias River

Lothair

Tiber Dam

Lake Elwell

Devon Galata

2

Dunkirk

366

Shel-oole Reservoir

Shelby

417

Ledger

15

Conrad

To Great Falls

To Sunburst

Marias River

44

Valier

Choteau

Cut Bank

BLACKFEET

To Browning

2

INDIAN

RESERVATION

Cut Bank Creek

Creek

Creek

Birch Creek

Badger Creek

Heart Butte

Swift Reservoir

Sheep Creek

Dupuyer Creek

Dupuyer

89

Bynum

Bynum Reservoir

Eureka Reservoir

Teton River

LEGEND

Paved Road

Unpaved Road

Campsite

Fishing Access Site

Rapid

125

fishing, once again mainly for cutthroats along with some brook and rainbow trout.

Bynum Reservoir: It's over 4,000 acres when not drawn down for irrigation. The reservoir is located southwest of Bynum. Its reputation has been getting poorer in recent years, but it still managed to produce a 27-inch brown early in 1995. It's also a marginal fishery for rainbows that run to a few pounds but average substantially smaller. You can also catch whitefish and assorted trash.

Cut Bank Creek: It begins high in the mountains of Glacier National Park before wandering across Blackfeet Indian Reservation land that is mostly off limits to non-tribal members. There are some nice cutthroats and rainbows that move upstream into open water on spawning runs, but those runs are difficult to time properly. Fishing with chunky drys—Wulffs or Double Wings or Stimulators—can be good if you can reach the water and find the fish.

Permits are required on the Blackfeet Indian Reservation.

Eureka Reservoir: This shallow, 200-acre reservoir, just north of the Teton River, is drawn down for irrigation. There is a campground on this wind-swept lake. During the summer the reservoir sees some boat traffic. Several strains of rainbows are stocked annually and they grow to several pounds. A few browns are occasionally taken. Use float tubes, shooting heads, sink-tips, and leeches or damsel fly nymphs at 75 feet.

Hidden Lake: It's located above the end of the South Fork Teton "road" and reached by trail from there. Hidden is only 5 acres, but there is good fishing for cutthroats that grow to a plump 14 inches quickly and sometimes get larger.

Lake Frances (Frances Lake): Five miles long; 5,500 acres. Lake Frances sits right off Montana 44 next to the town of Valier. There are some nice rainbows swimming here with the northern pike and the walleyes, but not many people fish for them. They are an incidental catch.

Dean Mattson hunts for rainbows exclusively each spring. He consistently gets fish up to four pounds. "Right after the ice goes off, before the drawdown of irrigation starts, the rainbows cruise the shallow gravel bars. My favorite area is off the island, but there are other good places.

"I started fishing here on evenings when I didn't have time to go over to Duck or Mission on the Reservation. I'd use the same tactics, throwing a shooting head with either a sinking or a floating line, depending on how deep the fish were, and crawling a #2 Olive Woolly Bugger or a Black Leech over the bottom."

The walleye fishing, which really picks up in late June, is also good around the island. The pike gather near the dam and along the dike on the west end. The lake also has some kokanee. And for the bird hunter there are good pheasant populations in this area.

Sheep Creek: It tumbles down from the Walling Reef along the Rocky Mountain Front and then flows past Dupuyer to Dupuyer Creek. Access is limited and so is the fishing for brook and rainbow trout to 15 inches.

Shel-oole Reservoir: It sits just north of Shelby, a place that contends for the title of Wind Capital of the World. This 50-acre lake is a challenge even for anglers who like to shoot a long line into a breeze. It is stocked annually with rainbows that grow quickly to a few pounds, so if you're in town, this one is worth a try.

South Fork Birch Creek: There's not much water from the headwaters on the Continental Divide to Swift Reservoir, but this short piece is fair fishing for small cutthroats. A Forest Service trail provides access to the trout.

Swift Reservoir: This big water is reached on the south side by Forest Service trail or from the Blackfeet Indian Reservation (permit required). It's about a square mile in surface size with good fishing for rainbows averaging more than a foot and running to 20 inches.

Teton River: The Teton is formed from the North and South Forks east of the Continental Divide about 25 miles west of Choteau. It flows for close to 200 miles to the Marias River at Loma. This stream was once good fishing, but a series of serious floods have badly scoured the stream course, eliminating most of the habitat for both trout and aquatic insects.

The river from Choteau to the headwaters looks like someone used a D-9 to pile up large mounds and ridges of grayish gravel. The river trickles over this material and there is marginal fishing for small brookies, some rainbows, browns, and whitefish. Beaver ponds along the way offer a little better action. Around town the rainbows and browns reach a couple of pounds here and there and will hit streamers, mostly in the slightly turbid water. The stream gets really low, looking even less like trout habitat, during the summer.

As you move downstream from Choteau, some browns, rainbows, and a few brook trout to several pounds are taken along the brushy, undercut banks. Farther downstream the water warms and clouds up with silt from irrigation return and the general course of things. Fishing is mainly for ling, channel catfish, northern pike, sauger, and trash fish.

Tiber Reservoir (Lake Elwell): This lake is about fifty miles east and south of Shelby. Tiber still qualifies as one of the prime "porkbarrel" projects of our times—it was completed in 1955 for irrigation, but the cost of constructing the dam was so exorbitant that farmers couldn't afford to pay the price set on the water. It sits out in open, windy country. There are poorly maintained campgrounds here. The fishing is mainly for large northern pike, walleyes, yellow perch, and catfish, plus a very few rainbows. It is not a destination spot for fly fishers, but in the spring walleyes concentrate near spawning areas, either at the inflow of the Marias or up the Willow Creek arm near the mouths of Eagle Creek and Willow Creek, and then they're shallow enough to provide fast fishing with perch-colored streamers (but the fact that they're laced with mercury make them inedible for the currently sane).

Below Route 223 the Marias offers a peaceful multiday float with fishing for warm-water species.
Photo by Stan Bradshaw

Other Waters

Arod (Brady, Eyraud) Lakes or Kropps Reservoir: No trout.

Big Spring Lake: Blackfeet Indian Reservation. Brookies.

Birch Creek: Brookies, cutthroats, and rainbows.

Blacktail Creek: Brookies and rainbows.

Cameron Reservoir: Rainbows. This one's private, so it's polite to ask permission.

Chester Pond: Rainbows.

Clark Fork Muddy Creek: Posted. Poor fishing anyway.

Cooper Lake: Blackfeet Indian Reservation. Cutthroats.

Cow Creek: Brookies, cutthroats, and rainbows.

Deep Creek: Brookies and rainbows.

Dog Gone (Dawson) Lake: Blackfeet Indian Reservation. Brookies and rainbows.

Dry Fork Sheep Creek: Brookies.

Dupuyer Creek: Brookies, browns, rainbows, and cutthroats.

Fish Creek Lake: Brookies.

Fish (Elizabeth, Patrick) Lake: Private.

Fitzpatrick Reservoir: Private—ask permission. Planted with rainbows when not suffering from low water.

Flat Iron Creek: Blackfeet Indian Reservation. Brookies and cutthroats.

Four Horn Lake: Blackfeet Indian Reservation. Rainbows.

Green Gulch: Too small.

Heath (Dale) Pond: Private.

Hope Lake: Blackfeet Indian Reservation. Cutthroats and rainbows.

Kipps Lake: Blackfeet Indian Reservation. Rainbows.

Kiyo Lake: Cutthroats.

Lenington's Reservoir: Private.

Little Badger Creek: Brookies and cutthroats.

Lower Two Medicine Lake: Blackfeet Indian Reservation. Brookies, rainbows, lake trout, and whitefish.

McCracken (Woody) Reservoir: Private.

McDonald Creek: Brookies, cutthroats, and rainbows.

Middle Fork Dupuyer Creek: Too small.

Middle Fork Teton River: Brookies, cutthroats, and rainbows.

Midvale Creek: Brookies and rainbows.

Mission Lake: Blackfeet Indian Reservation. Rainbows.

Muddy Creek: Brookies.

North Fork Birch Creek: Cutthroats.

North Fork Deep Creek: Posted.

North Fork Dupuyer Creek: Brookies, cutthroats, and rainbows.

North Fork Teton River: Brookies, cutthroats, and rainbows.

North Fork Willow Creek: Private.

O'Haire Reservoir: Private.

Railroad Creek: Blackfeet Indian Reservation. Brookies.

Romain Lakes: Posted.

Scoffin Creek: Brookies and cutthroats.

South Fork Cut Bank Creek: Blackfeet Indian Reservation. Brookies and cutthroats.

South Fork Deep Creek: Posted.

South Fork Dupuyer Creek: Brookies, cutthroats, and rainbows.

South Fork Little Badger Creek: Brookies and cutthroats.

South Fork Teton River: Brookies, cutthroats, and rainbows.

South Fork Two Medicine River: Brookies, cutthroats, and rainbows.

South Fork Willow Creek: Brookies and rainbows.

Spring Creek: Kid's stuff.

Summit Creek: Brookies, cutthroats, and rainbows.

Tomscheck (Robert) Pond: Brookies and rainbows.

Two Medicine Creek: Blackfeet Indian Reservation. Brookies, cutthroats, and rainbows.

West Fork Teton River: Brookies, cutthroats, and rainbows.

Weter (Roy) Lake: Blackfeet Indian Reservation. Kid's stuff.

Whitetail Creek: Blackfeet Indian Reservation. Brookies, cutthroats, and rainbows.

Willow Creek (Marias): Blackfeet Indian Reservation. Brookies and rainbows.

Willow Creek (Teton): Brookies and rainbows.

■ *Special thanks to Ray Buckley and Dean Mattson for their help on the Marias drainage.*

Milk River near Havre
Photo by Steve Helmbrecht

T H E   M I L K

From a fly fishing perspective, the Milk River is pretty slim pickings. Formed by the confluence of the North and South Forks (which head in the mountains of Glacier National Park), the stream flows for nearly 300 miles before joining the Missouri below Fort Peck Dam.

The 35-mile stretch on the Blackfeet Indian Reservation has some fair fishing for brook trout, rainbows, and a few cutthroats, but a tribal permit is required and access is limited. The banks are brushy and undercut and the stream grows some nice trout, but this is also grizzly country. Blackfeet guide Joe Kipp refers to this part of his land as "woolly" and rarely wanders here without a handgun of serious dimensions.

The Milk spends some time in Canada before crossing back into Montana. It's captured in long and narrow Fresno Reservoir before it reaches Havre. Below the dam it drifts nearly 250 miles through wide-open, arid country that is pockmarked with glacial depressions, reservoirs, and streams that frequently go dry in the summer. Most of the fishing in this stretch is for warm water species such as walleye, sauger, channel catfish, and some big northern pike. The state does plant Arlee rainbows in limited numbers and 20,000 smallmouth bass in the upper portion of this section. The bass provide some fine sport on streamers and they will even feed on the mayflies that hatch sporadically throughout the season. The trout and a population of whitefish, well, they swim in this water too, sometimes managing to get themselves stuck on a hook.

The Milk River drainage is not prime trout country, but it is some of the wildest, least-developed land in the state with large populations of upland birds, waterfowl, and big game. This is good country, worthy of anyone's time. Camping alone on the bluffs here will slam a sense of place and humility into a person in a hurry.

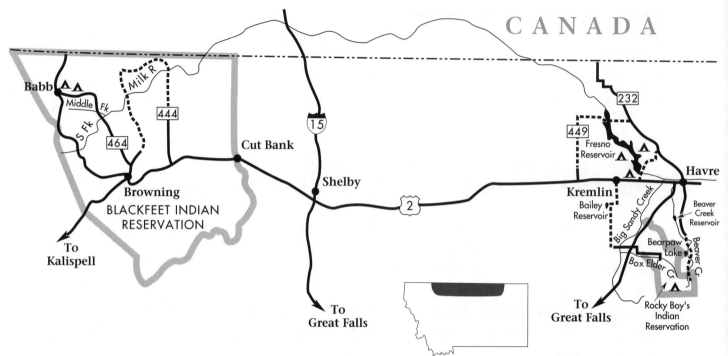

Fishing Waters in the Milk Drainage

Baileys Reservoir: Five miles south of Kremlin, this 70-acre private reservoir provides steady action for rainbows to a few pounds that hit scuds, damsel and dragon fly nymphs, leeches, and assorted other streamers early in the season. By midsummer the weeds get thick and the fishing gets tough, but a fly rod is better for picking the pockets than any other type of tackle. A large Dancing Caddis, an imitation where the hook rides up, is perfect for skittering across the vegetation. In the fall, after the weeds shrivel away, there is a another

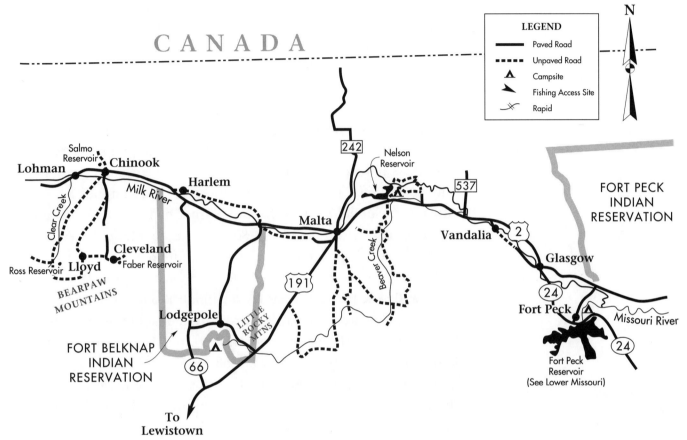

hot period of nymph and streamer fishing right up until ice-over. This one also has pike, crappie, yellow perch, and bass. Ask permission.

Bearpaw Lake: Rainbows, Yellowstone cutthroats, and smallmouth bass are planted in the 55-acre, fairly deep reservoir lying in the open hills beneath the Bears Paw Mountains south of Havre. There's a good campground and spring fishing is fast for hordes of stocked rainbows, most cookie-cutter 12-inchers. The excitement comes from the occasional holdovers to several pounds. The planted fish grow quickly here and by July they are silver and plump from gorging on plentiful food. Float tubes help, and boats with motors are not allowed. This is popular water, and a nice place to camp on the weekdays.

Beaver Creek (Bears Paw Mountains): This Beaver Creek runs for over 30 miles to the Milk just west of Havre along the Hi-Line (U.S. Highway 2). The fishing is relatively good all the way and accessible by road in most places. Brookies and rainbows hang out in the upper reaches, rainbows run the show in the middle section, and browns (some up to a few pounds) and rainbows cruise the slower lower reaches. There are good populations of hoppers and other terrestrials along this stream, especially in the open, grassy portions. This holds true for many streams out here, though a lot of them either dry up or hold only warm-water fish. Channel catfish sucking down hoppers is a strange sight. So, when in doubt, use terrestrials out here in the big open middle of wonderful nowhere.

Beaver Creek (Little Rocky Mountains): Beaver flows for more than 150 miles from the Little Rocky Mountains to the Milk River. It's crossed along the way by state and county roads. The upper runs in the hills are not bad action for brookies and rainbows that never get real big, but love to attack dry flies. This is out-of-the-way fishing that provides an excellent excuse to disappear for awhile with a sleeping bag, a jug of "Old Stump Blower," and a fly rod.

Beaver Creek Reservoir: Known as "first lake" locally, this is one of the better impoundments in what must be a population of 10,000 reservoirs, ponds, and lakes splattered across the Hi-Line countryside beneath the Canadian border. If you fished a pond every day for the rest of your life, you might get to half of them, but it's doubtful. The best among them, like this 180-acre piece of work on Beaver Creek north of Bearpaw Lake, have good numbers of fast-growing rainbows that take leeches, scuds, nymphs, streamers, terrestrials, *Callibaetis* mayflies late in the summer, and even a stray band of marauding caddis once in a while. If the first thing you tie on fails to provoke the trout, keep experimenting. Once you discover what works, you are often in for some steady (if not spectacular) action for big trout that have nowhere to run or hide. And most of the time, the still waters out here are all yours, particularly on the weekdays or in the fall.

Take the Beaver Creek Road south of Havre to reach this reservoir. It fishes well early in the year. The most popular fly in the spring is the Bloodsucker Nymph is size 8 or 10—of course, it imitates a small leech and should be fished in a slow, slow swim over the bottom. Halfback and Prince nymphs are good all summer. By early June the lake becomes fine dry fly water. Locally favorite patterns such as the Adams and the Mosquito have worked for years on Beaver Creek Reservoir. When the weeds get thick around the shoreline, usually by mid-July, the smart angler sits in a float tube or a canoe and casts back to the rim of vegetation.

Bowdoin Lake: Bowdoin is eight miles east of Malta along the Hi-Line (U.S. Highway 2) and better known for the staggering numbers of birds and other wildlife. The area consists of a number of lakes including Bowdoin, Dry, Drumbo, Lakeside Marsh, and Lakeside Marsh Extension. There are over 15,000 acres set aside just south of U.S. 2. Huge flocks of waterfowl move through there in the spring and fall. The bird list, resident and migratory, runs to 160 species. This is an impressive place, but there is little to attract the fly fisher. Look for a ranch pond.

Box Elder Creek: This stream is on the Rocky Boys Indian Reservation in the western Bears Paw Mountains and provides decent fly fishing for brook trout that occasionally top 12 inches. Check at tribal headquarters about accessibility and the possible need for permits. Reached south of Havre.

Clear Creek: Clear Creek joins the Milk River at Lohman after flowing for 35 miles from the flanks of the Bears Paw Mountains. It's followed by gravel roads most of its course. Clear Creek is good fishing in the upper pocket water for brookies, the middle section for rainbows, and the lower grassy, undercut bank stretch for browns of a pound or so. Irrigation hurts the water, but some good browns move up after the fall rains.

Faber Reservoir: A good piece of water sitting at the base of the Bears Paw Mountains just south of Cleveland (not that Cleveland). It's about 30 acres and planted yearly with 15,000 rainbows that grow up fast and chase all sorts of patterns. The highlight of the season is a really fine damsel hatch, the insects swimming to the shoreline and crawling out on the weeds by the millions every morning. On windy days the freshly hatched adults, a pewter gray color at first, get blown back onto the water and the trout slash and swirl in the shallows. A good nymph imitation works when the trout are out a bit deeper intercepting the migrating naturals. This one is private, so be sure you ask permission first.

Fresno Reservoir: Almost 6,000 acres of wind-swept water north of Havre in good mosquito country. Irrigation drawdown hurts the fishing for crappie, walleye, northern pike, and perch. A good dose of mercury contamination make even these fish risky for human consumption. If you like trout, this is not the place to fish, but the coves and bays on the western side of the lake, especially down by the dam, provide fine spring surface action for the pike after "good water" winters—after "bad water" winters the lake is so low that the spawning flats are high and dry.

Grasshopper Reservoir: This 20-acre reservoir south of Chinook is in range land north of the Bears Paw Mountains. Various strains of rainbows in varying size ranges are planted here every year—the mosquitoes, on the other hand, are a naturally reproducing, native population and they need no artificial enhancement. Get here in March, when the ice usually goes off, and the fishing is good off the gravel points. The lake goes through a period in late June when the fishing is very fast for 12- to 14-inch rainbows, with a few to 20 inches, but those mosquitoes are voracious by then. This "fast" time is good dry fly fishing—try a Mosquito for sentimental reasons, but the Black Ant and the Renegade are the local choices. Grasshopper is good fishing throughout the summer, but the trout drop deeper in the warm weather. Cast olive green damsel fly nymphs along the edges of the thick weed beds, allow them to sink to the bottom and strip them up and down in the water. Weeds make this one hard to fish after early July.

Middle Fork Milk River: This one is good for brookies and cutthroats on the Blackfeet Indian Reservation. A tribal permit is required, access is poor, the bugs are rough, and the grizzlies aggressive. So what? Live a little. Think of the stories they'll tell about you back home. "Yeah. That's right. Died on an Indian Reservation. Killed by a crazed 3,000-pound grizzly that ate him whole." They'll buy anything in Manhattan.

Nelson Reservoir: This is a special piece of pike water. There are warm, shallow bays up at the northern end, around Pelican Island. The fish move into one to three feet of water in these bays to spawn. They get very aggressive, nailing surface bugs and divers. This is great "polaroiding"—the angler spots his fish and casts to him. The strike is all visual in the clear water. This shallow water fishing is good through May. After that the fish drop back to deeper water in the main lake around drop-offs, points, and weed beds. The pike run from five to twelve pounds.

A 1994 study by the Montana Department of Health and Environmental Sciences found moderately high concentrations of mercury in the fish (translation: a cautious man wouldn't feed them to his dog). This puts a cloud on the fine walleye fishing here. They're still fine sport, a good fly rod fish with streamers at night in 5 to 10 feet of water, either before or after the hot spells of summer.

Ross Reservoir: This private pond is 12 acres up Wind Creek on the northern edge of the Bears Paw Mountains. It's planted yearly with Yellowstone cutthroats that are dumped in at 6 to 8 inches and quickly reach 14 or more inches and a couple of pounds on the abundant supply of food. The best fishing is from opening day until late June. Don't forget to ask permission.

Salmo Reservoir: Six miles northwest of Chinook, this small, shallow reservoir receives yearly plantings of several thousand Arlee rainbows. If they live more than three years, they are probably some other strain. But even in this brief time frame, the trout often close in on five pounds.

South Fork Milk River: This is a beautiful stream that begins in Glacier Park and runs out onto the Blackfeet Indian Reservation. Open in spots. Brushy in spots. Beaver dammed in spots. Buggy everywhere. Access is somewhat limited and a tribal permit is required for the brookies, cutthroats, and rainbows that sometimes reach a couple of pounds and love drys, hoppers, and Buggers stripped along beneath the banks. This is more of the "woolly" country Blackfeet Indian Joe Kipp talks about on the main Milk River. You are not going to outrun a grizzly in this stuff, but again, you only live once, and this is a pretty little stream in wild, electric country north of Browning.

Bird watching is one of the many pleasures of fly fishing.
Photo by Dan Abrams

Other Waters

Arnold Creek: Brookies.

Big Sandy Coulee: No trout.

Chain of Lakes: No trout.

Cole Gravel Pits: Rainbows.

Dry Fork Milk River: Brookies.

Ester Lake: No trout. It has nice-sized crappies that love Girdle Bugs. Tie this fly with a bead head, so that it jigs up and down on the retrieve, and the crappie will consistently grab it on the "drop." Ester is 30 miles southwest of Malta.

Fox Creek: Brookies.

Frenchman Creek: Northerns.

Gay Reservoir: Rainbows. Private—ask permission.

Glasgow Air Force Base Pond: Rainbows.

Hick's Reservoir: Private.

Hose Reservoir: Rainbows.

Kuhr-Newhouse Reservoir: Closed.

Laird Creek: No trout.

Lenhart Ponds: Private.

Livermore Creek: Brookies and rainbows.

Lodge Pole Creek: Too small.

McNeil Pond: Northerns.

North Faber Reservoir: Rainbows.

North Fork Milk River: Blackfeet Indian Reservation. Brookies and cutthroats.

People's Creek: Brookies and rainbows.

Porcupine Creek: No trout.

Reser Reservoir: Take U.S. 2 between Chinook and Havre; take Road 120 north to Reser. This is fun for bass that will jump all over Yellow Girdle Bugs on any late spring or summer evening.

Rock Creek: Smallmouth bass.

Sage Creek: No trout.

South Fork People's Creek: Brookies.

Thornley Dead River: No trout.

Toad Creek: Too small.

VR9 Reservoir: Rainbows.

Ward's Dam (Reservoir 82): No trout.

White Water Creek: No trout.

Willow Creek: No trout.

Wind Creek: Brookies.

■ *Special thanks to to Joe Kipp for his help on the Milk drainage.*

Misssouri River near Dearborn
Photo by Stan Bradshaw

T H E   M I S S O U R I

The Missouri River starts at Three Forks, not far from the speeding traffic of Interstate 90. Three famous trout streams—the Jefferson, the Madison, and the Gallatin—combine at the Missouri River Headwaters State Park. At their mouths, none of these famous waters is great fly fishing, however. The Jefferson, after receiving the muddy summer flow of the Beaverhead, is silty and warm; the Madison, coming out of Beartrap Canyon, suffers from fish kills during hot years; and the Gallatin is so dewatered in its lower reaches that if it wasn't for the inflow of its tributary, the East Gallatin, it wouldn't contribute any water in some summers. Not a very auspicious start for the mighty Missouri, but the situation improves downriver.

The Missouri takes its time as it winds through the Montana countryside, drifting through wide-open valleys defined by geologic structures with names like Giant Hill, Lava Mountain, Horseshoe Hills, and Hogback Mountain. On the bottom lands there are antelope, and up off the river, you can encounter grouse, deer, elk, coyotes, and, on rare occasions, mountain lions.

A series of dams slow the river even more, forming large bodies of water—Canyon Ferry Lake, Hauser Lake, and Holter Lake. Big trout hold in these lakes until the breeding drive moves them to upstream spawning gravels.

Along its course the Missouri becomes a geologic textbook. The river forces itself through twisted striations of sedimentary rock formations that were part of a vast inland sea 100 million years ago. It becomes canyon country. Interstate 15 and many lesser roads bend and swerve as they conform to walls of ochre, pink, red, and oxidized green.

Neither the brown trout nor rainbow trout populations are natural. Both species reproduce in the system, but the survival rates of young fish in the dewatered tributaries and in the main river are fair at best. The reservoirs are heavily stocked, however, and many of these trout wash over the dams in high water or through the turbines and accidentally populate the river. The most prevalent species in the river is a native—the whitefish populations reach an astonishing 15,000 per mile in some sections, and they reproduce quite well.

143

A Special Fly for the Missouri River

If there is a "universal" fly, especially for weedy, rich environments like the Missouri River, it is the Pheasant Tail Nymph. This pattern was developed specifically for spring creeks heavy with weed growth and full of small mayfly nymphs. Frank Sawyer, the great English river keeper on the Avon, designed this fly specifically to match the Blue-Winged Olives of that water. The same genera of mayflies, similar in color and form, are a major part of our insect fauna.

PHEASANT TAIL NYMPH

Thread: none (an important feature of the correctly tied PT)

Tail: three cock pheasant tail fibers—these are formed with the tips of the body herls

Underbody: fine copper wire with a hump at the thorax

Overbody: pheasant tail fibers wound with the copper wire and tied slightly fatter at the thorax

Wing Case: pheasant tail fibers doubled and redoubled

This is the dressing from Sawyer's 1958 classic, *Nymphs and the Trout*. Most commercially tied Pheasant Tails sold in fly shops are tied in a more conventional fashion, but they still successfully imitate a variety of mottled mayfly nymphs. On spring creeks and tailwaters, which harbor mainly smaller mayflies, the Pheasant Tail in sizes 16 through 22 is an indispensable pattern. It is the most consistent nymph throughout the season on the Missouri River.

It's often fished as a dropper dangling from 6 inches to a few feet off the back of a buoyant dry fly. A piece of monofilament is tied onto the eye or bend of the dry fly. The nymph hangs under the floating fly—an easy-to-see pattern that not only signals a strike on the nymph but also helps the sunken pattern drift drag free.

Three Forks to Toston Dam—There isn't much gradient to the river in this 23-mile section. It doesn't get squeezed by canyon walls until just above the town of Toston. It isn't classic trout water—it gets too warm in the summer and there is usually a brown tinge to the river. This doesn't mean that an angler willing to slam Woolly Buggers against the bank can't catch respectable trout, but neither the water nor the fishing methods are particularly pretty. The best times for dry fly action are in the spring, from March until the end of April, before runoff, when there's a good hatch of Blue-Winged Olive mayflies, and again in the fall, after the river cools down, and the lingering Trico mayflies or the late season Blue-Winged Olives become important to the trout.

This is a good section to float with a guide who knows the moods of this upper water. There is public access at Fairweather, about half-

way between Three Forks and Toston, and a boat takeout just above the Toston Dam. There are fly shops in this area that tout this water, but the key to fishing this section is knowing the "when" and "where" of it

Toston Dam to Canyon Ferry Reservoir—Toston isn't a "real" dam. It's a low irrigation facility that backs up a pool of water, and, in the last few years, generates a bit of electricity for the state. There's no cold bottom flow, and when the water in the pool warms up and spills over the top of the dam it can reach the high 70's. During midsummer these temperatures drive the trout down to Canyon Ferry Reservoir. The populations of full-time resident fish are pretty pathetic, less than a few hundred brown trout per mile in some parts of this 23-mile stretch.

One problem may be poor spawning rates in the few good tributaries in this area. The Montana Department of Fish, Wildlife, and Parks has instituted special regulations to help the trout. Parts of the Toston to Canyon Ferry stretch are closed in the spring (check cur-

144

rent regulations each season) to protect spawning rainbows, and three important tributaries—Warm Springs Creek, Dry Creek, and Deep Creek—have shortened general seasons. Parts of these streams have been opened to spawners and, with the cooperation of local irrigators, rehabilitated; and rainbows are already using these waters extensively.

This Toston stretch does change from scrub woman to princess in the autumn. Suddenly, this is a great place to catch large brown trout. Roughly 80 percent of the spawning female brown trout that run upstream from Canyon Ferry Reservoir are between 18 and 24 inches. So if 24 inches means a three- to four-pound fish, and many of the remaining 20 percent trout are larger than that, it's easy to understand the attraction the river has for the trophy hunter.

Methods vary widely on this stretch. Paul Heeny saw an angler there "using a two-handed rod, at least 13 feet long, and throwing heavy tube flies. He'd put the cast down and across, loop a big mend of slack to let the fly sink deep, and then let it swing in towards shore. He was catching fish, too, by working the fly exactly over a long, deep slot of river where the browns were holding."

Paul was working that same slot that November day, standing chest deep in the cold water and dead-drifting a tandem rig of an egg pattern and a scud pattern under a large yarn indicator. He was also catching brown trout, including two over 25 inches, and, in his words, "too many whitefish and even some suckers by scraping the bottom."

The deep methods, either streamers or nymphs, can work well in this stretch. For streamer fishing, use a Wool Head Sculpin, Hair Sucker, Egg-Sucking Leech, Double-Egg Sperm Fly, or a Crystal Bugger. For nymphing, use a Marabou Single Egg, Big Horn Scud, Rubber Legs Bead Head Squirrel Nymph, Brown/Orange Deep Sparkle Pupa, or Olive Hare's Ear.

You can fish shallow, too, but you have to concentrate on the lips of the pools at the heads of the riffles. The spawning females dig their redds in water so thin that it barely covers their backs. These fish will hit a small, unweighted wet fly better than they will a large streamer. A size-12 Partridge and Orange Soft Hackle or a Firecracker are proven attractors, used either separately or in a two-fly rig. Sneak into position, staying well back, and cast down and across. Try to "wake" the flies across the river just above the lip of the pool.

The brown trout don't start running heavy until mid- or late October. They stay in the river through November. The overcast, or even raining and sleeting, days are often the best. On sunny days the deep techniques prove most effective, but on the miserable days the active, shallow-water techniques take a fair share of the big fish.

Canyon Ferry Dam to Hauser Lake—Below Canyon Ferry the river dumps pretty directly into Hauser Lake. There isn't much of a tailwater fishery here, but the old river channel is shallow enough to trap the outflow from the dam for almost a mile. You have to move out from the shoreline flats until you find the current and the channel. Then work a fly, either a nymph or a streamer, deep to reach the fish. There's a good population of fat, 12- to 22-inch resident fish here all the time, more rainbows than browns, and in the spring and the fall there's an influx of spawners.

Hauser Dam to Holter Lake—There are roughly 1,500 trout per mile, 90 percent of them rainbows, in this 3-mile stretch. The old state record brown trout, a twenty-eight-pound fish, came from the heavy turbulence just below the dam. It's big water, and so varied in its 3-mile run that you can use just about any technique. And, if you're willing to do a little walking, you aren't likely to be bothered by crowds.

The huge fish of the early 70's just below the dam are either gone or very rare now, but there are still plenty of browns and rainbows up to five pounds here. They sit below the generators and gobble the chopped-up or injured fish that come through the turbines. This was where the Hair Sucker made its reputation as a big fish fly—on October 4, 1974, Bill Seeples caught five brown trout weighing between six and eleven pounds in four hours of fishing. He used a lead-core shooting head, short leader, and 3/0 weighted fly, casting as far as possible up into the turbulence of the outflow and mending repeatedly to let the line and fly sink as deep as possible.

Downstream from the dam the river is still big, but there are long riffles and flats that can be worked with a dry fly or nymph. Anthony Perpignano fishes this water a lot. "The secret is walking downstream from the dam," he notes. "There's no road along the

POPULAR FLIES

Dry Flies/Emergers

Buzz Ball

CDC Emerger

Clear Wing Spinner

Comparadun

Double Wing

Duck Butt Dun

Elk Hair Caddis

Emergent Sparkle Pupa

Fitzsimmons Adult Midge

Griffith's Gnat

Halo Mayfly Emerger

Henry's Fork Hopper

Humpy

Mohawk

Parachute PMD

Serendipity

Shroeder Parachute Hopper

Stimulator

Trude

Wulff

west side of the river, and floaters are rare on this stretch, so after a half mile you're pretty much alone. The fish, mostly rainbows averaging 14 to 17 inches, rise really well all summer during the evenings. There are big caddis hatches and an Emergent Sparkle Pupa is consistently effective on these trout."

Holter Dam to Cascade—This is the water most fly fishermen hear about when someone mentions the Missouri River. From Holter Dam to Cascade, roughly 35 miles of water, this is like a giant spring creek. The bottom is covered with weeds that harbor great populations of scuds and aquatic insects. Consistent hatches of midges, mayflies, and caddisflies bring trout to the top all year. Both rainbows and browns feed in pods, holding just under the surface and sipping mayfly duns and spinners.

The trout populations fluctuate a lot from year to year. The population of both rainbows and browns combined can run anywhere from 2,000 catchable (10 inches or larger) fish per mile to over 4,000 fish, depending on conditions. After a few seasons of low water the numbers of rainbows in the river drop off as spawning recruitment from dried-up tributaries declines—let there be one high water summer and the numbers increase sharply.

One explanation for this strong correlation between high water and high fish populations suggests that, in part, it comes from rainbows stocked in Holter getting washed into the river.

The rainbows in the Missouri are getting bigger, especially in the upper section near the dam. It used to be rare to catch a fish over 20 inches in the upper water. The Montana Department of Fish, Wildlife, and Parks used to stock Holter Lake with Arlee-strain rainbows, a short-lived hatchery fish that would grow quickly to 18 inches or so in three seasons and then die from old age, but recently the department has been stocking the lake with longer-lived strains, principally the DeSmet and Eagle Lake rainbows. And now the fish in the river are growing bigger.

The first dry fly fishing of the year starts with the winter midges on any warm day. These aren't necessarily small insects—there are

Nymphs/Wet Flies

Bead Head Hare's Ear

Big Horn Scud

Brown/Orange Deep Sparkle Pupa

Diving Caddis

Firecracker

Floating Damsel Nymph

Marabou Midge Larva

Marabou Single Egg

Olive Hare's Ear

Partridge & Orange Soft Hackle

Pheasant Tail

Prince Nymph

Rubber Legs Bead Head Squirrel Nymph

San Juan Worm

Streamers

Crystal Bugger

Double-Egg Sperm Fly

Egg-Sucking Leech

Hair Sucker

Marabou Muddler

Stub Wing Bucktail

Wool Head Sculpin

Woolly Bugger

big black buzzers matched with a size-14 fly. Other species of midges are smaller, and come in a full range of colors. Effective patterns include the Serendipity and Halo Midge Pupa for the emerger and the Fitzsimmons Adult Midge and the Griffith's Gnat for the adult. Another good pattern, the Buzz Ball, matches the clumped up, mating insects.

From mid-April through June, and again from September through mid-October, the Blue-Winged Olives will emerge from late morning until around four in the afternoon. The dun is probably the most important stage for the angler, but the nymph just prior to emergence, caught in the surface film, can also take trout. Bead Head Hare's Ears, Halo Mayfly Emergers, and CDC Emergers work well prior to and during the initial stages of the emergence. A Comparadun or a Duck Butt Dun matches the adult. A good generic pattern is a grizzly or olive parachute. The size range varies from 16 through 24, with the smaller patterns being more prevalent in the fall.

The Blue-Winged Olive hatch can sometimes be mystifying—fish rising everywhere to everything but your fly, no matter what it is. On these occasions, it can be effective to strip a small bead head or pheasant-tail nymph back through the working fish in short (6- to 8-inch) strips. Blue-Winged Olive nymphs are swimmers, and this action will often trigger a strike when nothing else will.

The PMDs start in early summer and they are so steady that, in truth, they could be called "Pale Morning, Noon, and Evening Duns." The fish get very selective after weeks of a steady diet of these insects. In fact, maybe more than any other hatch on the river, the PMDs, at one time or another will reduce you to distracted, mumbling gibberish. They'll ignore any presentation, no matter what the fly, if it has the least bit of drag. A good imitation, a Halo Mayfly Emerger or a Parachute PMD, for example, has to hit a feeding trout right in the mouth. Some days, it doesn't matter how precise you are or how good your pattern is—the fish don't care. On those days, your time might be as well spent in the cool recesses a local tavern, commiserating on the foul and fickle ways of trout.

Tricos hatch from July to September. Tricos provide plenty of action for the one- to three-pounders during the morning hours. These Tricos tend to run a little larger in the Missouri than elsewhere.

By "larger", this means sizes 18 to 20, instead of 22 to 26. The ambitious angler who gets out on the water before 7:00 a.m. will hit the emergence of Trico duns, and this stage can actually provide better fishing than the spinner fall that occurs later in the day. The spinners typically start swarming between 8:00 a.m. and 9:00 a.m. and on a windless day they hover in heavy clouds. That's the problem—once they hit the water there are so many of them that it's hard to get a fly to a fish with so many naturals on the surface. Good patterns include the Clear Wing Spinner and the Comparadun. Recognizing Trico spinners is relatively easy. They are small, of course. They have three tails with the male's about three times the length of its body and the female's the same length as her body. The wings are clear and there are no hind wings, unlike most mayflies.

Caddisflies are also important on the river. Every summer evening you'll see heavy hatches, with the mating flights cruising up the river. At times they're so thick you don't dare breathe through your mouth. Right at dark the egg-laying and the general emergence begins and the river boils with the slashes and splashes of rising fish. The trout could be feeding on the Spotted Sedge, which peaks in late June and early July, or the Little Sister Sedge, which spreads out over the summer. Or in June or July, the fish might be taking the summer Grannom (also called the Black Caddis). The following assorted color combinations should stand you in good stead: (1) brown wing and yellow body; (2) tan wing and ginger body; and (3) dark, almost black wing and very dark green body. All in sizes 10 through 16. You can match the hatching insect with an Emergent Sparkle Pupa. It will catch twenty to thirty fish on a good evening. Likewise, the Diving Caddis will imitate the egg-laying females of the Spotted Sedge and the Little Sister Sedge (both of which go underwater to oviposit). A dark Elk Hair Caddis usually works when the Grannoms fall and lay their eggs on the surface, but during the past few summers it seems as if the fish saw so much of this fly that they started to snub it. That might just be my imagination (or poor presentation), but it also seems that newer, more exotic imitations, such as Lawson's EZ Caddis, Mathew's X Caddis, or Mercer's Z-Wing Caddis, all of which give a very realistic profile on the water, have worked better during the heavy feeding.

The one perplexing phenomenon on the river are the random "explosion" rises. All around trout are sipping the prevalent insect and all of a sudden a big fish erupts through the surface. These rises are caused by one of three food forms—damsel nymphs, large emerging caddis, or minnows and fry. If the explosions are really random, and against the bank, then the trout are probably busting fry. A Marabou Muddler, a Stub Wing Bucktail or a Woolly Bugger, cast into the shore and swung out into the current, looks like a minnow escaping into deeper water. If the rises are swirls more than leaps, and happen with any consistency around the mats of shoreline weeds, the fish may be gorging on damsel nymphs—on a windy day they may even be taking the pewter gray, freshly emerged adult damsels that are getting blown back onto the surface. A Floating Damsel Nymph, cast from the shore out into the river and retrieved with spurts, fools these trout.

If the rises happen out in the main current, fish rocketing into the air, then the trout are feeding on large, emerging caddisflies. This happens more in the fall, when the large, case-making types hatch on the river. A sunken fly, such as a weighted size-8 Brown and Orange Deep Sparkle Pupa, fished dead drift over the tops of the mid-river weeds, works better than a surface pattern for these feeders. Most of the time, these explosive main-current rises are so random that your time is better spent working the more regular hatching activity.

Even when nothing is hatching the Missouri is a fine dry fly fishery. In low-water years especially, this is a shallow river and trout always seem aware of the surface. As a result, terrestrial imitations produce consistently all summer. Good grasshopper patterns, such as the Shroeder Parachute Hopper and the Henry's Fork Hopper, can bring trout a long way. A good trick is to put on two or even three Henry's Fork Hoppers, cast them into the bank, and retrieve them with hard strips that make them swim and dive. An ant or beetle pattern, fished as a trailer behind a big dry fly can be productive at times.

Even attractor dry flies have a place on the Missouri River. On this smooth, tricky tailwater the secret is often using very small attractors, 18's and 20's, or at the opposite extreme, very large attractors, 6's and 8's. The Wulff's, Humpies, Trudes, Stimulators, and Double Wings all have a place on this fishery. All too often first-time visitors to the Missouri resist using attractors. One formerly skeptical angler, James Carr, tells of taking a 24-inch, 7½-pound brown trout on a size-6 Double Wing.

Of course, you can always go subsurface when the trout aren't rising. Favorite nymphs on the river include not only the standards, such as the Pheasant Tail, Hare's Ear, and Prince Nymph, but also the types of flies that seem to work on tailwater fisheries all over the West, such as the San Juan Worm, Hot Pink Shrimp, Brassie, Marabou Midge Larva, and Bead Head Serendipity (in fact, a bead-head anything—possibly even on a bare hook—has become one of the most consistent producers year-round). Hanging the nymph off the back of a buoyant, visible dry fly, such as a Mohawk or a Stimulator, is a standard technique.

Visiting anglers need to master the "Missouri River lift." When a fish is hooked, either a rainbow or a brown, it might jump once or twice, but sooner or later it's going to dig into the heavy weeds. If too much line and leader gets wrapped in salad, the trout breaks off or pulls loose. To prevent this you have to lift your whole arm, mimicking the Statue of Liberty, as soon as you set the hook, and you have to keep that arm and the rod high throughout the fight.

The quality of the fishing, especially the dry fly fishing, depends on the amount of water released from the dam. Holter is not a peaking power facility, so the flow through the dam pretty much mirrors the flow into the lake. The reservoir can smooth the highs and lows a little, but during a low water year the river is going to run at roughly 2,500 cubic feet per second (cfs) and during a high water year it is going to run as heavy as 10,000 or more cfs. Above 6,000 cfs the Missouri is a vastly different river than it is at even 4,000 cfs. Wading becomes tough, and the holding water is neither so obvious nor as easily accessible as it is at lower flows.

At first glance, even in low-water years, the Missouri can be intimidating. It is hundreds of feet wide, but this can be rapidly reduced to pockets along the banks, long riffles, and channels around the islands. Look at the detail of the river right in front of you, and not the entire river. With this in mind, the Missouri becomes more accessible, and less inscrutable.

Cascade to Fort Peck Reservoir—Below the city of Cascade, and the mouth of the Smith River, the river begins changing from a cold-water to a warm-water fishery. There are good fly fishing opportunities for goldeyes, free-rising, insect feeders that reach 16 inches, and for smallmouth bass. There is also a scattering of trout down past Great Falls, until the river gets too warm, too sluggish, and too muddy. While this stretch may not be premier fly fishing water, it is nonetheless worth the trip. Below Fort Benton, the Missouri River Breaks is some of the wildest country left in the lower forty-eight states. An occasional fish on a fly is just a small bonus to a truly spectacular trip.

Hell Creek Badlands
Photo by L.A. Huffman
Courtesy of Montana Historical Society, Helena

The Missouri below Fort Peck Reservoir—Several hundred lonely miles to the east, below mammoth Fort Peck Dam, steelhead-like rainbows thrive in a fresh, clear tailwater fishery, mostly unknown and only rarely fished over with a fly. This stretch of the Missouri has rainbow trout that have been reported to exceed fifteen pounds. It is virtually unknown and unfished with fly rods. Less than two hours from the North Dakota border lies some tough, deep-water fishing for the diehard fly fishers.

Pat Clancey, who has worked for the Montana Department of Fish, Wildlife, and Parks at Fort Peck, says that there are rainbows in the tailwater that exceed five pounds, and adds that bait fishers consistently take trout over seven pounds. Most of these fish never find their way back into the river. This fragile population cannot stand this kind of pressure.

Fort Peck Dam is earthen and 6 miles long with a highway running across the top. When you pull over on top of the dam, you can look back west across much of the 189-mile length of Fort Peck Lake. Most of the time when you do this, the wind will try and blow you down the hill and into the Missouri flowing out onto the plains hundreds of feet below.

The river is big here. Too big to successfully fish the main channel. Again, as with the upper river, only more so, you must cut the water down to some semblance of fishable size. Do this by working a side channel, which is best done in the spring.

Rainbows are on the move at this time and there is sufficient flow to float you over some gravel bars. The water is anywhere from 100 to 200 yards wide. The trout hold out in deep (8 feet or more) runs and chutes. This is where you will fish your streamer. A one-mile section of prime spawning habitat is off limits to anglers. Big signs make sure you are aware of this fact.

Clancey says that the only aquatic insect life of any note is Chironomid and Dipteran, which more or less eliminates matching the hatch. The water is deep and the fish concentrate on forage species. Use size 2 to 2/0 Zonkers, Matuka Sculpins, Stub Wing Bucktails, and similar-sized streamers fished with a fast-sinking line and a short (four feet), stout (1X) leader. Even in the best of conditions, this is tough work. Factor in gusting winds that come with sufficient strength to force you to shift your feet to maintain balance and you're talking austere angling conditions, especially from a boat. You can handle some of the water from shore, but a stable flat-bottom craft will give you a decent casting platform away from bankside obstructions, and you can fish the water thoroughly.

La Barge Rock towers over the water of the Upper Missouri National Wild and Scenic River.
Photo by Merrill J. Mattes
Courtesy of Montana Historical Society, Helena

Eight-weight rods are not too much in this section of the river. So, to fish here, you really must be excited by the idea of fly fishing unknown turf for big, frequently uncooperative trout. If you measure enjoyment in terms of numbers of trout caught and released, don't come to this reach of the Missouri. But, if you like wild surroundings and the chance to connect with a big, powerful rainbow and can accept fishless days, the river below Fort Peck Dam might be worth at least a day or two of your life.

Fishing Waters of the Upper Missouri— Headwaters to Great Falls

Bean Lake: It is planted with 20,000 rainbows each year and provides good fishing in the foothills west of Augusta. Some fish survive the onslaught of their first season in this shallow pond, and there are some springs that prevent winterkill. The rainbows will reach a few pounds and take leeches and damsel nymphs from mid-July on.

Beaver Creek (below Hauser): This tributary is good fishing for rainbows and big brown trout up from the Missouri below Hauser Dam. It flows through canyon country, with good public access off the Beaver Creek Road on the lower and best-fishing sections. The upper reaches hold little brookies. This is a good fall stream for fat browns that will hit large streamers.

Beaver Creek (Sun River): Early in the year this stream has some good fishing for rainbow spawners up from the Sun River along with some cutthroat and brook trout. By summer, flows are too low to provide decent action.

Canyon Creek: This tributary of Little Prickly Pear Creek is on the Lincoln Highway (Montana 200). It offers good dry fly fishing for brookies and rainbows plus some nice fall-run browns. There are some good stretches right along the road—tough casting but nice water. Anthony Perpignano says, "The trick with Canyon Creek, in one line, is finding the deep pockets, but then you have to approach each pool very carefully and fish it gently to take more than one trout out of each spot. Hopper patterns work all summer, with the smaller sizes, 12 and 14, doing much better than bigger imitations."

Canyon Ferry Reservoir: This lake receives more fishing pressure than any other water in the state. It is a huge reservoir, about fifteen minutes east and south of Helena, and it's followed by state and county roads. This water is 25 miles long by 4 miles wide and has some good fishing all season around small islands at the southern end, mainly for rainbows but also for a few big browns in the fall. There are also perch, pike, walleyes (the gift of some slack-jawed bucket biologist), suckers (many from out-of-state), kokanee, and brook trout. The Montana Department of Fish, Wildlife, and Parks (FWP) plants hundreds of thousands of rainbows of varying sizes each year along with a good number of brown trout. In 1990 the state switched from Arlee strain rainbows to DeSmet and Eagle Lake strains. This has translated into larger trout among the holdover population. There are marinas, restaurants, campgrounds, homes, boat ramps, human sacrifices, and a little bit of everything else here. This place can be a serious zoo at midsummer. The best times to fish are in the spring for the rainbows and maybe in the fall for the browns that move quickly up into the shallows to spawn.

The easiest fishing is in the spring—at times it can be too easy and a fly fisherman can get jaded with catching two- to six-pound Eagle Lake rainbows. It can get so easy when the spawning rainbows congregate along certain stretches of shoreline that FWP has to close sections of the lake to protect the population. After the ice goes off Canyon Ferry, the better areas include the bays on the north end of the lake, around the dam, along Magpie Point, and near Kim's Marina. The peak of the shoreline concentrations vary from year to year, but it generally happens sometime in May. You can walk the shoreline and spot cruising fish. These fish, planted from docks in this area, have imprinted on the lakeshore and come back by the thousands, looking

When the Eagle Lake rainbows make their spring run at the north end of Canyon Ferry, you don't even need to get your feet wet.
Photo by Stan Bradshaw

for love. The problem is, it's in all the wrong places. Since there is no running water to incubate the eggs, all this energy is for naught. Talk about all revved up and nowhere to go . . .

Nonetheless, these fish put on quite a show. They nest and protect their territory with all the ardor of a Babine Steelhead. At times, they'll be rolling right at your feet, oblivious to you. The standard drill is to cast to them with a Woolly Bugger, a small nymph, or a small egg imitation below a strike indicator. Cast ahead of the cruisers

UPPER MISSOURI RIVER

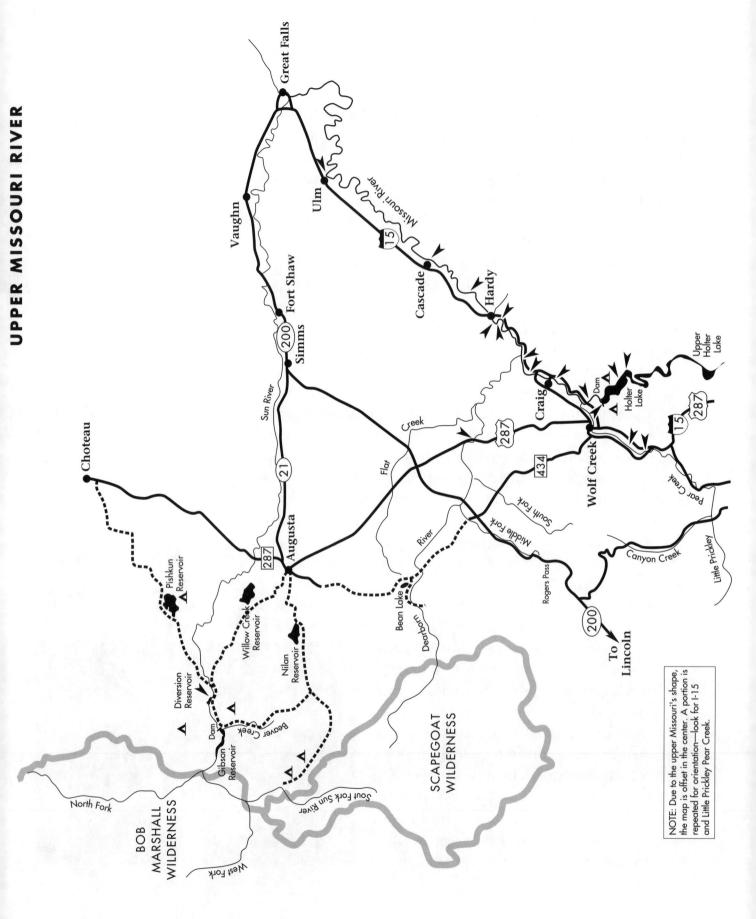

NOTE: Due to the upper Missouri's shape, the map is offset in the center. A portion is repeated for orientation—look for I-15 and Little Prickley Pear Creek.

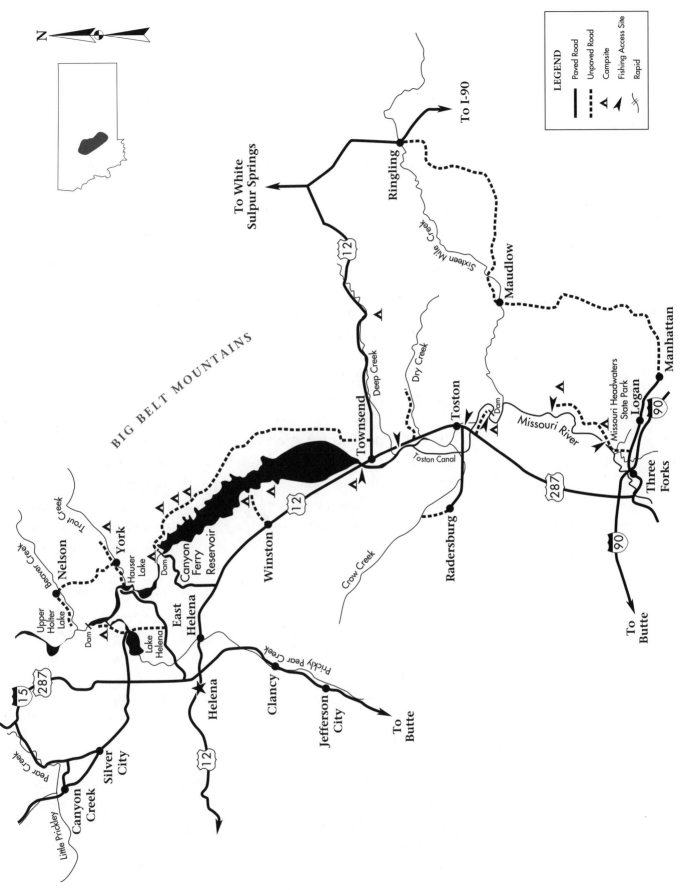

UPPER MISSOURI RIVER

LEGEND

Paved Road
Unpaved Road
Campsite
Fishing Access Site
Rapid

N

To I-90

Ringling

To White
Sulpur Springs

Maudlow

Sixteen Mile Creek

12

BIG BELT MOUNTAINS

Deep Creek

Dry Creek

Townsend

Toston

Dam

Missouri Headwaters
State Park

Missouri River

Manhattan

Logan

90

Three
Forks

287

Toston Canal

Trout Creek

Nelson

York

Hauser Lake

Dam

Canyon Ferry Reservoir

Winston

12

Radersburg

Crow Creek

Beaver Creek

Upper
Holter
Lake

Dam

Lake
Helena

East
Helena

287

15

Helena

Clancy

Prickly Pear Creek

Jefferson
City

To
Butte

90

To
Butte

Silver
City

Canyon
Creek

Pear Creek

Little Prickley

12

157

and let it dangle; or maybe impart a small twitch. This is not a finesse game, and, at times, it can run dangerously close to bobber fishing. As one Canyon Ferry regular put it, "This is a good time to kick back in a lawn chair with a six pack and just watch that indicator." On the other hand, these are hot, energetic fish, and a couple of days of 20-plus-inch fish in the spring can really take the edge off a long winter.

After the spring flurry the rainbows drop into deeper water, but early morning float tubing at the mouths of Goose Bay and Confederate Bay is still productive. Use sinking lines, but don't go too deep—search from the 6-foot to 12-foot levels until you find the trout (which hang just under the thermocline). The best flies are perch-colored and silver-colored streamers.

Crow Creek: This is a good fishery for rainbow, brook, and some brown trout. It enters the river near Toston. The stream suffers greatly, though, at the hands of irrigators and from mining pollution. Drive to Radersburg and start fishing upstream from there. There are more than 20 miles of good water in the Helena National Forest, but with easy access and public campgrounds this becomes a popular area during the summer.

It's a rich stream in the upper reaches, with lots of great deep-pool structure. When the mayfly and caddisfly hatches are happening, the trout rise freely to generally matching flies. At other times they'll take a Parachute Adams or an EZ Caddis eagerly enough. The smaller fish are so quick to rise that after a while the game becomes finding the trophies—rainbows up to 14 inches or brookies up to 10 inches.

Dearborn River: It heads along the Continental Divide in the Scapegoat Wilderness, flowing for over 60 miles to the Missouri south of Great Falls. The mountain section is good riffle, pool, and pocket water for cutthroat and rainbow trout averaging perhaps 10 inches. The middle section is often hit hard by irrigation demands but there are some brook and rainbow trout. In the canyon stretch north of Wolf Creek some nice browns to several pounds and rainbows of similar size are taken by those floating the river. The most popular put-in access is where Montana 287 crosses the river, and the shuttle required for the trip is time-consuming. Large nymphs and streamers work well until midsummer when water levels make floating difficult. Autumn precipitation raises the level of the Dearborn and this is the best time for the browns.

One notable hatch on the river is the Skwala stonefly in March and April. This pre-runoff insect creates some of the best dry fly fishing of the season. Anglers who hit this regularly have their favorite flies: Richard Rose—size 10 Olive Air Head; Anthony Perpignano—size 10 Black Stimulator; Payton Lear—size 8 Dark Green Fluttering Stone. The trout run bigger, with rainbows to 16 inches and browns to 18 inches, during the hatch.

Deep Creek: Much of this water is followed by U.S. 12. This is a pretty little stream east of Townsend that flows through open sage flats with willow-choked banks and then through rocky, narrow canyon land above. There are nice browns to maybe a couple of pounds below, but permission is required. Small brookies and rainbows take a little bit of everything—drys, wets, and nymphs—in the small pools and runs up above. This valley gets especially heavy infestations of grasshoppers, making a good hopper imitation a must in the summer.

John Barsness, who lives next to the stream, said about the grasshopper hordes of 1991, "It was scary. It was scorched earth. First they ate the leaves off the apple trees up to fifteen feet, then the onions down to the roots in the garden, and finally the insulation off the furnace pipes outside the house."

Dickens Lake: It is planted with rainbows that grow quickly and sometimes reach five pounds. This is typical "East of the Divide" reservoir fishing, not far from Gibson Dam (northwest of Augusta). The wind blows and the lake gets too weedy to fish by mid-July. Leeches, scuds, damsel nymphs, and assorted streamers produce, as do *Callibaetis* from August into September. Hoppers, ants, and beetles also work in the summer.

Diversion Reservoir: This lake is northwest of Augusta, impounded by a large concrete dam, and over a mile long by as much as 700 feet wide. It offers average fishing for rainbow and brook trout that average less than a foot.

Dry Creek: A small stream crossed by U.S. 10 north of Toston with a little bit of fishing in the upper reaches for rainbows and some brookies. The lower reaches are dry most of the year, but the Broadwater Irrigation District and a local landowner, working with FWP, has managed to maintain rearing habitat for rainbow trout fry long enough to get them back to the Missouri. Nice, open, and dry (really?) country.

Flat Creek: Flat Creek is a meandering, small stream that begins south of Augusta and winds through open, grassy land with lots of undercut banks that hold some brookies, fat rainbows, and big browns. Much of it is posted, making access possible only when crossed by county road or through permission from area ranchers.

Gibson Reservoir: Gibson is over five miles long by a quarter mile wide. You'll need a boat or float tube to reach rainbows and brown trout that will exceed 15 inches and smaller numbers of small brookies and cutthroats. The problem with this irrigation reservoir is the drastic summer drawdown (hurting both aesthetics and basic productivity). Working the creek inlets with streamers or nymphs is the best bet, especially early and late in the season. The estuary of the forks of the Sun River, at the upper end, is the only consistent area for rising trout.

Hauser Lake: This large impoundment on the Upper Missouri holds some large rainbows and browns. This one is about a dozen miles northeast of Helena and about 6 miles below Canyon Ferry and measures nearly 3,800 acres of surface area. There are public campgrounds, boating activity, and sapphires and garnets lying in narrow seams in the cliffs surrounding the lake. The fishing is best through the ice (which is tough with a Blue-Winged Olive), but there is also some action in the spring for the rainbows and in the fall for the browns. The lake also supports walleyes (which are fine sport in Wisconsin and Ontario, but have all the fighting qualities of a wet towel in Montana waters). Hauser has kokanees, which make the walleyes look like spectacular battlers, that average one and a half to two pounds and run up to four pounds. Suckers and perch provide forage for some large browns that rarely come up from the deep. There are also some truly huge carp if you're looking for a little different challenge.

Holter Lake: Holter covers nearly 8 square miles of water impounded along the Missouri above and below Gates of the Mountains 30 miles north of Helena. There are good numbers of rainbows and browns, some reaching five or more pounds, but these are usually taken by trollers working way down deep. There are also perch, which concentrate by midsummer over the weed beds in the river channel at the upper end of the lake, and suckers. Lots of boat traffic, too.

Lake Helena: This one is over 2,000 acres with tons of carp (for which there is a thriving commercial operation) and some nice rainbows that thrive on the small bugs lurking in the algae. FWP planted largemouth bass a few years back, but they don't seem to have taken hold very well. It is best fished in the spring with large streamers.

The lake itself might not be prime fly fishing water, but there is a whole system of irrigation ditches draining into it. The water is pumped out of Canyon Ferry and flows through the intervening valley. Anthony Perpignano, in his words, "hikes along every dirt-bottomed canal. They all hold trout, mostly below culverts in the wash-out holes. The browns run up to 16 inches and the rainbows run up to 14 inches. They take hopper patterns. The closer you get to Lake Helena, the better the fishing gets." If you decide to try ditch-hopping, make sure the land isn't posted or that you have permission. Montana law doesn't recognize irrigation ditches as public water.

Little Prickly Pear Creek: There's an inverse relationship—when the Missouri is fishing poorly, anglers come up here, but when the Missouri is prime, the stream is almost empty. One of the secrets then, for small-creek lovers, is to come here when the main river is sizzling hot.

There are three distinct sections. The upper reaches, from the mouth of Canyon Creek down to Sieben Ranch, meander through deep slow pools and undercut runs. The resident fish, rainbows up to 16 inches and browns up to 18 inches, feed on good hatches of mayflies and caddisflies. Fly selection in this low-gradient water gets more critical, however. The Emergent Sparkle Pupa and the Diving Caddis are standards for the caddis hatches; a Sparkle Dun works well when the mayflies are popping; a Goddard Caddis and a Stimulator are good searching flies when there aren't a lot of bugs on the water; either a small Joe's Hopper or a Mohawk makes a good terrestrial fly; and a Olive Flashback Hare's Ear or a Red Fox Squirrel Nymph are effective subsurface patterns. This is also prime rattlesnake country, so watch your step.

The middle reaches, from the Sieben Exit down to Wolf Creek, and the lower reaches, from Wolf Creek down to the mouth at the Missouri River, both get a lot of migratory fish. These trout, both rainbows and browns, stay in the stream long after spawning time. It's not rare to catch fish over 20 inches even during the summer on Little Prickly Pear. The water that runs parallel to I-15 has been rehabilitated and improved over the past decade to overcome the damage done by highway construction. There are some good pools and shelf water within walking distance of the road. The stream is closed in the fall to protect spawning browns from the Missouri.

This shallow little stream tends to get pretty hot by mid-July in most years, and the fish are easily stressed. In midsummer, give this one a break and try somewhere else.

McClellan Creek: This one has brookies, cutthroats, browns, and rainbows. Above the Northern Pacific Reservoir this is just a bouncing, small stream with bouncing, small trout. Below the reservoir there is only a quarter or so mile of stream before it empties into Prickly Pear, but this piece is a miniature tailwater. The bottom is coated with the little four-sided cases of Grannom caddis, and there are fine summer hatches of these insects. It is difficult casting with lots of overhanging brush, but an Emergent Sparkle Pupa rolled and tucked into the tight spots takes brookies to 10 inches, rainbows to 12 inches, and browns to 18 inches.

Middle Fork Dearborn River: It heads near Rogers Pass and it's followed by Montana 200 most of its length. It is fair fishing for cutthroat, brook, rainbow, and perhaps a stray brown trout up from the Dearborn. This is a fun stream to putter around with small fish on dry flies or nymphs.

Nilan Reservoir: Nilan is over 100 acres, goes to 50 feet deep, and is located about 15 minutes west of Augusta. Nilan is heavily planted with rainbows that quickly reach 15 inches and will top five pounds on occasion. It is a good streamer or woolly worm lake. There is occasionally some midge action where small gray or brown drys take the cruising trout. If you're in the area in August, don't pass up the Augusta Rodeo. Be prepared for a party that goes on "forever." And the rodeo isn't too bad, either. One of these affairs in the early seventies changed my outlook on life.

Northern Pacific Reservoir (Quarry Pond): Take U.S. 12 out of East Helena, turn right on McClellan Creek Road, and hit the short gravel connector to this 15-acre pond that butts up against I-15. It is "close-to-urban" fishing for small rainbows and brookies, and fun for those of us with no pride and no sense of aesthetics.

North Fork Sun River: The North Fork heads below Sun River Pass at nearly 8,000 feet and drops swiftly down through wilderness to 4,750 feet at Gibson Reservoir. There are pockets and pools filled with cutthroats and brookies and some chunky rainbows. It is hike-in water all the way, with a good trail following the river. After runoff an angler can stop anywhere and pop a good dry fly attractor on the river and consistently catch trout. There are outfitters that will take fishermen up the stream on horseback.

Park Lake: This is a popular spot for rainbows and grayling just 14 miles above Helena (take I-15 to Clancy and take the Lump Gulch Road to Forest Service Road 4009). In the spring this is a good float-tubing bet with small dry flies or emergers for hungry grayling.

Robert Smathers fishes it and says, "A size-16 Griffith's Gnat, with a trailer of a size-18 Brown Halo Midge Emerger on a 6X tippet, is my best combination."

Pishkun Canal: It has rainbows averaging 10 to 12 inches. It's an irrigation diversion off the Sun River. It dries up every winter (killing everything in it), but when the gates are opened in the spring it repopulates. With mostly grass along the banks, this ditch is good hopper water.

Pishkun Reservoir: Southwest of Choteau, Pishkun Reservoir is 1,550 acres with some drawdown in the summer due to irrigation. FWP plants it with rainbows that grow well. Also hundreds of thousands of kokanee salmon are taken here by trolling license plates with hooks attached to them. Fun fishing. There are also northerns to ten pounds (the fishing peaking in late June), some yellow perch, and maybe a holdover grayling or two. The rainbows have been recorded over ten pounds. Try working a perch imitation, fishing the thing in the lanes between the weed beds in deep water (but use a wire leader to keep from getting chopped off by the pike).

Prickly Pear Creek: This small stream flows into Helena from the south, running down from some low mountains past Alhambra and Montana City and followed by I-15. It still suffers from mining and smelting pollution, but Anthony Perpignano fishes it all the time and says, "People think it's dead, and to be honest, there seem to be long sections that are just about sterile, but certain stretches have large trout up to 22 inches. The lower water, below the ASARCO smelting plant in East Helena, has plenty of algae and lots of snails, but the bottom is sandy and there aren't a lot of hatches. The trout are here, maybe up from Lake Helena, and I've never caught a brown trout under 16 inches in this water. The rainbows are smaller, mainly 6 to 10 inches. Bigger flies, a Woolly Bugger or a Plain Jane, take the best fish.

"Above the ASARCO plant it is a different stream. The bottom is rocky and there's more gradient as it comes out of the Elkhorns.

There are brookies, browns, and rainbows. The best area is at and just below the mouth of McClelland Creek. It's good up to Clancy. Above Clancy there are some beaver ponds with small brook trout."

Sheep Creek: Only the lower half mile or so of this small stream entering the Missouri south of Cascade has any public access. That short stretch, however, affords some fishing for rainbows up to a pound and a few browns up to a couple of pounds.

Sixteen Mile Creek: Heads just west of the Crazies below Punk Mountain and flows for 50 miles through open, grassy country up by Ringling (I hear Jimmy Buffett on the airwaves even now) before dumping down through a canyon that really is full of rattlesnakes before entering the Missouri several miles above Toston at Lombard. The upper reaches are too small to bother with. The snakes make fishing for the rainbows and browns (plus a few brookies and white-fish) a risky proposition once the weather

Sixteen Mile Creek, circa 1910. Catch-and-release hadn't quite caught on yet. Courtesy of Mansfield Library, University of Montana, Missoula

warms. The stream is high and muddy in the spring, so fall is the best option after the hard frosts have calmed the rattlers to a certain degree. Access is difficult throughout most of the best reaches.

South Fork Dearborn River: Like the Middle Fork, this stream also begins near Rogers Pass and flows through pine forest and through cottonwoods and aspen. The fishing is similar to the Middle Fork, but it's not quite as good.

South Fork Sun River: It heads below Scapegoat Mountain and flows through wonderful, hike-in country to Gibson Reservoir. The upper reaches are barren, but below Pretty Prairie there is fine fishing for rainbows, brookies, and cutthroats. The water is very clear, running over the lightly colored gravel, and the trout blend with the bottom. They rush up, appearing like magic, to grab dry flies floating over their heads.

Sun River: It has its beginnings on the eastern edge of the Bob Marshall Wilderness and flows into the Missouri near Great Falls. Gibson Dam discharges dictate the amount of water in this river, as do diversions at Diversion Dam. Those erratic releases from the dam also hurt the productivity of the river. The Sun is about 25 miles west of Augusta, and the Rocky Mountain Front dominates the western horizon. The upper section of the Sun, above Diversion Dam, has 10-

Sun River west of Augusta
Photo by Steve Ellis

inch or so cutthroats, brookies, and rainbows. The river below has some good-sized browns, along with rainbows, brook trout, whitefish, and more and more northern pike. Caddis hatch off and on in this drainage and there are some stoneflies crawling along the fast-water stretches, but it's not a great dry fly river.

Ten Mile Creek: This is the water supply for Helena. The stream follows U.S. 12 out of town for a while and then curls up into the hills. The city takes its water out just above Rimini. Above this juncture it is better fishing, mainly for brookies and cutthroats up to 10 inches. From Rimini down to U.S. 12 there are brookies and a few rainbows, but the population is hammered by dewatering each summer. Below the Blue Cloud Ranch there are browns, brookies, and rainbows; also in this stretch, with the limited spawning areas that crowd the brookies and browns together, there are a few tiger trout, naturally produced hybrids between brook and brown parents.

Trout Creek: It's fair fishing for brookies, rainbows, and some browns in the upper reaches east of Helena above Hauser Lake. The lower section is lined with houses from the mouth to York, and house building is creeping up on the good stuff, too. For the moment good hatches make this a fun little dry fly stream.

West Fork of the South Fork of the Sun River: This creek joins the South Fork above Pretty Prairie Guard Station and is followed by trail to the headwaters. The lower stretches are good fishing for brookies and rainbows as the stream runs between timbered hills with plenty of pools and gravel drops holding the trout.

Willow Creek Reservoir: Over 1,500 acres with good fishing for the many planted rainbows that grow quickly in the rich environment. There is a lot of boating activity that can make float tubing adventuresome, but working streamers, leeches, and nymphs into and then away from shore is productive. The summer highlight is the *Callibaetis* hatch, but it starts earlier than usual on this lake. The peak emergence happens between 5 a.m. and 10 a.m. As the trout cruise over the weed beds, try to plot the course of these rising, gulping feeders.

OTHER WATERS
of the Upper Missouri—Headwaters to Great Falls

Alpine Lake: Cutthroats.

Auchard Creek: Too small.

Avalanche Gulch Creek: Brookies and rainbows.

Barr Creek: Brookies.

Barr Lake: Rainbows.

Battle Creek: Brookies.

Bear Lake: Cutthroats.

Beaver Creek (into Canyon Ferry Lake): Brookies and rainbows.

Big George Creek: Cutthroats and rainbows.

Biggs Creek: Brookies.

Big Muddy Creek: Brookies, browns, and rainbows.

Big Sheep Creek: Too small.

Big Tizer Creek: Brookies and cutthroats.

Blacktail Creek: Brookies, cutthroats, and rainbows.

Blubber Creek: Brookies and rainbows.

Boulder Lakes: Brookies.

Chamberlain Creek: Too small.

Clancy Creek and Dredge Ponds: Brookies and rainbows.

Confederate Gulch: Brookies and cutthroats. It runs into Canyon Ferry Lake and the opening is later than the regular season to protect the spawning rainbows (check regulations each year). There are some good beaver ponds right next to the road.

Cottonwood Creek (Canyon Creek): Too small.

Cottonwood Creek (Holter): Brookies and rainbows.

Crystal Creek: Too small.

Cutrock Creek: Brookies and cutthroats.

Deadman Creek: Too small.

Duck Creek: Too small.

East Fork McClellan Creek: Too small.

Elk Creek: Brookies, browns, and rainbows.

Elk Ranch (Swazee) Pond: Rainbows.

Elkhorn Creek: Cutthroats and rainbows.

Fairview Creek: Brookies.

Falls Creek: Brookies and rainbows.

Faulkner Creek: Too small.

Ford Creek: Brookies and rainbows.

Gates Creek: Brookies, cutthroats, and rainbows.

Glenwood Lake: Cutthroats.

Goss Creek: Brookies and rainbows.

Greyson Creek: Brookies.

Hanna Gulch: Brookies and rainbows.

Hay Creek: Brookies.

Indian Creek: Too small.

Izaak Walton Kid's Pond: For children.

Levale Lake: Cutthroats.

Little Sheep Creek: Too small.

Little Tizer Creek: Too small.

Little Willow Creek: Brookies.

Lowry Lake: Private.

Lump Gulch: Brookies.

Lyons Creek: Brookies and browns.

Magpie Creek: Brookies.

Marsh Creek: Brookies and cutthroats.

Maupin Creek: Too small.

Meadow Creek: Posted.

Medicine Rock Creek: Brookies.

Middle Fork Sixteen Mile Creek: Poor access.

Mill Coulee: Too small.

Moose Creek: Brookies and rainbows.

North Fork Willow Creek: Brookies.

Renshaw Lake: Cutthroats.

Rock Creek (Missouri): Too small.

Rock Creek (Sun River): Cutthroats and rainbows.

Rose Creek: Too small.

Runway (Malmstrom Air Force Base) Pond: Children's water.

Russell Fork Deep Creek: Brookies and rainbows.

Seven Mile Creek: Brookies and rainbows.

Silver Creek: Brookies and cutthroats. The cutthroats have high concentrations of mercury in their tissue. This little stream north of Helena is not the place to catch breakfast.

Six Mile Creek: Too small.

Smith Creek: Brookies and rainbows.

Sock Lake: Cutthroats.

Soup Creek: Too small.

South Fork Crow Creek: Brookies.

South Fork Crow Creek (Crow Creek) Lakes: Brookies and rainbows.

South Fork Little Prickly Pear Creek: Too small.

Split Rock Lake: Private. Perch and pike.

Stickney Creek: Brookies.

Sunny Slope Canal: Grayling, kokanee, pike, and rainbows.

Tillinghast Creek: Poor access.

Tizer Lakes: Brookies and cutthroats; crammed with them. Reached by a 4-wheel drive road. The perfect spot for kids—when they're tired of fishing, they can hunt for frogs and toads in the surrounding marsh.

Tunnell Lake: Cutthroats and rainbows. It's just a mile and a half below Pishkun Reservoir and excellent in the spring for pan-sized rainbows.

Virginia Creek: Brookies and cutthroats.

Warm Springs Creek: Brookies.

Whitetail Creek: Rainbows.

Willow Creek (Missouri): Brookies and rainbows.

Willow Creek: Posted.

Wolf Creek: Brookies, browns, and rainbows.

Wood Creek: Brookies and rainbows.

Wood Lake: Rainbows.

Belt Creek
Photo by Steve Oristian

Fishing Waters of the Lower Missouri—Great Falls to Border

Ackley Lake: About 250 surface acres fed by a canal from the Judith River, this lake is located southwest of Hobson and is popular locally with fishermen, boaters, picnickers, and other outdoor enthusiasts. The state plants 20,000 Eagle Lake rainbows in here each year that reach 15 inches with ease. Some big brown trout also find their way in here from the Judith—poor misguided souls. There are pike here, too, to eight pounds. Action slows down in the summer for all types of tackle, but in spring and fall even fly fishermen can have good fishing from the shore.

Belt Creek: This stream is formed in the thickly timbered Little Belt Mountains and flows for more than 50 miles to the Missouri below Great Falls. Followed by U.S. 89 and county roads, the best known water on this pleasant stream is called the "Sluice Boxes." These are large pools that derive this nickname from past mining operations that have also caused some pollution problems that linger even today. The Sluice Boxes and much of the rest of the upper 40 miles are good fishing with drys and wet flies for rainbows to 15 inches and averaging about 10. The lower reaches are best for brown trout—some moving up the river during fall spawning are quite large and susceptible to streamers. There are also whitefish in good numbers.

Big Horn (Brockton) Reservoir: Located in the northeast corner of the state, Big Horn is planted regularly with rainbows that grow quickly to several pounds. The trout will hit leeches, nymphs (especially dragon and damsel fly patterns), streamers, and olive scuds. This is just one of countless ranch ponds, lakes, and reservoirs that are lying out on the plains east of the Continental Divide. The fishing is generally good for fat rainbows. Many of these waters are private and off limits to all but family and friends. Others are planted with fish from state hatcheries and so open to the public. Because some of these waters winter-kill or become too alkaline to support trout, their

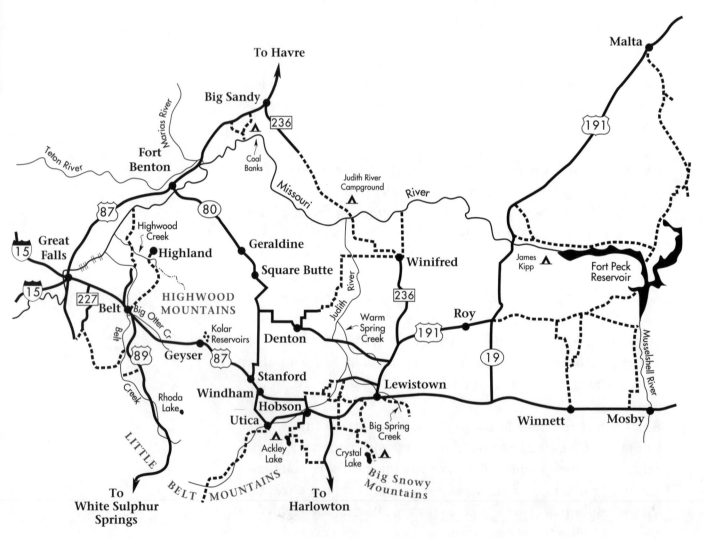

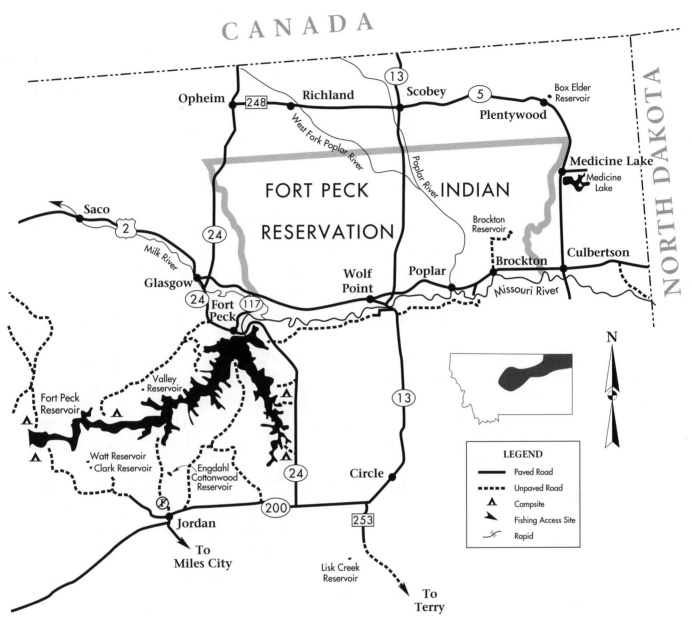

CANADA

NORTH DAKOTA

Opheim
248
Richland
13
Scobey
5
Box Elder Reservoir
Plentywood

Medicine Lake
Medicine Lake

West Fork Poplar River

FORT PECK
RESERVATION
INDIAN

Poplar River

Brockton Reservoir

Saco
2

Milk River

Brockton
Culbertson

Glasgow
24

Wolf Point
Poplar

Missouri River

24
117
Fort Peck

N

Valley Reservoir

Fort Peck Reservoir

13

Watt Reservoir
Clark Reservoir

Engdahl Cottonwood Reservoir

24

Circle

200

Jordan

253

To Miles City

Lisk Creek Reservoir

To Terry

LEGEND

────	Paved Road
┄┄┄┄	Unpaved Road
▲	Campsite
◤	Fishing Access Site
✕	Rapid

status is always changing. When traveling through the eastern portion of the state, the best way to locate these reservoirs or ponds is to call the appropriate Department of Fish, Wildlife, and Parks office (numbers are at the front of each regional section in the current regulations) and inquire concerning names of waters, location, accessibility, and current fishing status. The information the FWP has on waters is astounding and extremely accurate. A little prodding will often lead to some advice on the best patterns or prime time to fish. Calling the FWP is by far the easiest way to get onto some superb fishing for very big rainbows (or perhaps browns or brookies). A float tube is always a good idea, as is sunscreen and bug repellent.

Big Otter Creek: Another in the famed collection of Montana trout streams overrun with rattlesnakes. In the summer placing your hands or feet without looking can result in a very painful bite. Always keep an eye open for the reptiles, especially around rocks and cliffs where the snakes love to sun themselves. But don't be a whimp—this stream is worth the risk.

Otter has some fine fishing in its slow-moving miles of small water for browns that will average 12 to 14 inches but with many that will go over two pounds. Going west from Raynesford, on U.S. 87, the stream meanders back and forth from one side of the road to the other. Some of it is overgrown with brush and shrubs, but most of it is open meadows. The creek itself is plenty rich, with watercress and elodea covering the bottom, and tall grass on the banks contributes plenty of terrestrials to the food base. The best method is to crouch or kneel (eye to eye with those rattlesnakes) and move upstream, casting a dry fly or a nymph to the undercuts and deeper slots.

Big Spring Creek: It heads in the hills southeast of Lewistown and flows right through town. It runs 31 miles from its origin to its mouth at the Judith River. The soul of the creek is the spring that pumps out 64,000 gallons of water a minute. E. Donnal Thomas, Jr., writing about the stream in *The Big Sky Journal,* sums it up nicely, "For as spring creeks go, this is definitely a blue-collar version; beer rather than Chardonnay, bleachers rather than box seats, substance rather than style."

Big Spring Creek is famous for big rainbows that gather just below the hatchery west of town. The occasional one gets caught—eight pounds and up—but these fish are stuffed with the spillage from the hatchery and difficult to catch on flies. The real fishing starts a few hundred yards below the hatchery. Even there, however, it is not a "classic spring creek." It runs bank full and very fast; there are deep holes, but relatively few spots where trout can hold and leisurely sip insects from the surface. The key for the dry fly fisherman is not only knowing the timing of the hatches but also the backwaters and broad pools where fish will hold and rise steadily.

The section above town is a series of deep pools connected by riffles and runs guarded by brushy banks. This upper stretch has fewer trout (mainly rainbows) than below town, but is prettier, more accessible water, with fish averaging 15 inches and running to several pounds. These trout are spooky in the very clear water, so you need light tippets, low profiles, and delicate casting. This applies to the nymph fishing during the non-hatch hours as well as to the dry fly fishing. Pheasant Tails, Rubber Legged Hare's Ears, Bead Head Twist Nymphs, Gray/Olive Scuds, Palomino Nymphs, and Prince Nymphs do well. Even with a sink-tip line, you'll sometimes need weight to get down to the fish, who run for their lives at the merest suggestion of drag. The steadiest dry fly activity for hatch-matchers comes from the midge hatches during the winter on the Griffith's Gnat; the Blue-Winged Olive in the spring and fall on the matching Sparkle Dun; and the Pale Morning Dun all summer on the matching Sparkle Dun.

The demarcation zone between the upper and lower sections is the long concrete ditch that channels the stream through the middle of town. The progressive and sagacious people of Lewistown looked at their spring creek, and to protect the economic folly of people who had built right next to a stream that regularly floods, they took their wonderful heritage and trashed a beautiful section of it.

The lower stretch, with the Judith Mountains rising to the north, flows through rangeland and is marked by brushy and grassy banks. It's great water—better fishing even than the upper area. A large Woolly Bugger (olive) hammered along the banks will turn browns consistently, even along runs that look like poor habitat. Watch for shelves in the streambed that can wrench your knees or wet your

175

shirt. These are also prime places to dead-drift the Bugger or a big cranefly imitation. Two nymphs on the leader usually do better than one—the best combination is a big pattern, size 10 or larger, and a small pattern, size 16 or 18. This lower water gets the same hatches as the upper stretch; the secret is knowing areas where the stream slows down enough for fish to rise efficiently to small food forms. Grasshoppers, so abundant in the meadows along the creek, are not tidbits, and even in the heavy water both browns and rainbows rush the surface for them.

Access below town is at bridges off the city streets or off County Road 238. There are three public access points, but these aren't well marked on the main highway. There is camping southwest of town if you do not mind a spot with no amenities (like water and toilets) and can handle barking farm dogs and bright barn lights glowing all night. Access is being bought up and posted, but there are still adequate places to get on and off the water.

Big Spring Creek
Photo by Gary LaFontaine

The fish in Big Spring Creek are tainted with PCB's. A study by the Montana Department of Health and Environmental Sciences and the Department of Fish, Wildlife, and Parks recommended, "Children up to age 15, nursing mothers, and women of childbearing age should be particularly careful about consuming these fish."

Box Elder Creek Reservoir: This lake is within the Plentywood city limits and it's planted with 5,000 Arlee rainbows each year. Ninety acres of put-and-take (which happens quickly) fishing. To escape the normal hubbub around the reservoir, the fly fisherman can come out at dawn and enjoy a few hours of casting for rising and cruising trout.

Carter's Ponds: Upper and lower (the lower one is usually the best of the two, but the dam has been leaking and the fishing is deteriorating on this pond). They are planted yearly with rainbows that grow rapidly as they gorge on the tremendous numbers of olive scuds (sizes 14 to 16), damsel nymphs, and *Callibaetis* mayfly nymphs. A proven pattern here is the Rollover Scud, a fly with a distinctive motion that separates it from the hordes of naturals. The most consistent dry fly fishing is at dawn during spells of warm (not hot), stable summer and autumn weather—the fish cruise and indiscriminately sip drowned and crippled naturals from the previous night. They even work the shallow, mossy bays, feeding in the open lanes, and stalking these trout in the heavy vegetation feels like bass fishing. They stop feeding as soon as the sun hits the water. The shoreline is too weedy with cattails, reeds, and moss for easy wading. Either a float tube or a boat will help you get to the deeper water. There is a boat launch and a picnic area. The ponds are 7 miles north of Lewistown on U.S. 91.

Clark Reservoir: It's about 27 miles northwest of Jordan on a salmon-colored, dusty gravel road. This 20-acre lake, south of Fort Peck Reservoir, is planted with several thousand rainbows each year that grow quickly in the rich soup. The trout taste real strange by midsummer, but they provide good sport as they sometimes top 20 inches.

Crystal Lake: Crystal is about 40 acres in the Big Snowies (south of Lewistown) with a picnic area and campground. This pond provides average fishing for rainbows to 15 inches, but the real lure in this central Montana lake is the chance to catch trout in a mountain setting.

Engdahl Cottonwood Reservoir: North of Jordan, in some badlands country, this reservoir is planted with 5,000 smallmouth bass every other year. It's good fishing for fast-growing bass to a couple of pounds. You can have great fun with leeches during the day and poppers in the evening.

Fort Peck Reservoir: Well over 100 miles long with 1,600 miles of shoreline, it's surrounded by the 800,000-acre Charles M. Russell National Wildlife Refuge. It's planted with over 100,000 lake trout,

LOWER MISSOURI RIVER

100,000 northern pike, and millions of battling walleyes. This is the location of the exciting Governor's Cup Walleye (and competition license plate drowning) Tournament each summer, where teams of eager anglers race all over the place in metal-flaked, high-powered speed boats chasing the elusive species and the financial awards attendant with derricking the fish into a live well. Great fun. There are also chinook salmon planted here. Other species include some browns, rainbows, perch, burbot, smallmouth bass, carp, suckers, paddlefish, sturgeon, and goldeyes. Most of the fish taken in Fort Peck are caught either with bait or lures. One notable fly fishing opportunity is in the bays on the southern shoreline (especially near any creek inlet) with large streamers for schools of marauding northerns that average about seven pounds and run to over ten. Shooting heads help reach the fish when they are cruising way out. And watch out for muck and quicksand around the inlets. Hit this right and you can have some very exciting action. Another great target is the smallmouth fishery at the western end of the lake, especially at the mouth of the Musselshell (bass averaging four and a half pounds). The snakes, cactus, biting insects, and lack of available drinking water add to the experience. Bring a friend.

Highwood Creek: This stream is pretty good fishing for the open country. It pours out of the Highwood Mountains below Highwood Baldy Mountain and flows northwest to the Missouri about 20 miles below Great Falls. It's followed by Forest Service and county roads much of the way, and the upper reaches are fair fishing for brook and rainbow trout to a foot. The lower reaches, especially close to the Missouri, play host to some big rainbows in the spring (before the season opens) and to some even bigger browns in the fall. There are also some decent brook trout in this lower stretch that hold beneath the grassy, brushy, undercut banks and at the bottoms of slow pools. This is good streamer water all the time and nice hopper water from July into September.

Hoffman Reservoir: This is a private 6-acre lake northeast of Culbertson, and if you just happen to be in Culbertson on the

American Plan for a week or so, this is a good spot to know about. It's really quite pretty in the spring, and the fishing for rainbows (planted yearly) to 15 inches is very consistent and there is the occasional hold-over to spice up the day.

Judith River: The Judith flows out of the Little Belt Mountains southwest of Lewistown and runs for about 45 air miles north to the Missouri directly south of the Bears Paw Mountains. The upper reaches are good fishing for wild cutthroats and some rainbows, despite water shortages from irrigation demands. The return of the water also harms the banks. The Lost, Middle, Ross, and South Forks have good dry fly fishing for rainbows to 15 inches and a few cutthroats.

The middle sections of the stream flow through farm and ranch land. The stream is characterized by grassy or brushy undercut banks, a rock bottom, and fair numbers of rainbows and browns to perhaps 18 inches. There are also lesser numbers of brookies. Access is gained from country roads and state highways—take U.S. Hwy 87 to Hobson and go up the Judith River Road (which turns into gravel) past Utica.

Russ Vaughn skips past a lot of better known rivers to come up to this middle section of the Judith. "By midsummer the water is low and clear. The deeper runs and holes are separated by short riffles and the trout concentrate in the deeper pockets. This is not random, slap and dash fishing. It's a stalking and spotting game. The trout may be smaller but this is like New Zealand tactics. The rainbows run mostly 10 to 13 inches, but there are some to 20 inches. And there's always some nice, but very spooky, browns out in the open feeding. This is water for a 2-weight rod, a dark fly line, a 16-foot leader and a careful approach. You never even bother casting until you spot a fish and then you work on only him. It's all so visual that you can see the trout reject a fly, and you keep changing to different dry flies and nymphs."

Not far below the river's confluence with Big Spring Creek, bur-bot, channel catfish, goldeyes, and sauger take over as the water warms and turns turbid as it slides through arid, barren country. A few large browns are taken in this section, mainly by bait anglers looking for other species.

Kolar Reservoirs: Numbers 1, 4, 5, and 6 get anywhere from 250 to 2,000 4-inch rainbow trout yearly. Number 2 receives 1,500 3-inch, and 500 6- to 8-inch Yellowstone cutthroats. None of these ponds is more than 11 acres or all that deep, but the trout do well even with all the pressure they receive from area anglers. The first one is just north of Geyser, which is 45 miles southeast of Great Falls.

Lisk Creek (Kuhn) Reservoir: This private lake 17 miles out of Brockway receives annual plantings of rainbows ranging up to 9 inches and they grow quickly, if they survive the garlic-flavored marshmallow onslaught, in the fecund prairie waters. A number of trout reach two pounds in a hurry and a few others get much bigger, and they will hit streamers, leeches, scuds, damsel nymphs, midges, *Callibaetis* late in the year; and hoppers, ants, and beetles in the summer. The fishing here, great for the still water fanatic, is just like that found on hundreds of other prairie reservoirs.

Medicine Lake: This is another wildlife refuge with amazing numbers of waterfowl and plenty of other bird, mammal, and reptile species. The fishing found on the 31,000-plus acres of ponds and reservoirs in the northeast corner of the state can be very good for northerns to eight pounds or so, and for fat largemouth bass that hammer poppers that look like frogs. There are also smallmouth bass in lesser numbers.

Rhoda Lake: This little hike-in lake is in the Judith River drainage. Go south of Great Falls 70 miles on U.S. 89, along Belt Creek, and then turn left onto the Big Baldy Jeep Road. It's a stiff 3-mile climb from the end of the road up to Rhoda. The lake receives annual plants of Yellowstone cutthroats that survive but don't grow much beyond 15 inches in this 2-acre lake at 9,800 feet in the Little Belts. But this is a shallow body of water, with a maximum depth of 12 feet, and in this type of lake, where the fish can't really disappear into the deep, the fly fishing is very consistent. A good generic nymph, crawled slowly over the bottom, almost always takes the cutthroats here even if they aren't rising to the surface.

Valley Reservoir: Valley is about 30 minutes (they drive fast out here) southwest of Glasgow. It's only about 7 acres and not deep, but like most of the reservoirs in this part of the state, the fish that survive grow fast and big. The black soil on the plains is so fertile that any pothole that doesn't winterkill is potentially trophy water. Most of these lakes are managed for put-and-take because there is no natural reproduction, but any holdovers grow fat and silvery, reaching the two- to three-pound mark in one season.

Warm Springs Creek: Warm Springs begins in the Judith Mountains and flows for 25 miles to the Judith River not far from Denton. The upper reaches are planted with rainbows and the lower, open-prairie section is planted with small-mouth bass. Both species provide good fishing. Medium-sized streamers work for the bass, and general, searching dry flies and nymphs work for the trout.

Warm Springs Creek
Photo by Eileen Clarke

Watt Reservoir: It's way out in the middle of nowhere—and that makes this 10-acre, 20-foot-deep reservoir, located north of Brusett and south of Fort Peck Reservoir, a special still water fishery. It's planted annually with rainbows, just like the other prairie reservoirs, but this one is so remote that the fish don't get hammered by strange confections and baits. There are good numbers of two- and three-year survivors that will occasionally top several pounds.

West Poplar River: It flows over the border from Canada north of Scobey, and eventually joins the Poplar River, which twists and turns through grassy prairie and badlands country for 50 miles to the Missouri at Poplar. Much of the water is on the Fort Peck Indian

Reservation. It has northerns, walleyes, and smallmouths. Access is tough via "roads" that quickly turn impassable at even the hint of a rainstorm. There are a few sizable brookies and browns hiding out in this water, too. Don't forget your tribal permit.

OTHER WATERS
of the Lower Missouri—Great Falls to Border

Arrow Creek: Brookies.

Barta Pond: Rainbows.

Big Coulee: Brookies and cutthroats.

Big Muddy Creek: No trout.

Big Timber Gulch: Too small.

Birkeland Lake: Private.

Briggs Creek: Brookies and cutthroats.

Buffalo Creek: Too small.

Candee Reservoir: Rainbows.

Casino Creek: Brookies.

Castle Creek: Brookies and rainbows.

Cecil Coulee: Too small.

Chabot Reservoir: Rainbows. Permission required.

Childers Dam: Rainbows. Ask permission.

Cottonwood Creek (Geyser): Brookies and cutthroats.

Cottonwood Creek (Judith drainage): Brookies, cutthroats, and rainbows.

Cow Creek: Brookies.

Danelson Reservoir: Rainbows.

Dredge Cut Trout Pond: Few trout.

Dry Fork Belt Creek: Cutthroats.

Dry Wolf Creek: Cutthroats and rainbows.

Dyba Reservoir: No trout.

Eagle Creek: Brookies.

East Fork Big Spring Creek: Brookies, browns, and rainbows.

East Fork Creek Reservoir: Brookies, browns, and rainbows.

Edwards Ponds: Rainbows.

Elk's Country Club Pond: Kid's stuff.

Great Northern Reservoirs (Bainville Ponds): No trout.

Groh Reservoir: Northerns.

Hanson Creek Reservoir: Rainbows.

Harrison Creek: Too small.

Hassler Pond: Rainbows.

Hatfield Reservoir: Rainbows.

Highwood Creek: Rainbows.

Holgate Reservoir: Rainbows.

Hoover Creek: Too small.

Jefferson Creek: Too small.

Killenbeck Reservoir: Northerns and possibly some bullheads if they didn't winterkill. Ask permission.

King Reservoir: Rainbows.

Kirby Creek: Brookies.

Kuester Reservoir: Yellow perch, largemouth bass, and northerns. Private—be sure to get permission.

Lipke Pond: Rainbows.

Little Belt Creek: Brookies, cutthroats, and rainbows.

Little Otter Creek: Poor fishing.

Logging Creek: Brookies, cutthroats, and rainbows.

Lost Fork Middle Fork Judith River: Cutthroats and rainbows.

Louse Creek: Too small.

Martin Creek: Too small.

McChesney Reservoir: Northerns.

Middle Fork Judith River: Cutthroats and rainbows.

North Fork Cow Creek: Brookies.

North Fork Highwood Creek: Brookies and cutthroats.

North Fork Running Wolf Creek: Too small.

O'Brien Pond: Private.

Old Folks Ponds: Kid's stuff.

Olson Pond: Rainbows. Permission required.

Peck's Pond: Rainbows.

Peer Reservoir: Private.

Phillips County Reservoir #20: Largemouth bass.

Pilgrim Creek: Cutthroats and rainbows.

Pohlod Creek: Too small.

Poplar River: Northerns and smallmouth bass.

Prairie Elk Creek: No trout.

Raymond Dam: No trout.

Redwater River: Private.

Reimer's Pond (Harlow Reservoir): Brookies and rainbows.

Rock Creek: Brookies and rainbows.

Ross Fork Judith River: Browns and rainbows.

Roudebush Pond: Private.

Running Wolf Creek: Brookies and rainbows.

Sage Creek: Browns and rainbows.

Shonkin Creek: Brookies and rainbows.

Small's Pond: Private.

South Fork Cow Creek: Poor access.

South Fork Judith River: Cutthroats and rainbows.

South Fork Little Belt Creek: Too small.

Stafford (North Winifred) Reservoir: Rainbows.

Surprise Creek: Brookies and cutthroats.

Surprise Creek (Hutterite) Reservoir: Rainbows.

Thain Creek: Too small.

Troy Creek: Cutthroats.

URS Pond: Rainbows.

Weatherwax Creek: Cutthroats.

West Fork Lost Fork Middle Fork Judith River: Easy for you to say. Cutthroats.

Wheatcrofts Reservoir: Northerns.

Whitetail Reservoir: No trout.

Wolf Creek: Brookies and cutthroats.

Wolverine Creek: Too small.

Yaeger Pond: Private.

Yogo Creek: Brookies, cutthroats, and rainbows.

■ *Special thanks to John Barsness, James Carr, Pat Clancey, Paul Heeny, Payton Lear, Richard Micklish, Anthony Perpignano, Richard Rose, Bill Seeples, Robert Smathers, and Russ Vaughn for their help on the Missouri drainage.*

Upper Musselshell River
Photo by Gary LaFontaine

THE MUSSELSHELL

The Musselshell is another river that offers fly fishers some pleasant action, but should not be considered a "destination" river. True, there are some large brown trout holding here and the country is scenic and uncrowded. But access is poor and there really is not that much water to fish, especially during the height of summer when irrigation demands for adjacent fields suck the poor thing nearly dry. Just the same, if you are driving through the valley and have a few hours to spare, you've nothing to lose casting a streamer for the browns or just working small drys to the rising nine-inchers that are anything but selective.

After the spring runoff and before the Musselshell is drawn down from irrigation, the river here is classic big-brown water, bending and curving through open country, creating untold numbers of holding areas beneath the grassy and brushy banks. Water spills over sand and gravel shelves into deep pools shaded from the persistent sun by alders and cottonwoods. Riffles and silent glides swing lazily in soft arcs as the stream moves gently towards its rendezvous with the Missouri at Fort Peck Reservoir over 150 miles to the northeast. The setting is more agrarian than wild, but for background scenery Local Mountain, Bald Ridge, and the rest of the Crazies run away down south, with the Castle range showing in the west. From mid-July until mid-September, the fishing is normally poor due to irrigation.

The Musselshell runs for many circuitous miles but the stretch below Martinsdale, from the confluence of the North and South Forks down to Harlowton, is where you will experience the most "success." This section is perhaps 25 miles, and is reached by bridges and county roads that cross and follow the water here and there. The fish population is mostly brown trout in decent, but-not-close-to-Bighorn-River numbers, with far fewer rainbows and brookies. Large numbers of mountain whitefish are also present, probably in numbers that exceed the combined totals for all of the trout species put together.

In other words, the Musselshell is not a river to plan a vacation around for those who must travel long distances to reach Montana. Rather, this is a place to fish between trips to locations like Yellowstone or the Missouri River or Glacier National Park, way up by the Canadian border.

The river is easy to wade—not deep and rarely exceeding 20 feet wide—and your entrance is best planned well ahead by cautiously approaching the water to consider the tactical and logistical problems ahead. Usually by late June things have settled down to the point that some of the browns are visible holding along the bottom or when they make brief rushes out into the open to take a nymph or unwary minnow.

There are no crowds here, but the trout are spooky, perhaps from the many predators gliding in the air above. Quiet, low-profile movements are in order. The Musselshell is perfect for a 2- or 3-weight rod and a 9-foot (or longer) leader tapered to at the absolute maximum 3X, with 4X or 5X preferred. When hammering streamers, a heavier rod and a shorter leader, to 1X or 2X are okay, but the drys need the thinner material to do the job properly.

Streamers include Woolly Buggers, Marabou Muddlers, Matukas, and Matuka Sculpins. Nymphs might range from a Hare's Ear to a Prince to Cream Peeking Caddis. A Brown Olive or a Brown Serendipity are effective during emergence. The Deep and the Emergent Sparkle Pupa are standard caddis imitations. Drys could include Sparkle Duns, Clear Wing Spinners, Goddard Caddis, and a range of terrestrials that would include ants, beetles, and hoppers. The most abundant insect in the river is probably the Grannom caddis. You'll crunch the little four-sided cases under your feet when you wade the riffles. The finest hatch of the season on the river occurs in the late spring, from April through early May, when the water is clear and cold and those Grannoms fill the air. There are also good hatches of Blue-Winged Olives in April, July, and August, and again in September lasting into October. Sometimes nice browns over 15 inches can be taken on a size-18 or -20 Blue-Winged Olive in the fall. Trico spinners trigger a nice rise on summer mornings. The hoppers are excellent producers from July into September, in part because of the preponderance of hay fields next to the river. The patterns should grow larger as the season progresses—going from size 12 up to 8 or 6.

The Musselshell may be a "hit-and-miss" trout stream in the upper reaches, but in the lower water, from Roundup to Melstone, it is a good and consistent smallmouth bass river. The bass hit the same streamers that the browns hit on the upper river, but it wouldn't

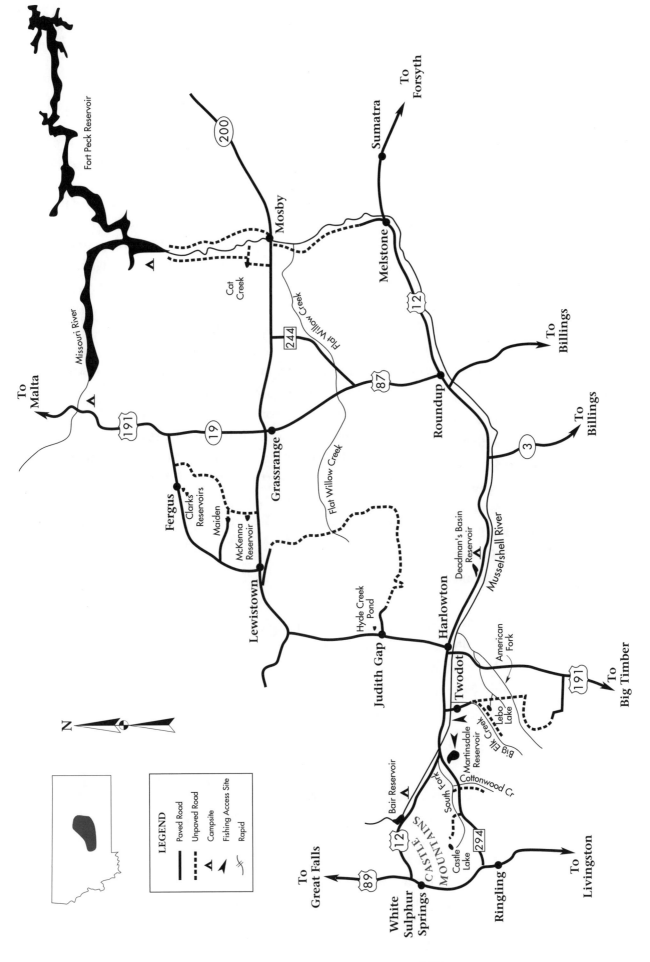

MUSSELSHELL RIVER

hurt to add a crayfish imitation, a bullhead imitation, and a few Slider-style cork bugs to your selection.

Mike Eva fishes the river for smallmouths exclusively with flies. "The best fish are in the big pools. They prefer a fly that hits with a soft splat and then struggles in the water. The more accurate the cast the better, especially around the brush and rock ledges. If the bass won't chase a fly, I'll put on a line with a 5-foot, sinking mini-tip and work a streamer under the cover. That usually works. The fish run from 11 to 16 inches on average, but there are larger ones even in the Harlowton to Melstone stretch. The angler who really wants a trophy should go all the way down to the mouth of the Musselshell, where it empties into Fort Peck Reservoir. On a good day the smallmouths there run from three to five pounds. And it's so isolated in that area that no one fishes for them."

Much of the land in this drainage is posted, but a polite request and a smile often gains access to some of the better water. Offer to pick up any junk you see and close all of the gates you pass through. Then thank the people at the end of the day and send them a bottle of bourbon at Christmas. Maybe they'll let you try your luck one more time the next season.

You don't need complicated hatches and elaborate pattern-selection dances on the Musselshell. The basics will always take the browns, provided you use extreme caution in your approach and presentation. Use the same care wading the stream. The smallmouths don't see enough anglers to get wise either, but the angler has to understand the association between bass and cover. In this fragile watershed, even with its limited access to visiting fly fishers, the fish demand some finesse.

POPULAR FLIES
Blue-Winged Olive
Brown Olive
Brown Serendipity
Clear Wing Spinner
Cream Peeking Caddis
Deep Sparkle Pupa
Emergent Sparkle Pupa
Goddard Caddis
Hare's Ear Nymph
Marabou Muddler
Matuka
Matuka Sculpin
Prince Nymph
Sparkle Dun
Trico Spinner
Woolly Bugger

Fishing Waters in the Musselshell Drainage

American Fork: The American fork has its beginnings in the Crazy Mountains to the south and flows for 30 miles to the main river east of Harlowton. The lower reaches are good fall fishing with limited access for good-sized browns. The upper section in the mountains is nice pocket water; use Royal Wulffs and the like for brookies to 12 inches.

Bair Reservoir: Deep and nearly 300 acres, it's right next to U.S. 12 about 15 minutes east of White Sulphur Springs in windy, open country. There are good numbers of big rainbows that often take streamers and nymphs near shore in the spring. Browns of size and some brook trout are also present. There is a campground and boat launch here. A float tube helps.

Big Elk Creek: This one begins in the Crazy Mountains and joins the Musselshell at Twodot. It's best for brookies, but access is controlled and the surrounding land is heavily posted. This stream, like all of the others on the upper river, can produce superb fishing for big browns in the fall. The fish will hit anything thrown in front of their faces at this time of the year. Catch a couple, play them quickly, then release them carefully. And use caution wading to avoid damaging the important spawning gravels that also support the insect and forage fish populations.

Castle Lake: Just three acres, it's below Elk Peak in the small range of hills known as the Castle Mountains southeast of White Sulphur Springs. Good fishing for Yellowstone cutthroats that grow to 15 inches or so.

Clark Reservoirs: These two small ponds are planted with rainbows regularly. They attracts enough local attention to qualify as a social highlight in the area for bait fishermen, but nobody gets out here early to drown worms and the fly fisherman can have the water to himself from dawn to about 8 a.m. The stockers rise well and these hours are the best fly fishing. It's located a few miles south of Fergus.

Cottonwood Creek: Cottonwood is a small Crazy Mountains stream that has decent fishing for small brook and rainbow trout with a few nice browns in the fall.

Deadman's Basin Lake: Nearly 2,000 acres and a 100 feet deep, Deadman's is about 20 miles east of Harlowton. It's pretty well developed as a recreation site and is quite a zoo in the summer. Still, there is some action for rainbows and browns to several pounds, plus some kokanee. It has a reputation as a fickle fishery: when the fish are on, they are really on. Active flies work best when the trout are aggressive. A team of three dapping wet flies, a single dry fly skittered fast over the top, or a weighted streamer pulled in long jerks from the bottom towards the surface all bring fish a long way. When the trout aren't feeding ravenously, the slower methods of presentation still catch a few fish. In the fall you can work this lake from a canoe or float tube without fear of being chewed up by the flock of speed boaters. About 100,000 rainbows are put into this water each year.

A typical eastside reservoir, Martinsdale can beat you up with wind. You'll need to bring a stout rod that can generate plenty of line speed.
Photo by Gary LaFontaine

Grebe Reservoir: Grebe is not too far from Sumatra or Roundup and fair fishing for this part of the prairie for rainbows that average a pound in this 4-acre pond.

Hyde Creek Pond: This one is right by a missile silo so you know you are safe from Bulgarian attack while you fish for foot-long rainbows in this 3-acre, spring-fed pond just north of Judith Gap.

Martinsdale Reservoir: Heavily planted with Yellowstone cutthroat and rainbow trout, this 985-acre impoundment is reached just south out of Martinsdale by dirt road. Lying in a broad dip in open country north of the Crazies, this one is over 100 feet deep with good fishing for rainbows and cutts up to 18 inches. Some very big browns lie near the inlet. Large streamers in the fall take these big boys. Scuds and leeches and damsel fly nymphs work on the rest of the salmonids. One hotspot is the little island located just south of the dam; fish between the island and dam and concentrate on the clumps of willows along that south shore. This area of the lake produced three rainbows over eight pounds on a single early June weekend in 1995 (two of those fish were caught with spinning equipment, but the third one was taken and released on a size-6 Red/Black Bristle Leech). Bring a boat or a float tube. The Mint Bar in downtown Martinsdale is a good place to escape the summer sun.

South Fork Musselshell River: Beginning a few miles west of Lennep, it is followed most of the way by county roads to the Musselshell northeast of Martinsdale. Access is tough. Ask permission or wade up from the main river for fair catches of browns to 18 inches and rainbows to 15 inches and brook trout that are smaller yet in this very narrow, brushy stream. Getting the fly on the water without scaring the fish or without drag is the problem here, not pattern selection.

Yellow Water Lake: Find the town of Winnett (an adventure in itself) and then go south for 7 miles to the turnoff for the lake. Drive 6 miles on gravel road to this 150-acre, irrigation reservoir. It gets drawn down in midsummer and is suitably ugly, but there are big trout here. There are plenty of rainbows to two pounds and the occasional trophy over five pounds. The nice thing about Yellow Water is that it gets so mossy in midsummer that fly fishing is easily the best method of taking fish. The secret is to cast a dry fly, a good still water pattern like the Devil Bug, the Shroud, or the Black Ant, to an open patch of water and then patiently let it sit there for what can seem like forever until a trout finds it and sips it under.

Other Waters

Agnes Creek: Posted.

Alabaugh Creek: Hits the South Fork of the Musselshell River near Lennep. Fast fishing for small brookies and rainbows. Much of the stream winds through agricultural land, but it's possible to get permission to fish this water.

Antelope Creek: Too small.

Ben Hill Pond: Rainbows. Twisted British humor.

Berg Reservoir: Brookies and rainbows.

Big Coulee Creek: Poor fishing.

Blacktail Creek: Brookies and rainbows.

Bonanza Creek: Too small.

Box Elder Creek: Too small.

Box Elder Dam: Rainbows.

Bozeman Fork Musselshell River: Brookies and cutthroats.

Broadview Pond: Rainbows, largemouth bass, crappies, and tiger muskie (hear them roar).

Burnett Reservoir: Rainbows.

Careless Creek: Brookies.

Castle Creek: Too small.

Checkerboard Creek: Brookies.

Christensen Pond: Brookies and rainbows. Permission needed.

Comb Creek: Brookies.

Crooked Creek: No trout.

Daisy Dean Creek: Poor access.

East Fork Haymaker Creek: Too small.

Finley Reservoir: Posted.

Fish Creek: Brookies to 10 inches. It's fun in the upper reaches, about 20 miles south of Twodot in the Crazy Mountains. It's crossed by county roads.

Flagstaff Creek: Brookies. Permission needed.

Flatwillow Creek: Brookies, browns, and rainbows.

Forest (Cottonwood) Lake: Cutthroats.

Half Moon Canyon: Cutthroats and rainbows.

Haymaker Creek: Posted.

Holiday (Flagstaff) Reservoir: Brookies and rainbows. Permission needed.

Hopley Creek: Brookies and browns.

Kincheloe Reservoir: No trout.

Kizer Pond: Rainbows.

Krause Pond: Private. No trout.

Lebo (Basin) Creek: Brookies and browns. Posted.

Lebo Lake: Private.

Lion Creek: Brookies.

Little Elk Creek: Browns.

Maginnis Creek: Brookies. Permission needed.

Maybee Reservoir: Rainbows.

McCurtney Creek: Brookies. Permission needed.

McKenna Reservoir: About 20 miles east of Lewistown on U.S. 87. This 3-acre pond has some rainbows.

Middle Fork American Creek: Brookies. Posted.

Miller Creek: Browns.

Morrisy Creek: Too small.

North Fork Flatwillow Creek: Brookies, browns, and rainbows.

Petrolia Lake: Rainbows, perch, and walleye.

Rindal Pond: Rainbows.

South Fork American Fork: Brookies.

South Fork Flatwillow Creek: Brookies and rainbows.

South Fork McDonald Creek: Poor fishing.

Spring Creek: Brookies.

Swimming Woman Creek: Brookies and rainbows.

Voldseth Reservoir: Brookies and rainbows. Permission needed.

War Horse Lake: No trout.

Warm Springs Creek: Brookies. Permission needed.

West Fork Cottonwood Creek: Brookies.

West Fork Flagstaff Creek: Brookies and rainbows. Some of those rainbows grow to 12 inches. Go up to the end of the Flagstaff Creek Road to hit the mouth of the this stream.

Willow Creek: Private.

■ *Special thanks to to Mike Eva and Ed Koppelman for their help on the Musselshell drainage.*

Red Rock River
Photo by Stan Bradshaw

The headwaters of the Red Rock River eventually find their way into the Gulf of Mexico almost 4,000 miles distant. Formed by waters from streams like Hellroaring Creek and Red Rock Creek in the Centennial Mountains along the Idaho border, this stream offers one of the last riverine refuges for Arctic grayling in the lower forty-eight states.

As the Red Rock flows through the Red Rock Lakes National Wildlife Refuge, then Lima Reservoir, and on beneath colorful cliffs to its final destination at Clark Canyon Reservoir, the river is guarded by the Madison, Gravelly, and Snowcrest ranges in the north and the Tendoys along the southwest.

The upper stretches of the river are excellent dry fly fishing for grayling that sometimes reach 15 inches and are not all that choosy about the pattern. Cutthroats display similar equanimity. As the Red Rock moves into the Centennial Valley, the stream slows a bit and takes on a marshy character as it wanders between large pools that are treated as lakes in their own right on the refuge. Brook trout, cutthroats, grayling, and even lake trout are taken along this section of the river. Trumpeter swans and large flocks of waterfowl are common sights.

According to officials at Red Rock Lakes National Wildlife Refuge, fisheries on the refuge suffer from low populations. As a result, the refuge has special regulations designed to improve fish numbers. Red Rock Lakes and the creek between them are closed to fishing.

The river from here to Lima Reservoir has suffered from cattle grazing and is too silted in and too warm to sustain a viable trout fishery. Once below Lima the river returns to a quality environment for trout, running through red-and-ochre-colored rock formations. Rainbow and cutthroat trout are the dominant species, with browns gradually increasing in numbers down to Clark Canyon. Access is severely limited except for some Bureau of Reclamation land just above the reservoir. Wading is the preferred approach, though a few hearty individuals drift downstream in float tubes. Permission on this prime water now comes mainly in the form of daily fee fishing. The angling is excellent on the restricted stretches, but if this is a trend for this river it is disappointing for local fly fishermen.

Blue-Winged Olives come into play, especially from late August into early October. Pale Morning Duns are seen from June through September. There is normally some form of caddis activity throughout the summer and into fall, matched by dry flies and emergers in sizes 12 to 18 in tan, gray, and brown. Grannoms are the earliest arrivals, showing up in May, followed by the Spotted Sedges and then Little Sister, Green, and Longhorn Sedges in late June. Sizes 12 to 14, for all but the Great Gray Spotted Sedge (6 to 8), are adequate. There are also Yellow Sally stoneflies, sizes 14 to 16, beginning in July.

The browns in the lower river will often top several pounds. Beginning in late September, these fish prefer large streamers like Muddlers, Woolly Buggers, Stub Wing Bucktails, Matukas, and Zonkers cast hard to the willowy, grassy, undercut banks and then pulsed back. Large wet flies in sizes 6 through 10 cast quartering upstream and worked along the current with slight action and then allowed to tail out at the end of the drift can also provoke some serious responses from the trout.

Matching the hatch is not so much the problem as is getting onto the best parts of the lower river. This is a matter of knowing a landowner or being willing and able to pay the daily fee. As abhorrent as the fee concept is, the money is well spent on the Red Rock. This is fine country to fish in for good-sized browns and rainbows in plentiful supply.

Fishing Waters in the Red Rock Drainage

Blair Lake: Blair is less than 10 acres and fertile for a lake above 8,000 feet. It's in a glacial cirque, and it's reached by a stiff march up from Hellroaring Canyon. Blair is good fishing for Yellowstone cutthroats.

Borrow Pits: Aesthetically, these ditches leave a bit to be desired, but they provide quality fishing right next to I-15 in open country not far from Dell for good numbers of brookies, browns, and rainbows averaging a foot and running larger.

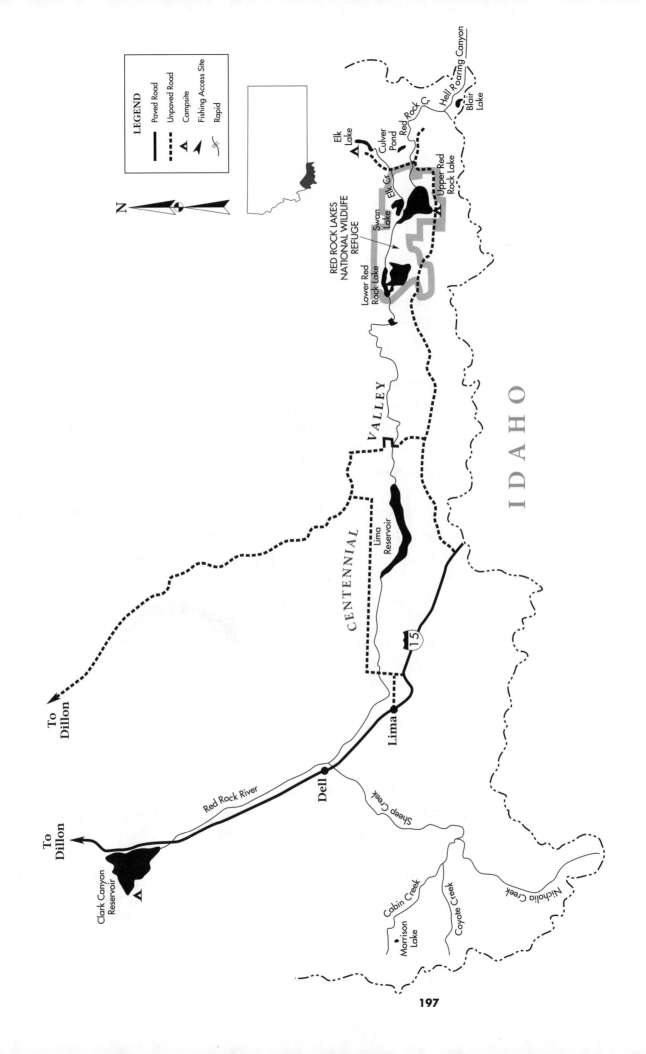

LEGEND

Paved Road
Unpaved Road
Campsite
Fishing Access Site
Rapid

N

RED ROCK LAKES
NATIONAL WILDLIFE
REFUGE

Elk Lake

Culver Pond

Red Rock Cr

Hell Roaring Canyon

Blair Lake

Elk Cr

Upper Red Rock Lake

Swan Lake

Lower Red Rock Lake

VALLEY

IDAHO

CENTENNIAL

Lima Reservoir

15

To Dillon

Lima

Dell

Red Rock River

Sheep Creek

To Dillon

Clark Canyon Reservoir

Cabin Creek

Coyote Creek

Nicholia Creek

Morrison Lake

Culver Pond (Widow's Pool): Nearly 30 acres and spring-fed several miles east of Upper Red Rock Lake with plenty of good-sized (read: BIG) brook trout that are tough to catch but will bite a Bigg's Special worked above the weed beds ever so slowly. There are also cutthroats, grayling, and rainbows. *Callibaetis* starting at midmorning from July through early September take fish, and Brown Drakes (*Ephemera simulans*) come off on occasion in the evenings in June and July. Try using Mike's Brown Drake sizes 10 to 12.

Elk (Elk Springs, Shitepoke) Creek: This is a small stream heading out of Elk Lake. There's good fishing in the beaver-dammed, swampy stretches in the Red Rock Lakes National Wildlife Refuge for brook and rainbow trout up to several pounds. Check the special regulations.

Elk Lake: Elk is one of the best grayling lakes in the state with fish to 15 inches caught each season. There are also cutthroats and lake trout to 20 inches on this popular water. The gamefish population is threatened by an illegal plant of Utah chubs, first discovered in 1986—the number of chubs is growing.

Hellroaring Creek: This is a good stream for cutthroats approaching the magic 20-inch barrier, especially in the lower reaches. Cutthroats are cutthroats. Don't get a headache trying to figure out what fly you think they will take. Except for the snobs in the Yellowstone River in Yellowstone Park, this species is not all that picky. Small brook trout also live here.

McDonald's Pool (Buck Pond): McDonald's is 7 acres below Elk Lake with rainbows over 20 inches and several pounds. In the summer this place is somewhat crowded.

Morrison Lake: Below Baldy Mountain at over 8,000 feet and 24 acres, Morrison reached by rough "road" for cutthroat trout that top a couple of pounds.

Red Rock Creek: This is one of the best (among the few) grayling streams in Montana with fish to 15 inches along with brook trout and cutthroats. It wanders down from Squaw Pass to Upper Red Rock Lake in the Centennial Valley. Access could be better, but this is a stream worth savoring, at least once. Be sure to check special regulations if you are on the wildlife refuge.

Red Rock Lakes: Closed to fishing in 1996. Check Red Rock Lakes National Wildlife Refuge special regulations.

Schultz (Warden's) Pond: This is on the Schultz Ranch with public access for rainbows that grow very large. There are no herds of the fat things roaming this fertile 2-plus acres in the Centennial Valley.

Though not common in this drainage, you might find bitterroot on the drier hillsides and ridges enroute to that secret pool.
Photo by Stan Bradshaw

Sheep (Big Sheep) Creek: Sheep heads below Eighteenmile Peak in the Beaverhead Mountains along the Idaho border. It enters Red Rock River just south of Dell and is followed by gravel road for much of its heavily fished length. Rainbows and browns over 20 inches are taken regularly with the best fish coming as soon as the general season opens, runoff permitting, and in the fall with egg-sucking leeches and Girdle Bugs and other ugly stuff work right up against the brushy, willow-choked, undercut banks.

Widgeon Pond: This one is on the county road between McDonald's Pool and Culver Pond with good fishing for cutthroats and brookies over 15 inches.

Golden stoneflies hatch when wild roses are in bloom.
Photo by Stan Bradshaw

Other Waters

Bear Creek: Cutthroats.

Beaver Creek: Brookies and cutthroats.

Breneman's Lake: Rainbows. Permission needed.

Cabin Creek: Too small.

Clover Creek: Brookies and cutthroats.

Corral Creek: Brookies and cutthroats.

Coyote Creek: Too small.

Deadman Creek: Cutthroats and rainbows.

Deadman Lake: Cutthroats.

East Fork Clover Creek: Brookies and cutthroats.

East Fork Little Sheep Creek: Too small.

Harkness Lakes: Brookies and cutthroats.

Kitty Creek: Too small.

Little Beaver Creek: Brookies.

Little Sheep (Middle Fork) Creek: Cutthroats.

Long Creek: Brookies, cutthroats, and rainbows.

Lower Red Rock Lake: Closed to fishing.

Middle Creek: Too small.

Muddy Creek: Cutthroats.

Nicholia Creek: Cutthroats and rainbows.

O'Dell Creek: Brookies, cutthroats, and grayling.

Picnic (Hackett) Creek: Brookies and cutthroats.

Poison Creek: Brookies.

Sage Creek: Brookies, browns, and rainbows.

Sawmill Creek: Cutthroats.

Shambo Pond: Closed to fishing.

Shineberger Creek: Too small.

Swan Lake: Clichéd ballet. Closed to fishing.

Tom Creek: Brookies.

Upper Red Rock Lake: Closed to fishing.

West Creek: Cutthroats.

West Fork Little Sheep Creek: Brookies.

■ *Special thanks to James Goodman and Tom Heinsinger for their help on the Red Rock drainage.*

Smith River at Deep Creek
Photo by Stan Bradshaw

S M I T H   R I V E R

Ask experienced Montana fly fishers what the most scenic float in the state is and many will say the Smith River. Throw in sometimes excellent fishing for browns and rainbows in the isolated 61-mile stretch of canyon river (a four- to five-day float) and you have the ingredients for a quality fishing experience.

Formed at the confluence of the North and South Forks in open meadow country west of White Sulphur Springs, the Smith flows for over 100 miles through some of the most spectacular canyon country in Montana. The upper 30 miles of the river wander across an open, rolling-hill mountain valley surrounded by the Castle, Big Belt, and Little Belt mountains. Brown trout to several pounds hide beneath the brushy, willowy banks, as do good numbers of smaller rainbows and brook trout. The pool-to-riffle-to-pool habitat in this gently flowing section is ideal for fishing an Elk Hair Caddis with an Emergent Sparkle Pupa dropper in the evenings, hoppers on a summer afternoon, or streamers, especially in autumn for spawning browns on the move.

The canyon section runs from Camp Baker to Eden Bridge with no public access in between. Twenty-two designated campsites are scattered along the way and that's it for amenities. Some private homes and ranches overlook the river in this section. The Smith gets a Skwala stonefly hatch, effectively matched with a brown wing/green body Trude or a dark-colored Air Head, in March and April. This is usually before runoff and the insects can trigger great surface action. Later in the spring, when the river is on the rise from runoff and rain, anglers can expect very slow fishing for browns that will take large olive or black Woolly Buggers or Girdle bugs either singly or together in a tandem rigging. Big ugly stuff draws the trout. These fish will be larger on average than fish taken later in the year when the weather warms and the water drops and clears. Perhaps this is because it takes a big fish to handle the swollen flow of the Smith. When the river begins to compress as runoff abates, the angling for browns and rainbows can be superb, again with the streamers, but also with caddis and stoneflies (especially large nymphs). The Smith gets good hatches of Salmon Flies and Golden Stone Flies.

Streamers and nymphs worked bank-tight to grassy pockets or between runs of broken rock and boulders can also be productive. Even after a tough winter the trout are firm and thick, though lacking the intense shadings attendant with autumn's spawning festivities. Downstream from Camp Baker rainbow populations can run to more than 1,300 per mile from 6 to 16½ inches.

The peak use period on the Smith runs from late May until levels are too low in mid- to late July (although in drought years floating can become impossible in mid-June). The majority of trout taken at this time will be rainbows, with some browns and a smattering of whitefish that frequently reach a couple of pounds. You may also take an occasional cutthroat.

Below Eden Bridge the river is a slow affair with riprap banks, undercut cottonwood-lined banks, and brushy banks, and trout populations drop off considerably. Large browns and rainbows, both resident and up from the Missouri, will take streamers and terrestrials cast close to the shore. This portion of the Smith is best worked in the spring and again in the fall to take advantage of migrating rainbows and browns.

Unfortunately, by late May, even on the wilderness stretches of the river, the solitude has been transformed into a riotous melange of canoes, rafts, driftboats, bikinis, halter tops, and tipsy aggregations of beer-sodden yahoos. Even in the often-rotten weather found early in the season, close to 100 people have logged in on the river.

In 1991, use figures by month were: May—253 craft and 2,219 user days; June—671 craft and 7,029 user days; July—191 craft and 1972 user days; and during August when the river was too low to float comfortably, the figures were 8 craft and 63 user days.

Comments from floater logs in the early 1990s are perhaps most revealing of the problems of recreational use at that time:

"Fishing was terrible compared to five years ago—too many people."

"Fishing has deteriorated over last 15 years."

"Need more campsites."

"Had the impression outfitters have taken over the river."

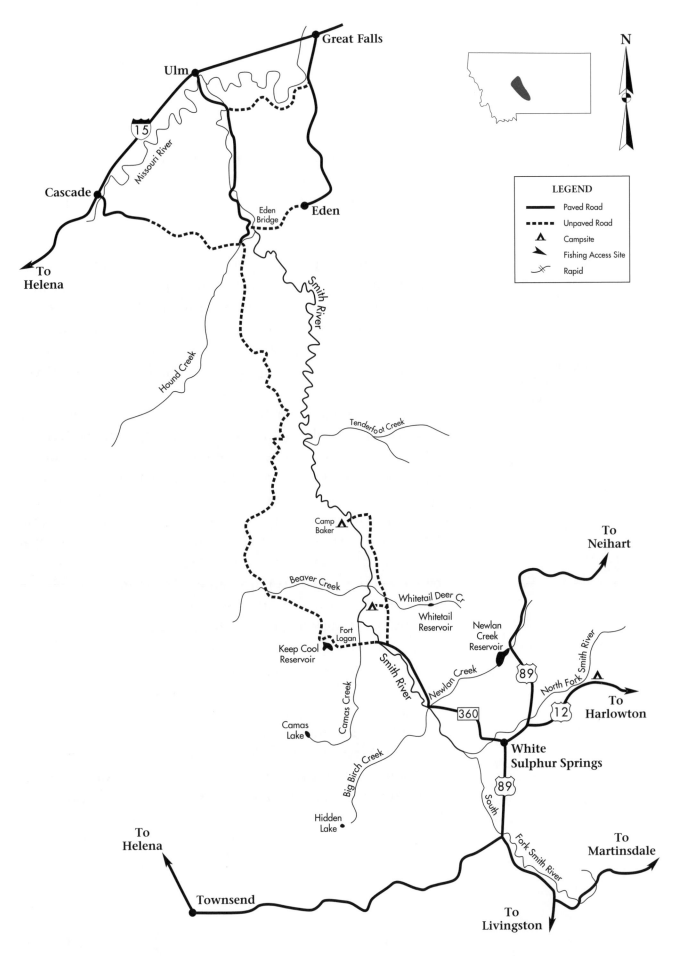

SMITH RIVER

N

LEGEND
Paved Road
Unpaved Road
Campsite
Fishing Access Site
Rapid

Great Falls

Ulm

15

Cascade

Missouri River

To
Helena

Eden
Bridge

Eden

Hound Creek

Smith River

Tenderfoot Creek

Camp
Baker

Beaver Creek

Whitetail Deer Cr.

Whitetail
Reservoir

Newlan
Creek
Reservoir

To
Neihart

Fort
Logan

Keep Cool
Reservoir

Camas Creek

Camas
Lake

Smith River

Newlan Creek

89

North Fork Smith River

12

To
Harlowton

360

White
Sulphur Springs

89

Big Birch Creek

Hidden
Lake

To
Helena

South

Fork Smith River

To
Martinsdale

Townsend

To
Livingston

205

"Outfitters and guides also need to be more courteous to those of us who are not among their party."

And from an outfitter, "Outfitters taking over campsites is also B.S."

These kinds of numbers, along with the attendant conflict between floaters, prompted the legislature to allow the Department of Fish, Wildlife, and Parks to regulate floater numbers and use. If you want to float the Smith these days, you must apply in advance for a permit, register at Camp Baker, pay a per-person fee of $15 (guides pay an additional $175 per trip), and declare intended campsites (you may only camp in designated campsites). While one result of these regulations has been that getting on the river at the peak season is no longer a lock, the quality of the experience has improved considerably.

Even with these regulations, however, the balmy days of late spring and early summer are still crowded. One alternative to the crowded peak season is to float in early spring or later in September and October, when water levels get too low to ensure an easy trip but also keep the crowds down. The downside of this alternative is that the weather is totally unpredictable. Spring and fall snowstorms, fairly common in this canyon country can quickly go from miserable to deadly. If you decide to go in these off-seasons, come prepared for the worst, no matter what the weather forecast.

Concerning the fishing, data indicates the numbers of brown trout from 18 to 22 inches has increased gradually over the past several years, while the number of 13- to 17.9-inch fish has held its own. Fish of 22 inches and larger are in short supply.

Notwithstanding its scenic qualities and fishing opportunities, the Smith is not immune to environmental insult. Noxious weeds (in the form of leafy spurge and spotted knapweed), first introduced through contaminated hay, have since spread throughout the drainage in epidemic proportions, helped along, in part, by recreational

Permits are required to float the Smith from Camp Baker to Eden Bridge.

users. Biological controls in the form of weed-eating insects have been introduced, but, as of 1995, it's still too early to tell the success of these efforts.

No less a threat is the proliferation of riverside "ranchettes". The growth of these second-home developments in the canyon have exacerbated landowner disputes in the past few years. Fortunately, one group, the Montana Land Reliance, has embarked on an aggressive program of acquiring conservation easements to limit riverside development. Their efforts have assured that many miles of private land will not be turned into housing developments.

Whatever its problems, the Smith, even at its overcrowded worst, is still one of the finest wilderness fly fishing experiences in the lower forty-eight states. Fantastic country, quality fishing, and good companionship are what fishing and the Smith are all about.

The bright yellow flowers of arrowleaf balsamroot often accompany spring runoff—good fishing can't be far behind.
Photo by Glenda Bradshaw

Fishing Waters in the Smith Drainage

Big Birch Creek: Big Birch is a few miles west of White Sulphur Springs. It provides solid action for exceptional numbers of brook trout to maybe 12 inches. The marshy, brushy country means hip waders and roll casts with dry flies or nymphs and the like.

Camas Lake: This shallow 5-acre pond is northwest of White Sulphur Springs. You can reach it by road and then 3 miles of trail to a small glacial cirque. The lake holds plenty of cutthroats to a foot or more, and it's a popular day trip.

Leonard Briggs fishes it, "The shallow water at the marshy south end is great in the spring. The fish cruise it looking for insects, and they'll aggressively charge a fly that crosses in front of them. A Shroud, fished with a twitch and pause, is a fun dry fly and a small Brown Hackle Peacock, no bigger than a size 16, is a consistent nymph."

Hidden Lake: Go up White Gulch and turn on the "microwave" road to get above Hidden Lake, and then hike down. Or go into the Big Belts, to the end of Big Birch Creek, and hike up to the lake. Either way, with pristine country and nice fishing for fat rainbows to 16 inches, this water is worth the trip. Hidden is deep, even though it's only 5 acres, and a sinking or sink-tip line puts a fly into the prime water at the drop-offs. Try weighted nymphs, such as the A. P. Muskrat, Gold Ribbed Hare's Ear, or Bead Head Twist Nymph, fished slowly up the slope.

Hound Creek: Hound Creek enters the Smith not too far above Eden Bridge and winds through open sage country that plays home to rattlesnakes and trophy mosquitoes. Access is poor but the fishing is good for plenty of browns to a foot or more and plenty of little

Smith River Canyon
Photo by Stan Bradshaw

brook trout. A Foam Beetle (or other beetle variation) is the most consistent fly, but a hopper pattern brings out the bigger fish.

Keep Cool Reservoir: It's about 20 miles northwest of White Sulphur Springs on private grazing land, but it's planted yearly by the state with Eagle Lake rainbows that grow fat and happy in this 5-acre, fecund environment. Try scuds and damselfly imitations fished *slowly* (often the key for slob trout on rich lakes).

Newlan Creek Reservoir: Here are 300 acres of water, 12 miles north of White Sulphur Springs, that are planted each year with thousands of Yellowstone cutthroats that grow to 18 inches. Big fish, easy access, and large water—a combination like that is bound to make this a popular place with anglers of all persuasions. Still, with so many acres a person can usually find his own bit of shoreline to work with a nymph. The cutthroats here do seem to be bottom grubbers. A size-10 to -16 Halfback is popular; so is a Green Disco Midge in size 18 or 20.

North Fork Smith River: The North Fork begins in the Little Belts and makes its casual way for more than 20 miles to the Smith not far from White Sulphur Springs. The upper reaches have lots of small brookies and rainbows. The lower sections, below Sutherlin Reservoir, are good fishing for nice browns along with lots of whitefish and some brook trout. Much of the land is posted, but access can be gained from county roads or often with a polite request and a smile.

Rock Creek: Rock Creek comes from the east side of the Big Belts Mountains through private rangeland, and then to the Smith north of the Old Fort Logan Military Reservation. Where you can get on it, it's good fishing for brookies, cutthroats, rainbows, and some fair-sized browns that are not all that concerned with what fly is cast upon the water. The roads, such as they are, are not in good shape and they can do a number on your vehicle or your tires. They also turn hazardous with the slightest suggestion of precipitation. When it rains, stay off of these roads.

Sheep Creek: A good fishing stream with dry flies for a mixed bag of brook, brown, and rainbow trout along with whitefish in its 30-plus-mile journey through forested valleys, canyons, rangeland, and grassy hills to the Smith northwest of White Sulphur Springs after beginning in the Little Belts north of Porphyry Peak. It is followed by country road much of its length, with Forest Service campgrounds in the upper reaches.

Sutherlin (Smith River) Reservoir: About 10 miles east of White Sulphur Springs on U.S. 12, over 270 acres, 80 feet deep with heavy drawdown from irrigation, Sutherlin is planted yearly with thousands of rainbows. This is popular with area anglers. There is a campground and other amenities.

Tenderfoot Creek: Reached by rough road on the east side of the Smith, 20 miles north of the Old Fort Logan Military Reservation. It's followed by both trail and logging road for good fishing for cutthroats, rainbows, and whitefish. The land at its mouth is posted, so if you are going to fish up from the Smith, stay inside the ordinary high-water marks.

Other Waters

Baldy Lake: Cutthroats.

Beaver Creek: Brookies and cutthroats.

Benton Gulch: Brookies and rainbows.

Black (Butte) Creek: Too small.

Bolsinger Creek: Cutthroats.

Camas Creek: Brookies and rainbows.

Deadman Creek: Brookies.

Deep (Dry) Creek: Cutthroats.

Dry Creek: Brookies.

Eagle Creek: Brookies and rainbows.

East Fork Hound Creek: Brookies and rainbows.

Edith Lake: Cutthroats.

Eight Mile Creek: Brookies.

Elk Creek: Brookies.

Elk Creek Reservoir: Brookies and rainbows.

Four Mile Creek: Brookies.

Freeman Creek: Cutthroats and rainbows.

Gipsy Lake (Gile Reservoir): Rainbows.

Grace Lake: Cutthroats.

Guise Creek: Brookies.

Hound Creek Reservoir: Rainbows.

Indian Creek: Brookies.

Iron Mines Creek: Cutthroats.

Jumping Creek: Too small.

Lake Creek: Brookies and cutthroats.

Lamb Creek: Too small.

Little Birch Creek: Brookies and cutthroats.

Middle Creek Lake: Rainbows. Permission needed.

Middle Fork West Fork Hound Creek: Too small.

Ming Coulee: Browns.

Moose Creek: Brookies, cutthroats, and rainbows.

Newlan Creek: Posted.

North Fork Rock Creek: Brookies, cutthroats, and rainbows.

South Fork Rock Creek: Cutthroats and rainbows.

South Fork Smith River: Brookies.

Spring Creek: Too small.

Thompson Gulch: Brookies.

Trout Creek (North Fork): Posted.

Trout Creek (Ulm): Posted.

West Fork Hound Creek: Poor access.

Whitetail Deer Creek: Brookies.

Whitetail Reservoir: Brookies and rainbows.

Willow Creek: Posted.

■ *Special thanks to Leonard Briggs, Richard Micklish, Paul Roos, Ward Ryan, and Jim Toth for their help on the Smith drainage.*

Old Indian signal point, Stillwater River
Photo by Kenneth F. Roahen
Courtesy of the Montana Historical Society, Helena

STILLWATER RIVER

The Stillwater River has its wild beginnings in the remote, rugged, and largely inaccessible Beartooth Mountains north of Yellowstone National Park. Wind-scoured plateaus lying thousands of feet above sea level are surrounded by jagged peaks that tower even more thousands of feet above. Snowfields and glaciers carve and crack the rock and provide water that drives the river. Waterfalls offer scenic diversion.

The Stillwater drains hundreds of square miles that hold more than 300 lakes that average less than 10 acres each in surface area. Nearly 40 percent of these waters hold trout of many species, including the rare and beautiful golden trout and Yellowstone cutthroat, rainbow, and brook trout. Grayling also show up in some of these clear, relatively sterile lakes. Many of them are at elevations over 9,000 feet, including an unnamed one at 10,400 feet. Lots of these lakes are unnamed, but a number of them contain trout, usually Yellowstone cutthroats.

The upper section of the Stillwater is a fast-flowing, pocket-water stream holding good numbers of brook, cutthroat, and rainbow trout averaging perhaps 8 inches and occasionally topping 12 inches. Attractor patterns take the eager fish. The middle section of the stream is accessible by road above and below the town of Nye with good fishing for browns to several pounds along with brookies and rainbows. The lower section runs out onto private and posted ranch land. This stretch has fair numbers of brook and rainbow trout and some big brown trout. Unfortunately, getting on the water is difficult.

In the middle and lower sections, nymphing the runs and riffles is a good ploy for catching rainbows. Streamers and large nymphs worked close to the banks always takes browns. Keep an eye out for caddis, especially around dusk as summer progresses. The caddis will bring all of the trout up to the surface as they begin to fall back onto the water during and after mating.

Fishing Waters in the Stillwater Drainage

Arch Lakes: You can reach these via the East Rosebud Trail above Elk Lake to Little Arch at nearly 10,000 feet below Phantom Glacier. This lake is planted regularly with Yellowstone cutthroats. The other lakes in the basin also have trout, some reaching a couple of pounds.

East Fiddler Creek: This one is followed by road above the West Stillwater–Rosebud Road for nice catches of browns and rainbows in the lower sections and cutthroats in the run below Fishtail Plateau.

East Rosebud Creek: The East Rosebud heads up on the Beartooth Plateau at Cairn Lake and flows for over 50 miles to West Rosebud Creek. To get there, take the road to East Rosebud Lake, and then the trail to the headwaters. You'll find good fishing in the middle sections for healthy browns and rainbows. Some big fish are taken down below in pasture land country, but permission is required.

East Rosebud Lake: This is a beautiful lake with mountain vistas all around. It's not a wilderness experience—there are summer homes and it is reached by good road. The fishing is fine for cutthroats and rainbows that top 15 inches and a very few browns that top several pounds. The lake is over 100 acres by 20 feet or more deep.

Emerald Lake: The West Rosebud road south of Columbus tracks right along the shoreline of this popular lake. It is 28 acres, but very shallow (maximum 7 feet). It is stocked with rainbows each year and, of course, these sacrificial lambs draw the crowds. Some of these fish escape the early slaughter and because of either intelligence or luck manage to grow larger, to 15 inches within a few months, and get more attuned to the natural environment. The lake also has some browns to a couple of pounds. Any fly fisherman with a speck of discrimination in his heart can ignore the splashy stockers and target the bigger fish. This is especially true at dawn every summer day when the trout dimple the surface.

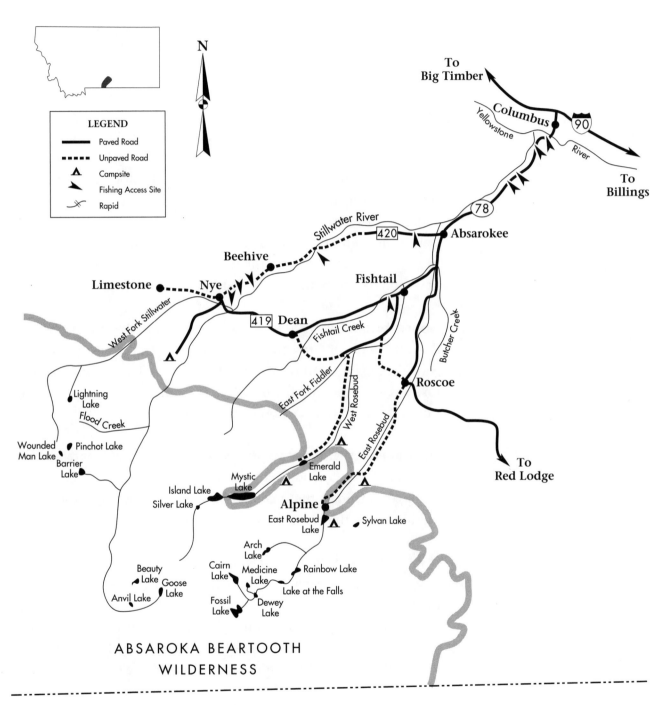

LEGEND

— Paved Road
- - - Unpaved Road
▲ Campsite
➤ Fishing Access Site
✕ Rapid

N

To
Big Timber

Columbus

Yellowstone

90

78

To
Billings

Stillwater River

420

Absarokee

Beehive

Limestone   Nye

Fishtail

West Fork Stillwater

419   Dean

Fishtail Creek

Butcher Creek

Lightning
Lake

East Fork Fiddler

West Rosebud

Roscoe

Flood Creek

Wounded
Man Lake   Pinchot Lake

East Rosebud

To
Red Lodge

Barrier
Lake

Island Lake   Mystic
Lake

Emerald
Lake

Silver Lake

Alpine

East Rosebud
Lake   Sylvan Lake

Arch
Lake

Beauty
Lake   Goose
Lake

Cairn
Lake   Medicine
Lake   Rainbow Lake

Anvil Lake

Lake at the Falls

Fossil
Lake   Dewey
Lake

ABSAROKA BEARTOOTH
WILDERNESS

WYOMING

Flood Creek: This outlet of Pinchot Lake flows for several miles to the Stillwater. There is good fishing for goldens (that love Goddard Caddis), rainbows, cutthroats, and all sorts of hybrid combinations.

Fossil Lake: It sits at nearly 10,000 feet and it is planted every three years with Yellowstone cutthroats that grow quickly enough, considering the elevation, to 15 inches. The access is from the Clarks Fork of the Yellowstone drainage—find Bald Knob Lake and from there it's a mile hike over to Fossil. The problem on this lake is the bad, almost constant, wind on the exposed plateau. Many anglers wait until evening and hope the cold, steady blasts will go away. When the wind does drop, the fish feed well on the surface, taking any good terrestrial imitation. Ants and beetles are good choices.

Goose Lake: Over 100 acres, deep, and reachable by four-wheel-drive rig south of Grasshopper Glacier out of Cooke City. Goose is good fishing for cutthroats up to a few pounds, but the angling pressure crops off the number of fish here. Sometimes a couple of nice trout are a good day on Goose.

Lake at Falls: This water is 50 acres of alpine splendor at over 8,000 feet on the East Rosebud Trail above Rainbow Lake. It's good fishing for large cutthroats that may have a slight golden tinge from cross-breeding with the goldens that used to swim here.

Lightning Lake: Over 60 acres and 120 feet deep at 9,340-feet elevation, this one probably holds a golden as big as anyone has ever caught. The big trout are almost impossible to catch unless they are in the connecting flow between Lightning and Little Lightning Lake. At these times a weighted Muddler or Stub Wing Bucktail worked repeatedly in front of the trout as they hold in the flow will provoke territorial strikes. Little Lightning is a nursery for goldens and is easier fishing. After the trout are done spawning, they head back to the deeps where reaching them with a small nymph is more than work. Finding your way to this water is not easy, but the best way in is around Chalice Peak from Lake Plateau.

Medicine Lake: Located at almost 10,000 feet in barren country above Dewey Lake, it's 30 acres and deep. Everyone should go up to the upper end to see the waterfalls (and the cliffs at the base of the falls aren't a bad place to start fishing). It's planted with cutthroats every eight years, but in spite of the long stocking cycle it always provides consistently good action for fish up to 15 inches. The fish really hug the littoral zone, cruising the edge looking for any easy meal.

Mystic Lake: It's over 400 acres and more than 200 feet deep when full. This reservoir is up West Rosebud Creek. Rainbows greatly out-number the cutthroats and hybrids. The wind howls on this water, making casting a difficult proposition, but for anyone who can handle the air (remember that the British still-water anglers *prefer* a stiff breeze) the fishing can be exceptional at the upper end for trout up to 16 or 17 inches.

Pinchot Lake: It's 54 acres by 30 feet deep in the Flood Creek Lake system. The fishing is mainly for rainbow-cutthroat hybrids that have a little sparkle from some golden trout genes. They'll go up to a couple of pounds.

Rosebud River: This is good fishing for browns and rainbows with the landowners' permission. There are some classic deep pools and undercuts here, and this is the water holding the better two- to three-pound fish. They can be caught, even during the middle of the day, but the method of choice is deep nymphing. A two-fly rig with a 9-foot leader, a large yarn indicator, and some serious split shot get everything down in the holes. The flies have to be subtle—a size-16 Pheasant Tail and a size-16 Pale Morning Dun Emerger work consis-tently all summer. The only other alternative to deep nymphing, with all of this fine holding water, is to hit the hatches and hope the trout come out to play. The Rosebud is followed by road to the Stillwater River.

Silver Lake: Over 70 acres with good numbers of rainbows and some cutthroats. It's located above Island Lake at 7,820 feet.

Sylvan Lake: Sylvan is in a glacial cirque reached by trail up Spread Creek from East Rosebud Lake. This is one of the better golden trout lakes around, with fishing for trout to 12 inches or a touch bigger. The goldens like small flies (very small flies) hanging motionless 18 to 24 inches below a yarn indicator. A size-20 Black Halo Midge Pupa or a size-18 Pearl Serendipity are proven patterns here. The hike in to Sylvan is long and steep but worth the effort.

West Fork Stillwater River: The West Fork is followed by road for a few miles, then by trail for 20 miles from the Stillwater at Nye up to the headwaters. It's good fishing in the lower reaches for browns and rainbows to 20 inches, but much of the land is posted. The upper section is good for cutthroats and rainbows.

West Rosebud Creek: It forms just below Grasshopper Glacier, flows through Silver and Mystic lakes, then courses for 25 miles to the East Rosebud. The lower section is heavily posted but good for browns. The middle portion is good for brookies, browns, cutthroats, and rainbows. The upper run has some rainbows.

Other Waters

Antelope (Morris) Creek: Brookies. Permission needed.

Anvil Lake: Cutthroats.

Arch Creek: Too small.

Bad Canyon Creek: Brookies, browns, and cutthroats.

Barrier Lake: Rainbow-golden hybrids.

Beauty Lake: Cutthroats.

Big Park Lake: Cutthroats, goldens, and hybrids.

Butcher Creek: Brookies, browns, and cutthroats.

Cairn Lake: Brookies.

Castle Creek: Brookies and browns.

Cirque Lake: Barren.

Crow Lake: Brookies.

Dewey Lake: Cutthroats.

East Fishtail Creek: Too small.

Echo Lake: Cutthroats.

Elk Lake: Brookies.

Favonius (Crow) Lakes: Cutthroats.

Fiddler Creek: Brookies.

Fishtail Creek: Browns and rainbows.

Froze-to-Death Lake: Cutthroats.

Huckleberry Lake: Brookies.

Hudson's (Ernie) Reservoir: Private.

Ingersoll Creek: Brookies, browns, and rainbows.

Island Lake: Cutthroats and rainbows.

Jordan Lake: Cutthroats.

Limestone Creek: Brookies and browns.

Little Goose Lake: Cutthroats.

Little Lightning Lake: Goldens.

Little Rocky Creek: Browns, cutthroats, and rainbows.

Lodge Pole Creek: Brookies, browns, and rainbows.

Lost Lake: Barren.

Middle Fiddler Creek: Browns, cutthroats, and rainbows.

Mutt and Jeff Lakes: Brookies.

Pentad (Crazy Mule) Lake: Rainbows.

Phantom Lake: Cutthroats.

Picket Pin Creek: Brookies, browns, cutthroats, and rainbows.

Rainbow Lake: Rainbows, goldens, and hybrids.

Rimrock Lake: Cutthroats and rainbows.

Shadow Lake: Brookies.

Sioux Charley Lake: Brookies.

Slough (Princess) Lake: Brookies.

Snow Lakes: Rainbows.

Sourdough Basin Lakes: Brookies.

Trout Creek: Brookies, browns, and rainbows.

Trugulse Lake: Cutthroats.

Tumble (Jasper) Lake: Cutthroats.

West Fishtail Creek: Brookies.

West Rosebud (Assure) Lake: Browns and rainbows.

Wilderness Lake: Cutthroats.

Wood Lake: Cutthroats.

Wounded Man Lake: Cutthroats and rainbows.

Zoetman (Pete No. 3) Pond: Private.

■ *Special thanks to Tony Ames and Daryl Stine for their help on the Stillwater drainage.*

Yellowstone River in Paradise Valley
Photo by Stan Bradshaw

THE YELLOWSTONE

The Yellowstone is spawned in the high mountains of the Yellowstone National Park caldera. It's fed by water melted from snow and ice clinging to jagged rock faces in Wyoming, from steaming geysers and mudpots in the park, and from runoff pouring out of the Gallatin Range and the Absaroka Mountains.

Despite constant proposals and threats from the Bureau of Reclamation to build a dam at Allenspur only a few miles south of Livingston, the Yellowstone still flows unsullied for 670 miles to the Missouri in North Dakota. How rare is this? It's the only major river in the lower forty-eight states that is undammed. This is a classic western river, ranging from ice cold headwater runs through deep, fast canyon stretches into wide riffled sections and finally into turbid, warm meandering flatland flows of deceptive power.

The Yellowstone offers a variety and abundance of water types. Combine this with a complex variety of food forms, hundreds of types of aquatic insects, terrestrial insects, crayfish and scuds, and an assortment of forage fish, and consider that the river is a "natural" environment, with flows changing daily, weekly and monthly, and it's easy to see why "local knowledge" is so important on this big river.

Gardiner to Yankee Jim Canyon—The first section of the river in Montana is the 18-mile stretch of water from Gardiner to Yankee Jim Canyon. Browns, cutthroats, and rainbows exist in roughly equal numbers in this big, deep, and powerful water. Look at a topographical map—all the lines are really close right down to both sides of the river. It's a canyon and that limits the amount of wading water, but this is a stretch where the best fishing is often against the banks and in the backwaters anyway.

The great fishing starts in the winter months. A number of hot springs, with LaDuke the most significant, warm up the water and keep the midges hatching even during the nasty spells. On nice days the trout rise well in slower areas to both the pupae and the adults. A Griffith's Gnat on a fine tippet is usually good enough to fool them, but when they get really critical about fly color, try variations in black, brown, and red.

By spring everyone is waiting for the Salmon Fly hatch. The adults emerge in late June, but the nymphs are growing big and rest-

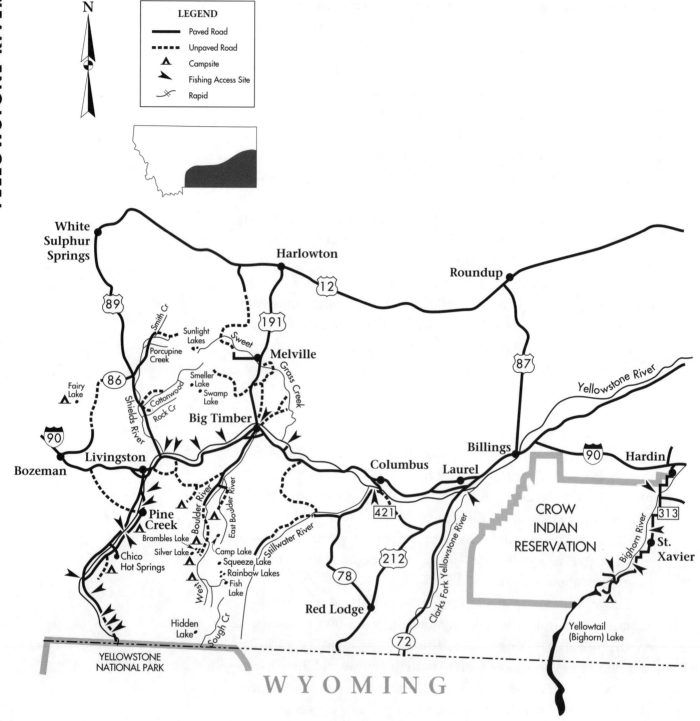

N

LEGEND
Paved Road
Unpaved Road
Campsite
Fishing Access Site
Rapid

White
Sulphur
Springs

Harlowton

Roundup

89

12

191

87

Smith Cr

Sunlight
Lakes

Sweet

Melville

Porcupine
Creek

86

Grass Creek

Fairy
Lake

Smeller
Lake

Swamp
Lake

Yellowstone River

Cottonwood

Rock Cr

Big Timber

Shields River

90

Billings

90

Hardin

Livingston

Columbus

Laurel

Bozeman

421

CROW
INDIAN
RESERVATION

313

Pine
Creek

Boulder River

East Boulder River

St.
Xavier

Brambles Lake

Bighorn River

Silver Lake

Camp Lake

Stillwater River

Squeeze Lake

Chico
Hot Springs

West Boulder River

Rainbow Lakes

212

Fish
Lake

Clarks Fork Yellowstone River

Hidden
Lake

78

Red Lodge

Rough Cr

Yellowtail
(Bighorn) Lake

72

YELLOWSTONE
NATIONAL PARK

W Y O M I N G

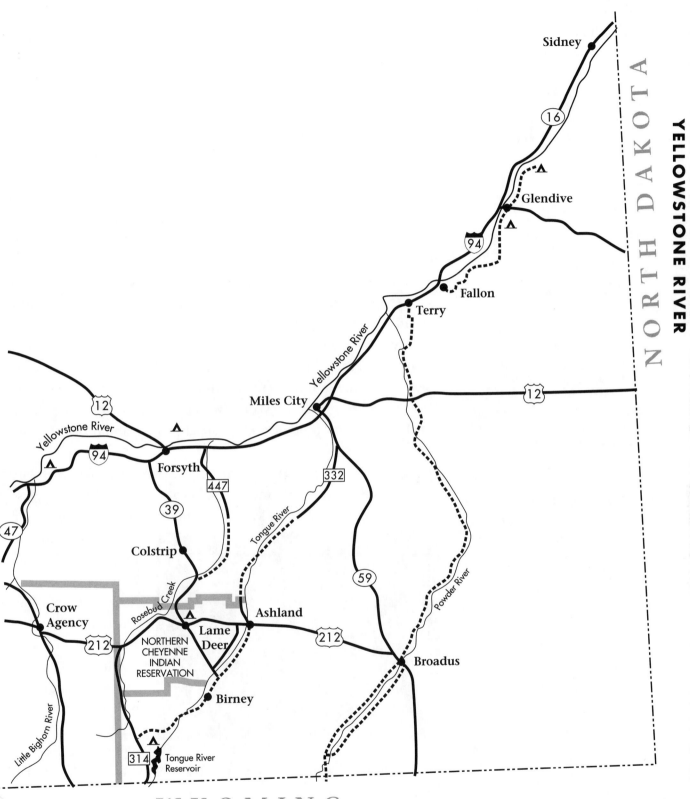

A Special Fly for the Yellowstone

The Spuddler ranks as one of the very best sculpin imitations. It comes from outstanding parentage. The fly was developed by Red Monical and Don Williams through Bailey's Fly Shop in Livingston—with the wide influence of Bailey's catalog it soon became popular everywhere. The pattern is a combination of a Muddler and a Spruce Fly. The Muddler, a Don Gapen pattern, is an all-around great imitation, mimicking a lot of different food items, wet and dry, in addition to the sculpin. The Spruce Fly is more of a mystery. The Light Spruce is form and color and the spitting image of a small whitefish; that explains its potency. But the Dark Spruce, even with the collar hackle of soft furnace fibers that clump around the shoulders and form a bulbous looking head, doesn't look much like a sculpin or any other minnow in Montana streams. It does, however, just like the Light variation, catch a lot of trout.

SPUDDLER MINNOW

Hook: 3X or 4X long shank (2–12)

Thread: gray

Tail: brown calf tail

Body: cream wool

Underwing: red fox squirrel tail hair

Overwing: four grizzly saddle hackles (dyed brown, tied flat on top of the squirrel tail hair)

Gills: a short band of red wool

Head: brown antelope spun and trimmed (wedge-shaped and flat on the bottom)

John Bailey speculates, "The effectiveness may be due to the flat head that makes the fly wobble and even spin in the water." (From his River Rap audio, "Fly Fishing Montana's Upper Yellowstone River")

less during the preceding months. It's possible to ignore other hatches during April and May, even the Mother's Day caddis (the early Grannom), because they are spotty in this stretch. Many anglers just concentrate on catching large trout on big nymphs.

Two anglers, Bill and Shelly Linden, spend the pre-runoff months each year fishing the water around Gardiner. They both use stonefly imitations, but they cover the water with two very different methods.

Shelly works the shoreline, "My flies are just as big as Bill's, but not nearly as heavily weighted. There are days when I never put a foot in the water. I'll stand on the bank and cast upstream, working the seams right next to the rocks. The steeper the bank, the better the fishing for me. My leader is 9 feet tapered to 1X and I don't need to put any weight on the leader. I don't use an indicator. The line tip tells me when to strike. My flies, which include Girdle Bugs, Bitch Creeks, Montana Stones, Dark Mossbacks, and Natural Drift Stones, are size 4."

Bill covers the deep slots farther out from the bank, "Shelly usually catches more fish and I usually catch bigger fish. I only use one pattern, a size-4 Dark Mossback, and when I tie them I wrap

goodly amounts of lead on the hook. The leader is short, no more than 3 feet, and I measure the tippet in pounds, not in diameter. I'll use twelve-pound nylon and that's as much for pulling flies off the snags as playing trout. The line is a 9-weight Teeny Sinking Mini-Tip and it gets down through the water column fast. The technique is a 'lift with the rod' and 'draw with the line hand,' a steady motion that keeps me in touch with the line. Since this is a feel method rather than a sight method, I'll set the hook when the rod tip doubles over."

The quality of the Salmon Fly hatch depends on the runoff. A number of upstream tributaries, especially the Lamar in Yellowstone

National Park, dump a lot of silt into the main river. Even during a normal year the Yellowstone can be brown soup, and this limits the dry fly fishing. During the occasional low water year, however, when the river is somewhat clear, the surface action with size-4 dry flies, including local favorites such as the Elk Hair Salmon Fly, Bird's Stone, Himenator, Tom's Adult Salmon Fly, Muddled Salmon Fly, Improved Sofa Pillow, and Orange Temptation Stone, rivals any Salmon Fly hatch in the West. For the best shot at big fish you have to float this stretch and pound the banks, particularly the areas with willows, with cast after cast.

Those willing to work nymphs will always take fish despite water that resembles a chocolate milkshake. Trout feed whenever possible (except for rare periods of satiation). They are opportunists. A large stonefly nymph bounced along the bottom will draw fish, which are not choosy in the fast current and cloudy water. Look for slower water at the end of riffles or along banks and work a dark pattern (black is best) hard and diligently even during the brightest hours of the day. The big fish are just where you would think they would be, in calm areas where they have shelter from predators. Muddy water turns off anglers far more than it does fish.

Both the Salmon Fly and the Golden Stone hatch last until mid-July. A ginger wing and light ginger body in sizes 6 to 8 handles the Goldens. There are other stoneflies in this part of the river. For the Yellow Sally use a wing of light straw with a yellow body. Yellow-bodied elk-hair caddis can be a good substitute in a pinch. For the Little Olive Stone tie a light gray wing and bright green body. Both of these are found in sizes 14 to 16, well into September.

By midsummer the crowds have disappeared from this water. There are summer hatches, but nothing that mesmerizes either fish or fishermen. The usual drill is to pound the banks with large attractors—Wulffs, Trudes, Double Wings, and Humpies, or grasshopper imitations—or slap the edges and creases with streamers such as Flash-A-Buggers, Spuddlers, Marabou Muddlers, and Hornbergs; or keep on working those big nymphs in the runs.

Yankee Jim Canyon to Tom Miner Creek—This is a short piece of water (and everything written about the Gardiner to Yankee Jim stretch applies here). It holds some serious trout, especially in the pockets and eddies found around large rocks and boulders. The water is sixty feet deep in places (use a lot of lead). The canyon has to be floated to cover it properly, but that means running through three Class III rapids. It's no place for amateur boatmen and wade fishing is limited.

Tom Miner Creek to Livingston—Browns and rainbows begin to outnumber the cutthroats in this stretch, but the cutthroats in this part of the river tend to run larger than in the upper section. Finding the cutts is relatively simple, too—look for the most featureless, currentless, uninspiring bits of river and that's where the cutthroats will be hanging out. The browns hold near obstructions and the rainbows use the current edges.

Casting near the mouths of the spring creeks along this part of the Yellowstone is productive (watch for some hatches not important in the main river, such as the Pale Morning Dun, in these micro-habitats). The land along the river flattens out, spreading into Paradise Valley. Hayfields along the stream edges give way to sage and grass covered foothills; and they in turn butt up against dark pine forests; and then even the forests yield to the lofty, ice-scoured, snow-capped peaks of the Gallatin and Absaroka mountains. It's a spectacular and humbling setting.

Prior to runoff, there is a hatch of Grannom caddis that is so predictable it is called the "Mother's Day Hatch" (also found on every major river in the West). "Predictable" is a misleading description, however, for fishing on the Yellowstone. By early May the river is ready to blow out with runoff. Show up on Mother's Day and you're likely to find a full flood with whole trees bobbing in the current. The best chance of hitting a fishable hatch of Grannoms on this river is in late April.

The fly to match the Grannom is tied in sizes 12 to 14, with a greenish-brown body and a gray wing shading to brown. Patterns can include a Deep Sparkle Pupa and an Emergent Sparkle Pupa for the hatching stage, and an Olive Elk Hair Caddis, Goddard Caddis, and Fluttering Caddis for the adult, egg-laying female (which conveniently collapses on the surface instead of going underwater).

One other significant hatch on the first 60 miles early in the season is the Blue-Winged Olive, sizes 16 to 20. These mayflies don't draw the largest trout to the surface, but they spark some steady feeding by rainbows and browns and ferocious gorging by whitefish. The Blue-Wings disappear by early April only to show up again from late July into mid-August, and one more time with feeling from late September through October. This last emergence can trigger some wonderful action for colorful browns. And by October, you'll have much of the best water to yourself.

Various species of mayflies are present on the Yellowstone, but this is not really a mayfly river. The far more abundant caddis and stoneflies make better selections. For working rough water a Wharry Caddis size 8 to 12 is a good choice, as is an Orange Bucktail Caddis. A couple of nymphs like the Peeking Caddis and the Brown/Yellow Deep Sparkle Pupa both in sizes 12 to 18 are nice to have, as are some Montana Stones (for many rivers around here) in 4 to 10, Golden Stones from 6 to 8, and George's Brown Stone in 6 to 10. Attractors should include Gray Wulffs (excellent on overcast days), Royal and Grizzly Wulffs, Humpies, and Royal and Coachman Trudes. Add some hoppers (always bring hoppers wherever you go—even to Beloit, Wisconsin). Some red and black ants round out the package.

For general mayfly activity, in addition to Blue-Winged Olives, include some Adams, Quill Gordons, Light Cahills, and Blue Duns, sizes 14 to 16. Also, pack some size 16 to 18 Meloche Duns for the PMDs around those spring creek outlets. A Pheasant Tail Nymph in 16 to 20, and a Hare's Ears from 8 to 16, handle the below-surface action.

Livingston to Reedpoint—As the river passes Livingston it picks up volume and speed. Wading becomes a bit more sporting and drift boats are common apparitions. Rainbows of over 13 inches are found in numbers approaching 1,000 fish per mile, along with a few large browns. Working current seams and down through deep holes is the best approach. From Livingston down past Big Timber to Reedpoint, the Yellowstone widens and slows, though there are long stretches of riffles flowing over gravel and bouldery streambed. There are also deep runs and pools. In the broken water, large attractor dry flies produce, as do stonefly nymphs. But the really big browns and rainbows are taken most often on the bottoms of the runs and pools. Think 2/0 sculpins and batting helmets. Casting these things all day is work and you may feel like someone has been doing a number on your skull with a rigging ax, especially on windy days. But these patterns, worked down deep, will turn some nice trout. The takes are predatory. Trout will rocket downstream with the current once they realize that there are strings attached to their meal. A survey near Big Timber turned up some trout closing in on ten pounds. Use heavy leaders.

Reedpoint to Billings—Gary LaFontaine and John Bailey report in their River Rap audio tape, "Fly Fishing Montana's Upper Yellowstone River," a hatch that occurs on the river from Reedpoint to the mouth of the Bighorn: "From late August through September it has an incredible mayfly hatch, never before listed or given a common name in angling literature. The creamy white Ghost Fly covers the flats of the lower river in such numbers that carp, sauger, and catfish join the brown and rainbow trout in a surface feeding circus. It's one evening act that an angler who hits it will never forget. . . ."

. . . Where's the first tee and what's the course record?

Both the Ghost Fly—best matched with a size-10 Vanilla Cone for the emerger and a Cream Mess for the adult—and the slightly smaller White Fly—matched with the same patterns in size 12—are worth a trip to this portion of the river. The hatch dates of these two species overlap, creating a white blizzard that turns the biggest trout into free-rising fools. The slurping sounds indicate a definite lack of table manners.

There are some heavy hatches of other mayflies on this stretch. The Blue-Winged Olive comes off three times a season—early, middle, and late. The Tricos form mating clusters in early morning clouds during August and September. The Yellow Drake, a size-16 Dun that hatches from late July through September, is very abundant.

There are also steady hatches of caddisflies. The two net-spinning genera, the Spotted Sedge and the Little Sister Sedge, hatch in heavy numbers on summer evenings. The caddis hatches bring up mainly trout.

The Yellowstone down into Billings gradually turns over to a predominantly warm-water fishery. But there are still some good-sized trout in this water that do well feeding on smaller sauger and catfish along with good numbers of other forage fish. Large streamer patterns, such as the Clouser Minnow, worked along brushy, undercut banks, off the ends of gravel shelves, and bounced through riffles are the best bets. Floating is a good, but tedious way to probe for these trout.

The Yellowstone is a complicated river. The best way to learn something of the water is to invest in a guide for at least a day (several days would be better) and float the section of water you are most interested in. Learn one or maybe two stretches of a river each year and concentrate your efforts. A scatter-gun approach might initially seem the best way to "have it all." Superficially this may hold true. In trout fishing, as in many of life's better pursuits, quality is always superior to quantity.

Some anglers focus just on the channels of the river. They discover "little trout streams" that fish much differently than the main Yellowstone. They can wade and cast to individual trout or read the water and fish blind with a nymph or a dry fly. The secret is knowing the good channels from the poor ones—the ones that have had water flowing through them all winter, and weren't blocked off by ice jams at the mouth or left dry by dropping flow levels, are the best summer fisheries. They have the insect life and the hatches that keep trout in them all the time. From year to year the channels change, some that were good becoming poor and vice versa. You'll need to retest a number of channels each year to find the best one that season.

Focus your attention on small pieces of the Yellowstone to discover what a truly fine trout stream really has to offer.

Fishing Waters in the Yellowstone Drainage

Armstrong Spring Creek: Armstrong is one of several spring creeks in the Paradise Valley south of Livingston on the west side of the Yellowstone River and east of U.S. 89. These spring creeks are considered to be some of the finest water of their kind, anywhere. (To fish these streams you pay a daily fee. From April into autumn, you'll have to make your reservations well in advance.) This means that there are fantastic numbers of trout living in an exceptionally fertile environment whose temperature and rate of flow remains virtually constant. Banks of these streams are lined with cottonwoods, with thick carpets of long grasses, and some bushes and brush. The creeks themselves are filled with thick beds of bright, emerald aquatic plants. There are smooth, silty stretches, slow slough-like (but cold and pure) runs, riffles running over broken rock, and gravel streambeds while peacocks and assorted other fowl cackle, squawk and, in general, proclaim to the world that they are indeed alive as they wander in nearby farm yard pens. Armstrong offers about two miles of challenging water.

In spring creeks, food is so abundant that several hatches are often taking place simultaneously. By the time you figure out what species is producing the most action and in what particular phase of its life, the trout have switched to another bug. And even if there is only one insect hatching, say for example the ubiquitous Blue-Winged Olive, the browns and rainbows and cutthroats are so selective that only a perfect presentation of something size 16 or less will cause the trout to take the imitation. Light tippets (7X is considered a bit heavy at times) make playing a three- or four- or five-pound fish in this water rather sticky. Most of the time when you catch a fish in one of these spring creeks you have earned it, though there are periods when even these finicky waters yield their trout with ease. Spring creek trout have their weaknesses and, at times, they are especially vulnerable to hoppers. At other times, Pheasant Tails drifted along the edges of current or worked slowly through slack water on the edges of the creeks will take the trout more or less consistently.

Compounding the difficulty of spring creeks is the fact that the trout see anglers covering the complete spectrum of skills nearly every day of the year. And the rainbows and browns have seen every pattern known to the western world many times over. Talk to those fishing the streams ahead of you—they may have some solid advice. And check the local fly shops—they are always in touch with the current hatching activity.

In addition to the Blue-Winged Olives, there are also Pale Morning Duns. The duns emerge around 10 a.m. Spinners fall in the morning and at dusk. Mid-July through early August, use PMD Thoraxes, Sparkle Duns, PT Emergers, and a PMD Spinner. When caddis are hatching, several patterns seem to have their moments, including the Z-Lon Caddis Emerger, Serendipity, PT Emerger, Emergent Sparkle Pupa, and the Electric Caddis (in the faster water).

Nymph fishing here can vary from easy to impossible. Ever fish a size-22 or smaller nymph? That's what the fish focus on at times in this water. At other times, they'll take a good scud imitation. In the spring, when the rainbows are spawning, a light-colored egg pattern is a winning fly. A little insect net, for seining the flow and sampling the bottom, can provide quick answers on all spring creeks.

Woolly Buggers in sizes 6 to 8 with olive bodies can also turn the fish. Cast the things bank-tight and strip like mad. If nothing takes by the third strip, pick up and cast again. Buggering the banks early in the morning or late in the afternoon can rev up your heart.

Big Bull Elk Creek: The word is that this is a good stream for browns and rainbows to a couple of pounds. It's on the Crow Reservation, however, which means only the daring among us would fish it, since it is off limits to non-tribal members. You can reach a small portion of the lower section by boat on Yellowtail Reservoir.

A typical Bighorn brown
Photo by Don Roberts

Bighorn River: One of the most fertile rivers in the West, the Big Horn is loaded with aquatic plant and animal life in cold, clear water. The Bighorn wanders through a gentle valley in the wide open high plains country way out west. A large mountain range that rolls away into Wyoming adds to the spectacle. There are good numbers of healthy trout here. Fish that willingly take a fly. Browns and rainbows weighing a few pounds or more are common. The river flows through a corridor surrounded by the

Crow Indian Reservation. While most other waters on the reservation are closed to non-tribal members, the U.S. Supreme Court opened the Big Horn to public access in 1981.

The Bighorn has received extensive coverage from the outdoor press and is very heavily fished from May through October. Literally hundreds of boats and rafts are launched on a typical summer day.

Ever since the water below the Yellowtail Dam was opened to fishing, angling writers have raved about the trophy browns and rainbows. When you have a river holding more than twice as many fish exceeding 12 inches in each mile than the Madison, the hype is not all that difficult to understand.

This publicity has translated into incredible fishing pressure on the first 13-mile stretch of water, known as the Upper 13. On a pleasant summer day you will encounter literally hundreds of anglers fishing from shore and a greater number working the river from drift boats and rafts. There are some things you can do to improve the odds for a pleasant and successful day adrift. For those who have little fly fishing experience or have never taken a good trout, the Bighorn is a good river to start out on—this doesn't mean that a beginner will catch a lot of fish, but he'll know that they're there, rising or visibly nymphing right under his nose, and he'll get a lot of chances at them. Many of the articles written in the past claim that fish are taken by the dozens and many of them are in the five-pound and up range. Tales of ninety-fish days with trout averaging three pounds or more abound. This can create some unrealistic expectations.

While the ninety-fish days occasionally occur, experience indicates something more modest for most fly fishers most of the time. But even these down-scaled expectations are optimistic. A person who fishes diligently will probably take a half dozen or more trout that should average around 16 inches in a day's fishing. Experienced anglers have a legitimate chance to catch a large trout. But don't expect five-pound fish on every cast.

In addition to the Upper 13, there are two other stretches of water of similar length—from Bighorn to Mallard, and from Mallard to Two-Leggins. These places are less crowded, but there are some trade-offs. These include low water and water quality problems from irrigation practices in the valley. This is often the case for the lower portion of these stretches from Rotten Grass on. Also, access is diffi-cult in spots and many of the outfitters prefer not to float this water. The lower two stretches have fewer fish, but they receive less angling pressure and the trout, on average, are larger.

If you wish to fish the Upper 13 from shore, from a rental boat, or with a guide, hit the water early. By 9 a.m. This will put you on the river before most other floaters. You'll be fishing over trout who have not been spooked by the casts of several anglers before you and you will have a much more peaceful experience floating a very pretty river in relatively serene surroundings. As summer gives way to fall the number of anglers declines slightly to more hard-core types whose main interest is in jumping large fish.

A 9-foot rod with a 6- or 7-weight line will handle all of the water. You want a rod that is light enough to make casting fun, but not so dainty that it lacks the backbone to deal with a stout breeze or to pressure a strong fish in the current. A longer rod will give you better line control.

There is a little bit of everything on the river: long, deep, glassy runs; deep holes; riffles; undercut banks; submerged logs; feeding lanes between clumps of aquatic plants; back-swirling eddies—all flowing down a relatively sedate gradient.

The Bighorn is pretty much an "all-season" river. Neil Selden, who lives close by in Billings, fishes it one day a year—the same day every year. "I used to fish the river seventy to eighty days a season, but the crowds are too much for me now. So I only go there on Super Bowl Sunday, and then, at least on that one day, I can move and fish anywhere that I want. I'll hunt 'noses,' looking for trout in the slower water rising to midges. A size-18 Olive Serendipity Emerger matches the insect that's on the river," says Selden.

The only time the Bighorn fishes poorly is in the late spring and early summer during years with high runoff. Normally the first thirteen miles of the river are fine even then (a tributary, Soap Creek, can mess up the clarity below that), but when Yellowtail Reservoir fills up and warm water spills over the top of the dam, coming off the top of the lake in the high sixty-degree range, it shocks the trout and stops almost all feeding activity.

Early spring, summer, and fall are consistently good fishing. The hatches are heavy and predictable and the trout seem to ignore the unending stream of boats going over their heads and rise for hours at a time. These fish don't mind someone casting to them, and even sloppy presentations won't put them down, but they won't take a fly that is dragging unnaturally. And they can get pretty critical about the imitation.

You can make pattern selection as complicated as you wish, but you should carry at least a basic selection of flies. The nice contradiction about most tailwaters (and spring creeks) is that the insect populations may be incredibly large but they aren't particularly diverse. It's a simple equation that means one thing—there may be only a handful of hatches but they will be really heavy. The hatches include: Blue-Winged Olives from April through May and from mid-September through mid-December; Pale Morning Duns from mid-July through late August; Yellow Sally stoneflies from mid-July through early September; summer Grannoms (also called the Black Caddis here) from mid-August through mid-October; Spotted Sedges from mid-August into early October; Tricos starting in mid-August and lasting into mid-October; Summer Flier Sedges in September; Tiny Blue-Winged Olives overwhelming other species during the evenings in September; and midges all winter.

"A lot of the insects on the Bighorn are a size smaller than they are on other rivers," advises John Gregg. "That's probably because of the colder, year-around water. For midges I like the Palomino series in various colors, but the Serendipity Emerger is popular, too. I'm convinced with the Blue-Winged Olive that a standard hackled fly, sitting perky on the surface, is better than a flush floating pattern, so for that hatch I'll carry standard, size-18 Blue-Winged Olive dries. But for the Pale Morning Duns I find that a No-Hackle PMD, size 16, works better than a Compara Dun or a standard, hackled fly. The Yellow Sally is matched perfectly by size-16 or -18 Little Yellow Stone. The Black Caddis, or Grannom, hops around on the surface to lay its eggs, and a size-14 Black Dancing Caddis is good for twitching and skating. For all the caddisflies, including the Spotted Sedge, a size 12 and 14 brown-winged and yellow-bodied insect, and the Summer Flier, a size 10, speckled cinnamon sedge that brings up big fish, an

Emergent Sparkle Pupa and a Henryville style dry fly always work for me. For the spinner fall of the Tricos I use a size-18 or -20 Black Poly-Wing Spinner. The Tiny Blue-Winged Olives, the *Pseudocloens*, are size 22 and 24, and a standard hackled fly seems to do the best for them, too. That list of imitations is personal with me, and I've tried just about everything old and everything new on the Bighorn hatches. Someone else might have an entirely different list of flies, and they'll be catching fish, too."

Nymphs are best during non-hatch periods. They may be the primary method—almost every drift boat that goes down the stream with a guide and clients has a couple of strike indicators bobbing on the surface. Popular patterns include Sow Bug and the Big Horn Shrimp. One fly that may be the best trout catcher in the bunch is also the most controversial. This is the infamous San Juan Worm, which imitates the red worms found in the river bottom detritus. All trout, especially the big ones, eat these worms. Many purists in fly fishing abhor the use of the San Juan Worm. The choice is yours. Many of these "purists" have no problem using leeches on Blackfeet Indian Reservation lakes or foam-rubber inch worms. There must be an ethical difference here somewhere.

Because of the relatively small size of most of these patterns, you will want to use at least 9-foot leaders (12 feet would be better) tapered down to 4X, 5X, and even 6X. Some other nymphs would include a Gold-Ribbed Hare's Ear size 12 to16, Pheasant Tail size 14 to 22, and Red Squirrel Tail size 14 to 18. These need to be fished right along the bottom and a twist-on or two of lead will sink these down where they can do their best work.

Streamer fishing demands heavier tippets, 1X or 2X. Woolly Buggers, Zonkers, Muddler Minnows, and Spruce Flies, all in the size 2 to 6 range, work well on the big trout, but a subtler, smaller Plain Jane, in sizes 10 and 12, cast tight to the overhanging grass banks, usually takes more fish.

Black Canyon Creek: This is another potentially good trout stream closed to non-tribal members on the Crow Reservation, but with some limited access from Yellowtail Reservoir. It holds decent browns and rainbows.

Boulder River: This is one of the prettiest trout streams in the state, offering excellent fishing for browns and rainbows to 24 inches in the lower reaches, and brook and rainbow trout in the upper, wilderness reaches. There is one problem, though. The best big-trout water flows almost entirely on heavily posted land owned by famous writers (nasty people as a whole), musicians, and film stars who believe it is their right to keep the rest of us poor mortals off of "their" water despite the state's stream access law. This lower river flows through ranch land and is characterized by undercut, brushy and grassy banks, good holes, silent runs, and enough riffle water to bring out the rainbows on a sunny summer day to pick off stonefly nymphs and caddisfly pupae. Excellent hatches of caddis take off beginning in midsummer, especially around evening, and hoppers are a superb play from July until the killing frosts of September, as are beetles and ants.

Boulder River south of McLeod
Photo by Stan Bradshaw

Streamers will take the hefty browns; these include Buggers, Matuka Sculpins, Spruce Flies, Hair Suckers, Marabou Muddlers, and the like. Use a 9-foot 5-weight with stout leaders for the streamer action.

The Boulder is followed by state and county roads into the Absaroka Range almost to the base of Mount Rae. From here you take a trail past a spectacular 70-foot falls that serves as a natural barrier to the downstream rainbows and browns. Above the falls, brookies and rainbows to 15 inches will come to Royal-anythings in the pocket water. Elk Hair Caddis also take in the pools and glides. Wet flies like Gold-Ribbed Hares Ears, Royal Coachmen, Black Gnats, and Henricksons, worked along the edges of current or swung through pools, will take some of the better fish in this wild stretch that heads in the heart of these mountains beneath 10,988-foot Monument Peak. Access on this part of the Boulder is good since the river runs through national forest 30 miles south of Big Timber. Runoff until July makes the river a bitch to wade, but after this the work is easy and enjoyable. As for the lower water, put Montana's stream access law to work and strike a blow for fly fishing's proletariat masses.

Bramble Creek Lakes: These four lakes are 3 miles up Bramble Creek from the Boulder River road below Fourmile Guard Station. Three of the lakes have fish. The best is #3, which is five acres at nearly 9,000 feet and planted every eight years with Yellowstone cutthroats that provide good fishing from the second year of the cycle through perhaps the fifth or sixth.

Camp Lake: At 9,000 feet, this one lies east of Contact Mountain and can be reached by trail roughly 4½ miles east from the Falls Creek campground on the Boulder River. It grows fair numbers of Yellowstone cutts running less than a foot. They take ant imitations from the surface with a satisfying rush and swirl. There's too much competition for food here for the fish to hesitate.

Cottonwood Creek: Cottonwood heads in the Crazies and flows for 17 miles to the Shields River with good fishing for brookies, browns (especially in the lower reaches), cutthroats, and rainbows. Parts of it are dewatered, and if you're not catching anything in one section, it might be smart to move to a new piece. It's followed by county and private roads and then Forest Service trail.

Cottonwood Lake: This is the origin of Cottonwood Creek (no kidding) in the Crazy Mountains at 8,550 feet. It's 9 acres, chilled by the melt of Grasshopper Glacier, and reached by a steep, 4-mile trail from the end of the Cottonwood Creek Road. All that huffing gets you decent fishing for cutthroats that average a foot or so but may go to two pounds.

DePuy's Spring Creek: DePuy's is another in the famed Paradise Valley spring creeks (see Armstrong discussion for fishing details). This was originally a trout hatchery and is now a well-managed stream with good populations of fat and picky rainbows and browns. Some whitefish, too. A fee fishery, it's 7 miles south of Livingston on U.S. 89.

If you come to the area to fish the Mother's Day caddis hatch, and the Yellowstone River is blown out with runoff, try to get a day on DePuy's (or Nelson's or Armstrong's). The spring creeks also have good hatches of the early Grannom and they fish well in May.

East Boulder River: This one's about 20 miles of 20-foot-wide water running out of the mountains and onto the sere foothills south of the Yellowstone River. There is fair fishing for some decent browns. There are also good populations of cutthroats, rainbows, and mountain whitefish that love nymphs, as is their destiny. You'll find access by road here and there.

East Fork Main Boulder River: This one is a little mountain stream with fair fishing in some pretty country several miles above the main river. There are brookies, cutthroats, and rainbows along with browns in the lower, meadow stretches. The meadow section is good hopper water, but the fish prefer smaller, size 8 to 14, flies.

Fairy Lake: In the Shields River drainage, it's 35 miles north of Bozeman. You get there on a poor road and you'll find good numbers of average-sized cutthroats. Fairy is 12 acres by 40 feet deep, but there are extensive shallows where the fish love to roam. The lake has a campground.

Fish Lake: This 18-acre lake is up the South Fork of Rainbow Creek, in the Boulder River drainage, in a beautiful setting with naturally reproducing cutthroats that grow to perhaps a foot. The odd thing is that these wilderness fish have a reputation for being tough to catch—they ignore big flies or fast-moving flies, but they'll suck in size 16 or 18 nymphs swimming *slowly* through the water.

Hidden Lake: Hidden lies in the Absaroka Primitive Area north of Yellowstone and offers typical (quite good) wilderness lake fishing for rainbows. You'll want to fish nymphs several feet beneath the surface with the slightest of twitches (this works on cutthroats, too, in these alpine waters). Hare's Ears and small Olive Woolly Worms are easy and obvious selections.

Lower Deer Creek: This one flows from the Boulder Plateau to Big Timber and the Yellowstone River. The upper reaches, mostly followed by trail, are fair for brookies, cutthroats, and some nice brown trout. The lower sections are hammered by irrigation, but can have a few browns in them during the fall.

Mill Creek: Mill Creek spills from the Absaroka Mountains west to the Yellowstone, the last stretch across a well-defined alluvial fan about 20 miles south of Livingston. The FWP has leased water rights on this stream to provide rearing habitat for cutthroat fry in midsummer.

The middle reaches with a nearby campground are popular for brookies, cutthroats, rainbows, and whitefish. The lower stretch is good for browns in the spring and again after the first rains of autumn.

Mission Creek: Mission flows into the Yellowstone 10 miles east of Livingston and it's followed upstream by road and trail to its origins below Elephanthead Mountain. The lower reaches are good for browns and some rainbows. As you move up the drainage, the browns drop in numbers and size and cutthroats take over. Whitefish are ever-present.

Mol Heron Creek: Mol Heron hits the Yellowstone not far from the Church Universal Triumphant (CUT) compound near Corwin Springs. Drive past the CUT whackos (being firm believers in the individual, they all dress in purple. One year they built bomb shelters for everyone because of imminent attack from the Soviet Union). The lower reaches have some spawning cutthroats early in the year and some browns in the fall. The upper sections are mainly pocket water action for small cutthroats.

Nelson Spring Creek: Yet another in the Paradise Valley hit parade of world-class spring creeks (see the discussion on Armstrong Spring Creek), this one is 4 miles south of Livingston and has a mile or so of fishing for lots of browns and rainbows. A few of these fish get very big. It's a fee fishery and during prime months reservations are locked up a year in advance.

One prominent feature of Nelson's is the pond on the lower end. The currents empty into this deep pool and curl devilishly around. It's almost impossible to get a fly to sit out there drag-free, but that's exactly what the trout demand. These fish, some of the biggest in the stream, cruise leisurely around this slow-water hold. The only way to get a decent presentation to them is to wade upstream to the dam, stand right there, and cast right on the current line.

Porcupine Creek: Porcupine flows to the Shields River north of Wilsall. It's hit by irrigation but there is plenty of brushy, bankside cover above as the creek meanders across an open valley. Brookies, browns, cutthroats (in the upper sections), and whitefish take streamers and nymphs and occasionally caddis near evening when the egg-layers drop out of the sky.

Rainbow Lakes: This group includes three main lakes and four smaller ones from 2 to 18 acres with rainbow-cutthroat hybrids, rainbows, and cutthroats growing to perhaps 15 inches. They are at

Rainbow Lakes country
Photo by Stan Bradshaw

the head of Rainbow Creek, in the Boulder River drainage, at over 9,000 feet in unspoiled mountain country with some pines here and there that provide wood for those few still willing to risk the wrath of the environmentally correct and have a small campfire. It's a 6-mile hike, but horsepacking is popular on this water.

Rock Creek: This particular Rock Creek flows out of the Crazies to the Shields River at Clyde Park. It's a little "tailwater" out of Rock Lake. While it doesn't get as much enrichment from it's high-mountain source as the big rivers do from their giant reservoirs, the fertility does jump up for a short ways below the dam. There are six miles of canyon water, followed by a good Forest Service trail, and by concentrating on the deeper holes you can catch some fat, wild brookies and cutthroats to 12 inches or so. There are 12 miles of lower gradient water below the canyon, but access is a problem on this section.

Shields River: The Shields has its headwaters in the Crazy Mountains, then flows west, then south for 60 miles to the Yellowstone River east of Livingston. The upper reaches of the river hold fair numbers of Yellowstone cutthroats. The rest of the river, flowing through open ranch and pasture land, is good water for some sizable brown trout, especially those migrating up the river from the Yellowstone in the fall. One consistent plan is to work the brushy, undercut banks or many logjams and brush piles with large streamers like Woolly Buggers, Muddlers, and Spuddlers. Access is from U.S. 89, county roads, and through private land where permission is definitely needed. There are some brook trout in the middle reaches and some good rainbows in the lower runs up from the Yellowstone. The river is often slightly discolored and dark streamers almost always work best, especially with some erratic pulsing action away from the banks and brush piles.

Silver Lake: It's a 7-mile hike up Fourmile Creek (a tributary of the Boulder) from the Fourmile Guard Station. For the serious high-country fly fisherman, that 6- to 8-mile distance is perfect. The lakes that can be reached by 2- to 4-mile hikes are day trips; only the dedicated backpacker, equipped for an overnight stay, is likely to walk 7 miles. As a result, Silver, being fairly fertile, doesn't get too much pressure and can grow some decent trout. It's planted by air on occasion with Lake DeSmet rainbows, and some of these fish grow to several pounds but average around a foot or so in this 10-acre lake at 9,046 feet.

Slough Creek: Slough Creek has its beginnings high in the Absaroka Range and flows for 15 miles south to Yellowstone National Park where it is one of the best big-trout waters in the park. You can reach the meadow section north of the park by a Forest Service trail. There is some good fishing for truly large cutthroats in the sapphire pools and beneath the undercut banks protected by thick mats of grass. Hoppers come into play about mid-July, as do ants. Look for caddis activity, especially towards evening.

Smeller Lake: This one's over 30 acres and 100 feet deep at 9,500 feet in the southern Crazy Mountains. It's a wicked 6-mile climb from the end of the Rock Creek road in the Shields River drainage. There are cutthroats that grow to several pounds here, but there are not a lot of the real big ones. For the big ones, put on your polaroids and wait for a large cruiser to pass along the shoreline. Cast precisely to that one fish with a good still-water pattern, such as a Timberline Emerger, Twist Nymph, or small Carey Special.

Smith Creek: Go to beautiful, downtown Wilsall on U.S. 89, turn up the Shields River Road, and drive 15 miles to Forest Service Road 991 to reach this nice, small-stream fishery. What makes it nice? The element of surprise. There are goodly numbers of trout up to 16 inches. Any fish over 10 inches in this brushy habitat, whether a brookie, cutthroat, or nice brown up from the Shields River, is a tough battle. There are some beaver ponds on the lower end and 5 miles of fine stream fishing.

Squeeze Lake: Squeeze is 7 acres, 45 feet deep at over 9,500 feet at the end of Hawley Creek in the Boulder River drainage. It's planted with Yellowstone cutts every eight years that do well for a few seasons, then fade away until the next air lift.

Sunlight Lakes: These two lakes are 5½ miles of trail above the end of the Sweet Grass Creek Road (take U.S. 91 north out of Big Timber and go left on Road 26). Both lakes are planted with Yellowstone cutthroats that do very well here (some trophy specimens in the upper pond). Neither lake tops 3 acres and they are both shallow. The fish can't hide, but they are well fed in these fertile waters. These are places that still-water specialists love to figure out—one of the answers here is a bottom cluttered with large cased-caddis larvae. A matching fly, crawled slowly over the debris, catches some of the nicest fish.

Swamp Lake: Swamp is in the Crazy Mountains. Access is difficult due to private land guarding the way. The creek it dumps into may be swampy, but the lake itself isn't the least marshy. It is above timberline, 15 acres, and deep. It used to have huge brookies, but it's now managed for Yellowstone cutthroats. Go north of Big Timber on U.S. 91 and take Road 23 to upper Swamp Creek. It's a 3-mile hike into the lake. Better visit this country soon. The state's wilderness bill failed to protect this fantastic country and the loggers can't wait to scalp what's left of the timber up here. The Crazies and Swamp Lake (too high) will survive, but will we?

Sweet Grass Creek: Sweet Grass heads in the Crazies and is followed by trail, private road, and county road for 50 miles to the Yellowstone east of Big Timber. The upper reaches are good for small brookies and some rainbows. The lower reaches get hurt by irrigation, but can be good for nice browns later in the fall after the rains return. Whitefish swim here, too.

Tongue River: The headwaters lie in Wyoming, then it flows through the Tongue Reservoir in Montana just north of Sheridan, Wyoming, and on to the Yellowstone near Miles City. This is coulee and bluff country with quicksand, rattlers, few people, some crazed Merriam's turkeys, and even crazier hunters. Great country if you like to stay lost and alone. Some large browns and rainbows are taken with heavy streamers down deep in the first 9 miles below the dam. After this, some nice smallmouth are found in the river (and they love Clouser Minnows) before catfish, sauger, bullheads, walleyes, and other warm water species take complete control.

Tongue River
Photo by Stan Bradshaw

West Boulder River: Formed by the junction of the East and West Forks above Beaver Meadows, it flows 25 miles to the Boulder River in the north. The stream is followed by state and county roads and then trail. There are browns and rainbows in the lower reaches but there's only limited access. There are cutthroats up above in the pocket water. It's a good stream to hit early in the season. Usually it is fishable when the main river is blown out with runoff.

Willow Creek Reservoir (Lodge Grass Reservoir): West of Lodge Grass, this one has some big trout but is on the Crow Indian Reservation, and they do not let non-tribal members fish the water. There is some deeded land on the Reservation that you can hunt (for staggering numbers of sharptails) and you can fish in some of the creeks for huge browns if you are lucky enough to know some of the ranchers.

Yellowtail (Bighorn) Reservoir: This reservoir lies within the Bighorn Canyon National Recreation Area in both Wyoming and Montana about an hour and a half south of Billings. This is mostly managed for rugged walleyes that fight like rising bread dough, but there are some big browns and rainbows.

There is a "big lips" fly fishing tournament held here every year for carp—some nice specimens over five pounds are caught and these fish fight plenty strong. And, believe it or not, they'll come to hoppers. Those that have tried this say these fish fight like Hell, and, on occasion, will take you into your backing.

There are also lesser numbers of lake trout, crappie, perch, ling, sauger, and channel catfish. There's very pretty canyon country, almost 200 miles of it surrounding the lake, and it is worth seeing and camping in via boat.

OTHER WATERS

Aldridge Lake: Cutthroats and rainbows.

Alpine Lake: Cutthroats.

Anderson Creek: Too small.

Bangtail Creek: Too small.

Basin Creek: Brookies, browns, and rainbows.

Bear Creek: Browns, cutthroats, rainbows, and whitefish.

Bennett Creek: Too small.

Big Creek: Cutthroats and rainbows.

Big Drop Reservoir: Rainbows.

Big Timber Creek: Brookies, browns, and rainbows.

Big Timber Trout Ponds: Rainbows.

Billman Creek: Brookies, browns, cutthroats, and rainbows.

Blacktail Lake: Cutthroats.

Blue Lake (Boulder): Cutthroats.

Blue Lake (Yellowstone): Cutthroats.

Brackett Creek: Permission required. Brookies, browns, and cutthroats.

Bray's Pond (Trout Lake): Cutthroats and rainbows.

Bridger Creek: Brookies and browns.

Bridge Lake (Boulder): Cutthroats.

Bridge Lake (Yellowstone): Cutthroats.

Buck Creek: Cutthroats.

Buffalo Fork Creek: Cutthroats and rainbows.

Burnt Gulch Lake: Barren.

Cache Creek: Cutthroats.

Camp Reservoir: Rainbows.

Campfire (Hindu) Lake: Cutthroats.

Canyon Creek: Browns and cutthroats.

Carpenter Lake: Cutthroats.

Castle Rock Lake (Colstrip Surge Pond): No trout, but some nice, hand-sized bluegills. During the summer months the bass, pike, and walleye fade, but the hotter it is the better the bluegill hit. Fish around the weed beds.

Cave Lake: Cutthroats.

Cayuse Creek: Browns and rainbows.

Charlie White Lake: Cutthroats.

Chico Lake: Private.

Chrome Lake: Grayling.

Cinnabar Creek: Rainbows.

Clark's Reservoir: Rainbows and green sunfish.

Clear (Alkali) Creek: Brookies, browns, and rainbows.

Cokedale (Miner) Creek: Brookies and cutthroats.

Cottonwood Reservoir: Private.

Cow Creek Pond: Rainbows.

Crandall Creek: Rainbows.

Crazy Lake: Cutthroats.

Crisafulli Reservoir: No trout.

Crooked Creek: Brookies and rainbows.

Crystal Lake: Cutthroats.

Cutler Lake: Rainbows.

Daily Lake: Rainbows.

Davis Creek: Cutthroats and rainbows.

Davis Lake: Cutthroats.

Deep Creek: Cutthroats.

Deer Creek: Brookies and cutthroats.

Dredge Hole: Brookies.

Druckenmiller Lake: Barren.

Dry Head Creek: Crow Reservation. Closed.

Duck Creek: Browns.

Dugout Creek: Too small.

East Bridger Creek: Too small.

East Fork Mill Creek: Brookies, cutthroats, and rainbows.

East Fork Sweet Grass Creek: Too small.

Eight Mile Creek: Brookies, cutthroats, and rainbows.

Elbow Creek: Cutthroats.

Elk Creek (Boulder): Browns, cutthroats, and rainbows.

Elk Creek (Shields): Brookies, browns, cutthroats, and rainbows.

Elk Creek (Yellowstone): Cutthroats.

Elk Lake: Cutthroats.

Erickson Pond: Private.

Fairy Lake Creek: Cutthroats.

Falls Creek (Boulder): Brookies and rainbows.

Falls Creek (Shields): Too small.

Falls Creek (Kaufman) Lake: Cutthroats.

Fish Lake (Boulder): Cutthroats.

Fish Lake (Yellowstone): Cutthroats.

Five (North Bear Creek) Lakes: Cutthroats.

Flathead Creek: Brookies, browns, cutthroats, and whitefish.

Fleshman Creek: Brookies, browns, and cutthroats.

Fourmile Creek: Cutthroats and rainbows.

Friedley Creek: Brookies, cutthroats, and rainbows.

Gardner Reservoir #2: Walleyes and crappies.

Gartside Reservoir: Smallmouth and largemouth bass, yellow perch, walleye, pike, and crappies.

Glass Lindsey Lakes: No access.

Graham Creek: Cutthroats.

Granite Lake: Cutthroats.

Grosfield (Louis) Reservoir: Private.

Haughian Trout Pond: Private.

Helicopter Lake: Cutthroats.

Hellroaring Creek: Cutthroats.

Hollecker Pond: Rainbows.

Homestad Reservoir: Largemouth and smallmouth bass.

Horse Creek (Shields): Too small.

Horse Creek (Yellowstone): Cutthroats.

Horseshoe Lake: Cutthroats.

Intake Dam: No trout. Caught a few sauger here once on a small, white marabou streamer. It's an irrigation dam on the Yellowstone near Glendive.

Johnson's Dam: No trout.

Killen (Needlebutte) Reservoir: Rainbows.

Knox (Castle) Lake: Brookies.

Labree Reservoir: No trout.

Lake Abundance: Cutthroats.

Lake Abundance Creek: Cutthroats.

Lake Kathleen: Barren.

Lake Raymond: Barren.

Lake of the Woods: Cutthroats.

Landers Reservoir: Private.

Lindsay Dam: No trout.

Lisk Creek Reservoir: Rainbows.

Little Bighorn River: Crow Reservation. Closed.

Little Cottonwood Creek: Too small.

Little Mission Creek: Browns and cutthroats.

Little Timber Creek: Browns and cutthroats.

Lonesome Pond: Cutthroats.

McNight Lake: Goldens.

Meatrack Creek: BBQ Ribs and cutthroats.

Merrell Lake: Private.

Middle Fork Flathead Creek: Too small.

Middle Fork Hellroaring Creek: Cutthroats.

Middle Fork of Sweetgrass Creek: Cutthroats.

Mill Creek: Poor access.

Moose Lake: Rainbows.

Muddy Creek: Cutthroats and rainbows.

Mud Turtle Reservoir: Planted with rainbows in 1995. Also a few largemouth bass.

North Amelong Creek: Too small.

North Fork Bear Creek: Cutthroats.

North Fork Brackett Creek: Brookies, browns, and cutthroats.

North Fork Deep Creek: Cutthroats.

North Fork Elk Creek: Too small.

North Fork Flathead Creek: Brookies, browns, and cutthroats.

North Fork Six Mile Creek: Cutthroats.

North Fork Sweetgrass Creek: Cutthroats.

North Fork Willow Creek: Poor access.

O'Fallon Creek: No trout.

Otter Creek (Crazies): Brookies.

Otter Creek (Tongue): Catfish.

Passage Creek: Cutthroats.

Pear Lake: Rainbows.

Pine Creek Lake: Cutthroats.

Powder River: Browns, catfish, rainbows, sauger, and sturgeon.

Ringstveidt (Pete) Dam: Rainbows.

Rock Creek: Brookies and cutthroats.

Rock Lake: Cutthroats.

Rodgers Reservoir: Rainbows.

Rush Hall Dam: Rainbows.

Sacajawea Park Lagoon: Rainbows.

Sage Creek: Brookies, cutthroats, and rainbows.

Schaak (Adolph) Pond: Private.

Shooting Star Lake: Cutthroats.

Silvertip Reservoir: Largemouth and smallmouth bass.

Six Mile Creek: Cutthroats.

Skunk Creek: Browns and cutthroats.

Soda Butte Creek: Cutthroats.

South Fork Elk Creek: Brookies.

South Fork Shields River: Brookies, browns, and cutthroats.

South Fork Willow Creek: Too small.

South Sandstone Reservoir: Large walleyes, pike, small perch, and some bass and crappie.

Speculator Creek: Too small.

Sunlight Creek: Too small.

Swamp Creek: Brookies.

Tauck Reservoir: Private.

Ten Mile Creek: Brookies.

Thompson Lake: Cutthroats.

Thunder Lake: Rainbows.

Tom Miner Creek: Poor access.

Tongue River Reservoir: Northern pike, Koi, walleye, sauger, crappie, smallmouth bass, Great Whites. The peak for crappie (great eating) is in late May and early June during the spawn, and they love the jigging action of a Clouser Minnow on a slow retrieve. The best smallmouth action is in late June and early July along the shoreline in the brush.

Trail Creek: Browns, cutthroats, and rainbows.

Trespass Creek: Too small.

Tronrud (Adolph) Ponds: Private.

Twin Lakes: Cutthroats.

Upside-down Creek: Barren.

West Boulder Lake: Cutthroats.

West Bridger Creek: Brookies.

West Fork Duck Creek: Brookies, browns, and cutthroats.

West Fork Little Timber Creek: Brookies.

West Fork Mill Creek: Cutthroats.

Westrope Dam: Private.

Wibaux Fish Pond: Bullheads, green sunfish, and pike.

Willow Creek: Browns and cutthroats.

Wounded Man Creek: Cutthroats.

■ *Special thanks to John Gregg, Shelly Linden, Bill Linden, Geoff Nelson, Neil Selden, and V. E. Smith for their help on the Yellowstone drainage.*

Treat them gently when you show them off.
Photo by Don Roberts

Negotiating your way around Montana is easy. Routes from interstate high-ways all the way down to some gravel roads are marked on the state road map. Adequate signs make navigation a straightforward proposition.

Gravel roads are accorded the status of main thoroughfares in much of the state, but once you leave the unmarked systems you enter the exciting world of "Where in the hell are we?" Topographic maps help and so does asking directions. Montanans, for the most part, are friendly and helpful. They are used to misguided souls, so they know how to give good directions. You just have to know how to listen. If you run out of gas, they will normally offer you a gallon or two and frequently seem offended at the concept of payment. This is still honest country. May it always be so.

For those new to the state, a little pretravel preparation will make the adventure run quite smoothly.

First, contact Travel Montana at 800-541-1447 (or write to them at Capitol Station, Helena, MT 59620) and ask for a travel package that will include the current Travel Planner, Vacation Guide (full of stuff that is not very exciting for anglers but may amuse others), and a state highway map.

The Travel Planner has comprehensive listings of motels and hotels, bed and breakfast inns, ranches, resorts, hostels and hot springs, licensed outfit-ters, and private and public campgrounds. Further information includes local chamber of commerce contacts. If you know what area of Montana you will be visiting, contacting the appropriate chamber(s) will result in even more detailed information.

Next, call the Montana Department of Fish, Wildlife, and Parks (FWP) at 406-444-2535 (or write to them at Capitol Station, Helena, MT 59620) and request their fishing guide, state parks guide, and fishing regulations. They will give you a sampling of places to go, campgrounds, fishing access sites.

The Travel Planner, highway map, FWP materials, and this fishing guide offer a lot of information—more that enough to plan an extensive fishing vacation. The only way to fine-tune your trip, would be to hire a guide.

When you purchase your fishing license (for out-of-staters around $50) be sure and pick up a copy of the current fishing regulations (or get it in advance from FWP).

As for driving, the powers that be did repeal the federally mandated 55 mile-per-hour speed limit late in 1995. But don't interpret that as "the sky's the limit" (not even in Big Sky Country). "Reasonable and prudent" rules daytime speeds and nighttime limits are 65 on interstates and 55 on two-lane highways. Be especially careful when sailing around that Winnebago on the two-lane—vehicles coming the other way may be traveling as fast as you are.

During spring and fall, all-weather tires or four-wheel-drive are good ideas for the mountain passes. And when the highway department states that a certain pass is closed due to rough weather, believe it. You will be risking your life on a grand scale if you ignore the warnings. And keeping your gas tank topped up is prudent. Off the main roads stations often close early or do not open some days. The boys at the local Cenex like to go fishing, too.

ADDITIONAL INDIAN RESERVATIONS

There are five other reservations in Montana east of the Continental Divide in addition to Blackfeet—Rocky Boys (south of Havre), Fort Belknap (west of Malta), Fort Peck (northeastern corner), Crow (south of Billings), and Northern Cheyenne (east of Crow).

The first three are located along the Hi-Line near the Canadian border and offer limited angling potential and serious access problems because of tribal regulations and restrictions. The only fishing of note is provided by ranch ponds and these are private, for the most part, and off limits. There are some on the Fort Peck Reservation that are managed by the Montana Department of Fish, Wildlife, and Parks and they are open to fishing and will be discussed in the appropriate river sections, as well as any streams and creeks holding catchable populations of trout. There is so much other prime water in Montana that to risk a hassle or ticket to catch a ling or sauger or catfish approaches folly or worse.

The Northern Cheyenne Reservation has similar access limitations, but access to the Tongue River can be gained along the river's eastern shore, which is off the reservation.

As for the Crow Reservation, there are reports of ponds, reservoirs, and lakes with tremendous trout in them, but they are closed to all but tribal members for the moment, unfortunately. The only waters available to non-tribal members are Bighorn Lake and the Bighorn River in the Bighorn Canyon National Recreation Area. Everything else is out-of-bounds. Perhaps someday the tribe will recognize the potential of this resource in terms of their own financial welfare. But when we feel excluded, we must remember that we have not exactly done these people (or the other tribes) any favors in the past.

The bottom line is that there is some wonderful fishing for trophy trout that is available to only a lucky few on these eastern reservations.

REAL AND PERCEIVED DANGERS

Marauding, red-eyed bears lusting for a taste of human flesh and eighteen-foot-long rattlesnakes as thick as your hip with six-inch fangs dripping milky venom are the deluded creations of Hollywood and not the stuff of everyday Montana reality.

Yes, bears do attack us and snakes do bite us, but these rare encounters are even more rarely fatal. Far more dangerous are threats from lightning, wind, and cold.

Lightning kills more people each year than rap concerts, and a fly fisher waving a graphite rod is a superb conductor of this static electricity. When heavy electrical weather looks imminent, get off the water, look for low ground, discard your rod, and wait for the storm to pass. Undercut banks, caves, and isolated trees are not safe locations. Nor are overturned aluminum boats. When lightning shows up, always think invisible. Try and become the lowest-profile object in the immediate area.

The combination of cold, wind, and moisture can quickly lead to a deadly condition known as hypothermia, a condition in which the body's core temperature drops low enough to cause blood to rush from the extremities to the vital organs. Numbness in the toes and fingers progressing into the arms and legs is an obvious symptom as are shaky fingers. Shivering is another early warning sign. The real danger is the loss of reasoning (in many of us this may be extremely difficult to detect) and the ability to make rational decisions. Paddling around in an ice-cold lake in a float tube is an easy way to become hypothermic, and if early warnings are not heeded, an angler could just stop moving and die. If you start to get cold, get to shelter —tent, car, cabin, etc.— and get warm and dry. Don't try to tough it out. Pay attention to your fishing partners. If they show any signs of hypothermia, get them off the water, to shelter, and warm them up.

Insects are another problem. Mosquitoes, black flies, and deer flies can make life hell. Repellent works well against the first two and a .28-gauge handles the third. Taking B-complex vitamins each day for a couple of weeks also works. Afterwards the body secretes a compound that insects find offensive. Ticks are another matter and Lyme disease and Rocky Mountain spotted fever can cause acute illness or death. Tick patrol at the end of each day during tick season is mandatory. Be sure and remove the head. This may require tweezers.

Most spider bites are locally painful but not life threatening. Treat with cold compresses and perhaps aspirin. If the victim exhibits nausea, vomiting, or diarrhea followed by weakness and disorientation, a systemic reaction is underway and you need to get immediate treatment by a doctor unless you are capable of injecting a syringe of epinephrine (synthetic version of adrenaline). An antihistamine such as Benadryl can help prevent further reaction to histamine and rebound effect.

Rattlesnakes really do try to stay out of our way. The most common places to encounter these gentle reptiles is in rock piles, cliffs and walls, and the dry grasses of eastern Montana. The sound of a rattle will turn even the most graceful among us into a world-class spastic whirling from toe to toe in a desperate attempt to reverse direction.

If bitten, one or two puncture marks will be visible. If venom has been injected swelling and pain will be immediate. Transport the victim as quickly as possible for antivenin treatment. Pain may be severe, but the victim can usually walk to transportation. Splint the affected part if possible. Remove any constricting items such as rings and clothing from the bitten extremity before swelling makes it difficult. The sooner a person reaches medical help the better. Bites are rarely fatal in healthy adults, but the symptoms can be awful.

Most medical experts agree that traditional field treatments, such as tourniquets, pressure dressings, ice packs, and "cut and suck" snakebite kits, are ineffective and often dangerous. Treatment in the field is a waste of time.

The almighty Montana sun can cook your brains and fry your hide in a hurry. Wear a hat, sunglasses, and plenty of sunscreen. Drink cool liquids constantly. A gallon of water per person is the minimum and a cooler full of ice and preferred beverages is a godsend. If dizziness, weakness, or a rapid pulse occur, seek shelter. If you stop sweating and get flushed, cool down fast. You may have heat stroke.

Another problem, especially in the back country, is avalanches. Even in July tons and tons of snow and ice remain on steep rock walls and packed into bowls. Avoid crossing these areas of exposure. A peaceful looking snow bowl with well-defined cornices is an invitation to disaster. If you absolutely must cross such an area, do it one at a time. If caught in an avalanche try and swim with the flow and, as the avalanche starts to slow and the snow starts to pile up, ball up and get one hand in front of your face to create an air pocket and thrust the other hand as high as possible (if it ends up above the snow you'll be easier to find).

Wading swift rivers can also be deadly. Losing your footing can mean being swept under a logjam or into midstream boulders. On slippery, freestone streams, wear stream cleats and even carry a wading staff. Always look ahead and choose footing carefully. Caution is definitely the better part of valor here.

As for bears and other wild animals (read the first part of the section on Glacier National Park in Volume I), make noise to alert animals of your presence. Keep your eyes open and always leave an area immediately whenever a bear or bison or moose is spotted. Yelling, eye contact, and bluffing often provoke attacks and are last resort (like when a charging grizzly is ten feet away) measures. Most big game animals avoid humans like the plague. Attacks are almost always a result of moving into an animal's territory unannounced or threatening its food supply, such as a buried carcass.

The number of anglers injured or killed by these real and perceived dangers is insignificant compared to those that suffer at the hands of car crashes and heart attacks. So do not fear the natural world, just give it a good deal of respect.

SUGGESTED GEAR

Successfully fishing in Montana does not require truck loads of equipment, although most fly fishers are collectors, hoarders, and gadget freaks, often foregoing the monthly house payment in favor of purchasing a new rod. Most experienced anglers have their own preferences, but for those who have never fished Montana or are new to the pursuit, the following, while subjective, is representative of tackle and related gear needed to enjoy fishing in the state.

Rods: If you bring just one pick a five- or six-weight. These have enough strength to handle some wind and big water and still fish smaller streams halfway decently. If you bring two, an ideal combination would be a 9-foot, seven-weight and an 8-foot, four-weight. The seven-weight will fight the wind that blows crazily along the Rocky Mountain Front and out onto the plains and also will work well nymphing and fishing heavy streamers. The four-weight will fish smaller rivers and streams along with quiet ponds quite nicely. Others might include a two-weight for spring creeks, a five-weight for medium rivers, and an eight-weight for the hurricane conditions often found around places like the Blackfeet Indian Reservation.

Reels: While the current cliché is that reels are now much more than a con-trivance for holding line, the need for disk drag is almost nonexistent. So if you cannot afford one, do not despair. The chances that a trout will smoke your reel are unlikely. On the other hand, purchase the best equipment you can afford. It can't hurt.

Lines: Use either double-taper or weight-forward lines and match them to your rods or go maybe one step up in weight (say a seven-weight line for a six-weight rod) to cheat the wind a bit. Definitely bring at least a 6-foot sink-tip for nymphing, streamers, and lake action. A 10-foot sink-tip is nice, too. Stick with floaters for two-weights and three-weights. A little weight above the fly works fine. Optional lines would include intermediate and fast-sinking lines for working deep in lakes. Shooting heads are nice and will give you a few more feet, but this is trout, not tarpon, fishing we're talking about. Backing of twelve pounds is adequate.

Patterns and Leaders: A few suggestions are: Blue-Winged Olives, Tricos, Pale Morning Duns in emergers, duns, and spinners; Stonefly Nymph, Pheasant Tail Nymph, Hare's Ear Nymph, Zug Bug, Sheep Creek, Scud, Kaufmann's Damsel Nymph, LaFontaine Antron, Prince Nymph, Partridge & Peacock; Muddler Minnow, Woolly Bugger, Zonker, Spruce Fly, Marabou Leech, Elk Hair Caddis, Royal Wulff, Adams, Humpy, Goddard Caddis, Royal Trude, Hopper, Sofa Pillow, Girdle Bug, and Bitch Creek. A fair investment to be sure, but also a pretty good all-around selection for the rest of the country.

Whatever you have, bring, but be sure and stop at the nearest fly shop or sporting goods store to stock up on a few recommended patterns. The days of proprietors selling you everything in the store are pretty much over. You can buy with confidence in Montana.

Nine-foot leaders tapering to 3x or 4x are basic tools. You can add tippet material for finer work or cut the leaders back for heavy-water nymphing. Or, best of all, you can tie your own.

Clothing: Even in summer bring clothes for cold weather. Snow and sleet, especially in the high country, is a twelve-month-a-year situation. Rain gear is a must as is a hat to protect you from the sun. Boots are helpful. For fall, winter, and spring fishing be prepared for anything weather-wise. This can be very cold country.

Miscellaneous accouterments: Obviously bring your vest. Hip and chest waders will give you added versatility and comfort. If bringing only one pair, bring chest waders. Stream cleats are great for freestone streams. You need sunglasses and sunscreen as well as insect repellent. A small camera for trophy photographs is handy. If you have room bring a landing net, float tube and fins, and a fly tying kit.

STREAM ETIQUETTE

Catching the largest or the most fish should be far down the list of fly fishing priorities. Certainly, it is more fun catching fish than not catching them, and most of the time taking big fish is more exciting than hooking little ones. Unfortunately the drive to take the most or largest has led directly to some boorish if not downright obnoxious behavior on Montana's rivers, streams, and lakes.

It has become all too common to have some inconsiderate jerk walk right in next to someone who has been carefully working a pool, and begin casting to the same pod of fish. Others throw rocks into pools to drive away anglers from "chosen" spots. Still others float over and in front of wading anglers. Obscene language, gestures, and even fist fights seem to be on the rise. The growing lack of consideration is ruining fly fishing for many of us on a number of rivers. The observation of a few basic rules would go a long way toward eliminating some contentious scenes.

Perhaps most importantly, respect another angler's desire for space and privacy. Don't plunge right into water another person is working and crowd the poor soul. If this is your idea of pleasure, take up tournament bass fishing. Enter the water as far below and behind as possible—out of sight is best—of an angler working upstream. Do the opposite (above and behind) for an angler working downstream. Just don't step into the stream ahead of someone else. Avoid crowding those in canoes or float tubes on lakes and keep your voice down. Sound travels quite well over water.

On busy waters, wait until an angler finishes a stretch of water before entering. On opening day in some parts of Montana the crowding may be excessive on popular waters, but, like New Year's Eve, this date is reserved for amateurs. While you wait, observing another's technique can have its own pleasures, but many of us are uncomfortable with being watched. Try to play the invisible man while waiting—out of sight, out of mind.

All good guides, when floating a river, will steer well clear of other boats on the water. They will also pull far away from wading anglers, leaving them the water they are fishing. This sometimes means that the clients in the boat have to stop casting for a minute or so, but the floaters have the whole river and can afford to pass up a short stretch. A nod, a friendly word, or even an exchange of information on the day's fishing is the norm between floaters and waders on Montana's rivers when both parties respect each other's rights.

In some parts of the country in the past few years the concept of fellowship among anglers has taken an awful beating. Just saying "Hello" and receiving a friendly response is now an occasion worthy of log-book notation.

One of the true virtues and assets of fly fishing is (or was) the friendliness and willingness of anglers to share information and a little small talk. Who cares if another manages to connect with a trout you were unable to fool? Competition in fly fishing is an obscenity.

If you're crossing private land, treat it with respect. Close any gates you open; don't harass the livestock; and if you take your dog, keep it under control. If you can't control it, leave it home.

In Montana the penalty for littering can be a good thumping if the wrong person catches you in the act (and few juries, in spite of all the DNA evidence, are going to convict the attacker). But with the growing number of slobs in our midst, it's no longer enough to simply not litter. If you find other people's leavings in the form of cans and candy wrappers, pick them up and stow them in your vest. This concept of littering also applies to throwing "trash" fish up on the bank to die—Don't. Most of those "trash" fish are natives to our rivers, and don't deserve that kind of treatment.

Finally, catch-and-release has done more for preserving and improving trout fishing in Montana than anything else. It may be more important in Montana than anywhere else because of our state's reliance on wild fish populations in our streams and rivers. Catch-and-release is the ultimate form of etiquette—preserving the resource for others to enjoy. It's not the end-all and be-all for every water (in many lonely places it doesn't hurt to keep a few), but on our best known and hardest hit fisheries it is the last hope for quality angling. For this concept to be successful trout must be played fairly but quickly. Work a fish too long and lactic acid builds up in its muscle tissues. Even an apparently successful release will eventually result in death. Releasing that first 20-inch trout is tough, but after a season or two, watching them swim off to cover is reward enough.

All stream etiquette amounts to is the Golden Rule—Do unto others as you would have them do unto you. (As Jimmy Buffett once said regarding another matter, "The concept was so simple, it plum evaded me.")

WHIRLING DISEASE IN MONTANA
With special thanks to Paul Sihler

A little-known parasite that infects members of the salmonid family may have a devastating impact on Montana's rainbow trout fishery, and apparently there is no cure in sight.

Myxobolus cerebralis, the parasite that causes whirling disease, was first discovered in 1994 in the fifty-mile stretch of the Madison River above Ennis Lake, and the first reports are frightening. The rainbow population in this world-famous stretch of water has declined by more than 90 percent since 1991, from approximately 3,400 fish per mile to less than 300, according to Montana Department of Fish, Wildlife, and Parks (FWP). Since then, it has been found in twenty-two other locations within the Clark Fork, Jefferson, Madison, Beaverhead, and Swan river drainages. State officials predict that eventually it will spread into every major watershed in the state where both salmonids and the parasite's alternative host, tubificid worms, are found. Nonetheless, the potential effects of the disease in watersheds other than the Madison remain uncertain.

According to Marshall Bloom of Montana Trout Unlimited, whirling disease endangers Montana's wild trout populations. "Montana is the only state in the lower forty-eight that relies nearly exclusively on natural reproduction rather than hatcheries to populate its rivers and streams with catchable trout." While hatcheries are able to grow fish through the disease—food is provided and there are no predators in hatcheries—some wild trout populations have been decimated.

The threat is especially great to Montana's native trout species such as red band rainbows, Westslope cutthroats, Arctic grayling, and bull trout. Populations of these species are greatly diminished from habitat loss and hybridization. While the effects of whirling disease on native trout species is still unknown, 90 percent population declines such as happened on the Madison could drive these species to extinction.

Myxobolus cerebralis has a complex life history. Trout are infected by the parasite when the *triactinomyon* (TAMS) form of the parasite is released into the water column by tubificid worms. In the few days of their life, TAMS can attach to a trout's mucus cells or on its skin. Once attached, they can inject a pre-spore material which migrates to the trout's cartilage. Once in the cartilage, spores which consume cartilage develop. In Colorado, researchers have found some heavily infected fish with as many as 500,000 spores.

The most common signs of infection are cranial deformities, black tails in young fish, "bug-eyes", and spinal deformities. Only occasionally is the tail-chasing swimming motion that gives the disease its name ever witnessed in wild trout. These symptoms are caused by the destruction of cartilaginous tissues and subsequent deformities of the skeleton. The black tail results from inflammatory pressure on the nerves controlling the pigment cells. In the wild, these stresses may cause direct mortality and most certainly cause secondary mortality by increasing the trout's susceptibility to predation and by inhibiting its ability to feed.

The spores remain in the fish until it either dies or is consumed by a predator. When the fish dies, more spores are released into the environment. The spores are especially hearty. They can survive in frozen fish at -20 degrees Fahrenheit, and for up to twenty years in dried mud. Once released into the water, the spore is consumed by tubificid worms. The spore then attaches to the worm's gut where it metamorphoses into a TAM and the life cycle begins again.

Nobody knows how whirling disease spread to Montana. The primary cause of its spread across the nation has been through the transportation and stocking of live infected fish—often by state fish and wildlife agencies. In 1995, however, all federal, state, and private fish hatcheries in Montana tested negative for whirling disease. Other possible vectors for its spread include escaped fish from private fish ponds, illegal stocking by "bucket biologists", the disposal of whirling disease–contaminated fish in a kitchen disposal (conventional sewage treatment will not kill whirling disease). "Once it's there, it's there," said state fisheries biologist Mark Lere. Biologists first noticed a decline in rainbow-trout numbers in the Madison near the West Fork in 1991. By 1993 the reduction in rainbows had reached Varney Bridge.

Brown trout are not as severely affected by whirling disease, perhaps because North America's original brown trout stocks came from Europe, where the disease originated. It was first reported in central Europe in 1903, but the complete life cycle was not described until the early 1980s. Whirling disease now occurs across Europe and was accidentally introduced into the United States around 1955, when its presence was found in Pennsylvania and Nevada. To date it has been detected in seventeen additional states, including Alabama, Colorado, California, Connecticut, Idaho, Massachusetts, Michigan, Montana, New Hampshire, New Jersey, New York, Ohio, Oregon, Virginia, Washington, West Virginia, and Wyoming.

The Madison River is one of the world's best wild trout fisheries, with a significant rainbow population, particularly in its upper reaches from the West Fork upstream to Quake Lake. Once the elimination of stocking took place (in 1973), the number and size of wild trout rose dramatically on the Madison, to the point where the river could provide a sustained quality fishery despite experiencing 140,000 angler fishing days per year, with summer catch rates on rainbows on some upper Madison stretches running as high as four fish per hour.

Rainbows used to make up 80 percent of the Madison below Quake Lake. Browns were the next largest population. Should the rainbows be wiped out in this section of the river, biologists do not look for a dramatic rise in the number of brown trout.

I'm an alarmist by nature. I asked several biologists and guides what they thought were the chances for a worst-case scenario. None wanted to be quoted by name, but all but one felt the chances for such a disaster were greater than fifty-fifty. One guide said the outbreak could seriously harm his business.

Despite the bleak outlook, Montana officials say all is not lost and there are several signs of hope. First, brown trout populations on the Madison have not been affected, and the Madison still offers world-class fishing for brown trout. This may hold true for other rivers as well.

Second, FWP biologists are not certain that trout in all rivers will suffer the same declines as the Madison rainbows. The states of California and Idaho, for reasons that no one understands, say they have some streams where whirling disease is present and the impacts on fish populations are minimal.

Third, Dick Vincent, FWP fisheries manager in Bozeman, believes that the Madison rainbows will eventually develop a disease-resistant strain. Currently he has found about a 5 percent survival rate among rainbows subjected to the disease in the infected area. "That's not much, but it's better than nothing. It may take a decade or as long as a century for resistant strains to develop. We don't know." If these fish are surviving because of a behavioral trait such as spawning time or location, then there will be strong selective pressure for a population of fish with these characteristics.

Fourth, little is currently known about tubificid worms. As more is learned about their distribution, life history, and interaction with *Myxobolus cerebralis,* more management options may emerge.

Finally, researchers are looking for species and strains of trout that are immune to the disease. If one can be found, then infected steams may be repopulated with resistant fish.

In 1995, to underscore the state's commitment to dealing with whirling disease, Governor Mark Racicot convened a multi-disciplinary Whirling Disease Task Force to try to identify immediate research needs and available resources to meet those needs.

STREAM ACCESS IN MONTANA
contributed by Stan Bradshaw

Imagine that you're floating one of Montana's blue-ribbon trout streams, like the Beaverhead. It's a perfect day for fishing, cool, slightly overcast, and bugs are up on the surface. Even better, you're in your brand new customized fishing raft with all the latest doodads. As you come around a bend, a low bridge looms up. Low, but not too low to clear. But, as you start under it, and too late to respond, you spot the strands of barbed wire, hidden in the shadows of the bridge, strung taut across the entire river at raft height. Before you can react, your boat is swept into it, the tubes are torn, and the boat sinks. Within seconds, you and most of your fishing gear are strewn downstream. Question: Do you have any recourse against the jerk who strung the barbed wire?

Or imagine another day on Little Piddly Creek. It's a small creek, too small for floating, but, with runs, riffles, and undercut banks, a good small stream fishery. You get on the creek where it goes under a state highway, and wade upstream, staying in the water all the way. A half mile upstream from the highway, a pickup roars across an adjacent hay meadow, pulls up opposite where you are fishing, and a big beefy fellow jumps out, veins popping out of his neck, and proceeds to read you the riot act for trespassing and tells you that you have to get the hell off the creek. Question: Just what are your rights to fish the Little Piddly?

Both of these hypotheticals occur, in one form or the other, each year in Montana. Prior to 1984, the answers to these questions were anybody's guess. In 1984, two Montana Supreme Court rulings went a long way toward answering these questions. In 1985, legislation enacted to clarify the court rulings further defined the rights of recreationists to use Montana's rivers and streams. At the end of this chapter, we'll revisit those examples and apply the current law to them to provide some answers.

In the early 1980s, a coalition of recreationists and sportsmen's groups, the Montana Coalition for Stream Access, filed lawsuits against landowners on two rivers, the Beaverhead and the Dearborn, to establish the right of recreationists to use them. While there were some differences in the historic uses of these two rivers (the Dearborn had been used to float logs to market; the Beaverhead had not), the issue was the same in both cases—whether recreationists had the right to float, wade, and fish on these rivers. The Supreme Court decided both cases within months of each other, and the basic ruling was the same in each.

The court said that any surface waters capable of recreational use may be used by the public regardless of who owns the streambed, and regardless of whether the river is navigable. This ruling marked a dramatic departure from the law in most other states. With the exception of Wyoming, in every other state the right of public use hinges on whether a waterway is navigable by some kind of craft ("navigable" is one of those chameleon terms in the law that changes meaning according to how it's used, so take care to know in your home state what the term means). After 1984, in Montana, if a stream held some recreational value, landowners could not keep recreationists out of the stream.

The court, and later the legislature, placed some limits on this right of access, however. First, the law limits your right to use a stream to the land between the "ordinary high water marks." What is the ordinary high water mark? It is:

> The line that water impresses on land by covering it for sufficient periods to cause physical characteristics that distinguish the area below the line from the area above it. Characteristics of the area below the line include, when appropriate, but are not limited to deprivation of the soil of substantially all terrestrial vegetation and destruction of its agricultural vegetative value.

The legislature was careful to caution that a floodplain is not considered to be within a stream's ordinary high water mark. Is that clear as mud now?

Actually, the ordinary high water mark is pretty clear most of the time. If you stay below any visible shoreline vegetation, you're probably okay. Otherwise, if you are in doubt about where the mark is, err to the narrowest possible interpretation. Better to narrow your range of movement some than to risk a trespass charge.

The second major limitation to public use is that it does not include a right to cross private lands. You can enter a waterway at some point of public access, such as a highway right-of-way or a fishing access site, but a landowner may post his land against trespass (more about trespass below) above the ordinary high water mark.

The statute also allows landowners to petition the Fish, Wildlife, and Parks Commission to close or restrict waters to public use if the stream does not support any recreational use, public use is damaging the banks and land adjacent to the stream, the public use is damaging the landowner's property under or next to the stream, or if the public use is causing other environmental damage. In the year after passage of the law, there was a spate of closure petitions. Most of these were denied. Only two, one on Nelson Spring Creek, and one on a part of the Musselshell River, were granted.

On Nelson Spring Creek, the commission simply prohibited wading in the stream during cutthroat spawning (June 15 to September 15) to protect spawning beds. Since the landowner on this stream charges a fee, this has the practical effect of keeping uninvited people off the stream during that period.

On the Musselshell, the Fish, Wildlife, and Parks Commission closed the river to public use through the landowner's bison pasture for safety reasons. In both cases, the closures are marked by signs.

An Infestation of Orange

Anywhere you go in Montana, you are likely to be struck by the profusion of fluorescent-orange-topped fenceposts. Those orange monuments are the moral equivalent of trespassing signs in Montana. No, it doesn't really mean that we Montanans can't read. It's simply an offshoot of the stream-access battles of the mid-eighties. One concession to landowners was the simplification of a previously obscure posting requirement by allowing the use of fluorescent orange paint to signify that land is posted, and describing what constitutes adequate posting (a landowner simply has to post his land at gates going into his land and on stream banks where they pass into his land).

Orange paint aside, however, Montana law requires some specific notice that land is closed to trespass before you can be cited for criminal trespass (The one exception to this is big-game hunting—if you plan to hunt big game on private land, you need the landowner's permission even if the land is not posted). This notice can be made by use of signs, orange paint, or even verbally ("Get the hell off my land" will do), but the burden is nonetheless on the landowner to notify you that you are not welcome on his land. If you pass onto land that is not posted and you haven't otherwise been notified that you are not welcome, you can go above the ordinary high water mark. Use this right judiciously, however; landowners have been quite rightly outraged by careless recreationists who have abused the land, and in some instances have simply closed their land off to public use.

When the legislature first amended the law to allow orange paint for posting, word quickly circulated that anyone who posted their land with orange paint couldn't let anybody—even their relatives—on it. Wrong. Just because land is posted does not mean that you can't ask permission. The orange paint simply means that you cannot use the land without express permission (On the other hand, if the landowner posts a sign that says "No trespassing, don't ask," you can take that as a hint about the value of asking permission). If you're not sure about whether you can cross private land to get to a reach of stream, find the landowner and ask permission. The worst you can get from the landowner is a "no."

Now back to those hypothetical problems.

As to the jerk whose barbed wire destroyed your raft, a number of possibilities exist. First, it is not illegal to run boundary fences or stock fences across rivers and streams. But Montana law does make it a criminal misdemeanor to impede navigation on a public stream (Section 45-8-111 MCA). This carries with it a possible fine of $500 and possible jail time. Not exactly a capital crime, but a clear statement of public policy against this kind of shenanigan. The trick here may be in determining whether the fence is a legitimate boundary or stock fence, or whether it is a spite fence. As a practical matter, the criminal statute has rarely, if ever, been used in Montana, perhaps because most people, including county attorneys (who would have to prosecute any violations under it) are unaware of it.

A second possibility would be a civil suit. While civil liability in a case like this always requires close scrutiny of the specific facts, the law generally does not countenance the deliberate placement of hazards such as this. In fact, the stream access statute says that a landowner is liable to a recreationist only for "willful or wanton misconduct"—basically intentional acts. If this happens to you, and you and your camera survive it, get pictures—not only of the damage, but also shots of the hazard from every angle, especially the upstream side.

A couple of other observations about this situation are in order. First, if you are able to see the hazard before you get to it, Montana law allows you to leave the ordinary high water marks and portage around it "in the least intrusive manner possible." This does not mean that you can leave the river at the slightest excuse and call it a "portage," but where an obstacle makes the river genuinely unpassable, you may get out and go around it. Curiously, the legislature has specifically allowed you to portage around artificial obstacles, but is silent as to natural obstacles. So if you come to a waterfall or some other natural obstacle and the adjacent land is posted, you are on your own.

Hypothetical number two: The answer to this one is simple. As long as you keep inside the ordinary high water mark, you may lawfully fish Little Piddly. Whether you want to brave the wrath of a big brute who seems dangerously close to commiting mayhem is a judgment call that you have to make. But let's embellish the facts a little.

What if, when you got out of your car on the state highway, you could see no orange paint or other indications of "no trespassing" on the land adjacent to the creek? Then, you could cross the field to get to the creek, at least *until* the land-owner came out and yelled at you and told you to get off. At that point, you either have to leave his land or stay inside the ordinary high water mark.

Despite the variations described above, staying legal under Montana's stream access law is not all that difficult. Likewise, staying on an amicable footing with landowners and your fellow anglers is fairly easy. If you follow the basic rules below, you should have no trouble using our rivers and streams with a minimum of hassle. Just use a little common sense and courtesy.

Rules of the River

1. If in doubt about your right to get onto a given stream, ask permission.

2. Make sure you know the current regulations for the water you are fishing.

3. Don't litter. If you see litter, pick it up and take it out. Leave the river cleaner than you found it.

4. If you take a dog, keep it under control. If you can't control it, leave it home. If you want it to survive your trip, don't let it harass livestock.

5. If you are camping, don't leave a trace.

6. Take extreme care with fire. If things feel dry to you, don't build one.

7. If there are other anglers on the stream, give them a wide berth.

8. If you're crossing private land, leave all gates as you find them, and leave all fences intact.

Fly fishermen have basically three choices with insect hatches: Ignore them, accept them, or hunt them. The hatch charts are designed to help all of these strategies (even "ignoring them" works best when it isn't practiced in ignorance). These charts are not complete. The expanse of the state, with its diverse terrestrial and aquatic environments, makes that impossible. The charts identify the major insect hatches, the ones heavy enough to trigger consistent and often selective trout feeding. The dates for these hatches, covering a number of waters, are broad, too, but the references in the write-ups to individual rivers or lakes give more specific time periods.

The waters mentioned in the hatch chart are rivers unless otherwised noted.

CADDIS	JAN	FEB	MAR	APR	MAY	JUNE	JULY	AUG	SEPT	OCT	NOV	DEC
Grannom				• •	• •							

Brachycentrus sp. size 12–16, wings=dark gray to almost black, body=medium to very dark green

The early Grannom (*B. occidentalis*) is also known as the Mother's Day hatch. The summer Grannom is *B. americanus*.

Beaverhead, Big Hole, Bighorn, DePuy's Spring Creek, Grasshopper Creek, Madison, Marias, McClellan Creek, Missouri, Musselshell, Nelson's Spring Creek, Poindexter Slough, Red Rock, Yellowstone

CADDIS	JAN	FEB	MAR	APR	MAY	JUNE	JULY	AUG	SEPT	OCT	NOV	DEC
Green Sedge					• • •	• • • •	• • • •	• • • •	• • • •	• • • •	• •	

Ryacophila sp. size 12–16, wings=mottled brown or gray, body=bright green

There are many important species hatching throughout the summer months on fast-water streams and rivers. Madison, Red Rock

CADDIS	JAN	FEB	MAR	APR	MAY	JUNE	JULY	AUG	SEPT	OCT	NOV	DEC
Great Grey Spotted Sedge						• •	• • • •	• • • •	•			

Arctopsyche grandis size 8–10, wings=mottled dark gray, body=green

Sometimes it is a "hidden hatch." Trout feed on it and ignore the Salmon Fly, but fishermen don't notice.

CADDIS	JAN	FEB	MAR	APR	MAY	JUNE	JULY	AUG	SEPT	OCT	NOV	DEC
Speckled Peter						• •	• • • •	•				

Helicopsyche borealis size 16–18, wings=speckled brown, body=straw yellow
Poindexter Slough

CADDIS	JAN	FEB	MAR	APR	MAY	JUNE	JULY	AUG	SEPT	OCT	NOV	DEC
Little Tan Short Horn Sedge						• • • •	• • • •	•				

Glossosoma sp. size 14–18, wings=tan, body=greenish brown

The larvae make the turtle-shell cases found on rocks in riffles. Madison

CADDIS	JAN	FEB	MAR	APR	MAY	JUNE	JULY	AUG	SEPT	OCT	NOV	DEC
Ring Horn Microcaddis						• • •	• •					

Leucotrichia pictipes size 20–24, wings=spotted black, body=brown

This is a tiny insect, but there are larval densities of 5,000 per square foot on the Madison. Madison

CADDIS	JAN	FEB	MAR	APR	MAY	JUNE	JULY	AUG	SEPT	OCT	NOV	DEC
Spotted Sedge							• • •	• • • •	• • • •	• •	

Hydropsyche sp. size 12–14, wings=spotted brown, body=dirty yellow

Major species include *H. oslari*, *H. occidentalis*, and *H. cockerelli*

Beaverhead, Big Hole, Bighorn, Grasshopper Creek, Madison, Missouri, Red Rock, Ruby, Yellowstone

CADDIS	JAN	FEB	MAR	APR	MAY	JUNE	JULY	AUG	SEPT	OCT	NOV	DEC
Little Sister Sedge						• •	• • • •	• • • •	• • •			

Cheumatopsyche campyla size 16–18, wings=tan, body=ginger

There are massive evening hatches on major, rich rivers.

Beaverhead, Big Hole, Grasshopper Creek, Missouri, Poindexter Slough, Red Rock, Ruby, Yellowstone

CADDIS	JAN	FEB	MAR	APR	MAY	JUNE	JULY	AUG	SEPT	OCT	NOV	DEC
Little Plain Brown Sedge						• •	• • • •	• •				

Lepidostoma pluviale size 14–16, wings=brown, body=light brown
Madison

CADDIS	JAN	FEB	MAR	APR	MAY	JUNE	JULY	AUG	SEPT	OCT	NOV	DEC
Vari-Colored Microcaddis							• • • •	• • • •	• •			

Hydroptila sp. size 18–22, wings=gray to brown, body=yellow to brown

Abundant in spring creek environments
Poindexter Slough

CADDISFLIES

	JAN	FEB	MAR	APR	MAY	JUNE	JULY	AUG	SEPT	OCT	NOV	DEC
Long Horn Sedge							••••	•••				

Oecetis avara — size 12–14, wings=ginger, body=ginger
Beaverhead, Red Rock

	JAN	FEB	MAR	APR	MAY	JUNE	JULY	AUG	SEPT	OCT	NOV	DEC
Little Western Weedy Water Sedge							•••	••••	••			

Amiocentrus aspilus — size 16–18, wings=very dark brown, body=dark green
An especially important midsummer hatch on the Bighorn (mixes with the summer Grannom in a Black Caddis hatch)
Bighorn, Poindexter Slough

	JAN	FEB	MAR	APR	MAY	JUNE	JULY	AUG	SEPT	OCT	NOV	DEC
Summer Flier Sedge								••	•••			

Limnephilus sp. — size 8–10, wings=cinnamon, body=dark ginger
Bighorn

	JAN	FEB	MAR	APR	MAY	JUNE	JULY	AUG	SEPT	OCT	NOV	DEC
Giant Orange Sedge									••••			

Dicosmoecus sp. — size 8, wings=mottled dark brown, body=burnt orange
Big Hole, Smith

CRANEFLIES

	JAN	FEB	MAR	APR	MAY	JUNE	JULY	AUG	SEPT	OCT	NOV	DEC
Orange Crane Fly							••••	••••	•			

Tipula sp. — size 6–10, wings=light veined, body=orange
Beaverhead

DAMSELFLIES

	JAN	FEB	MAR	APR	MAY	JUNE	JULY	AUG	SEPT	OCT	NOV	DEC
Various species							•••	••••	••••	••		

size 8–12, wings=clear in most species, body=bright blue or green in most species
Bailey's Reservoir, Bean Lake, Bighorn Reservoir, Carter's Pond, Deerhead Lake, Dickens Lake, Faber Reservoir, Grasshopper Reservoir, Lisk Creek Reservoir, Martinsdale Reservoir, Mission Lake, Missouri, Pintlar Lake, Rat Lake, Wade Lake, Willow Creek Reservoir

MAYFLIES

	JAN	FEB	MAR	APR	MAY	JUNE	JULY	AUG	SEPT	OCT	NOV	DEC
Blue-Winged Olive			••••	••			••••	•		••	••••	•

Baetis parvus and *Baetis tricaudatus* — size 16, wings=slate gray, body=olive
Armstrong Spring Creek, Beaverhead, Benhart Creek, Big Hole, Bighorn, Big Spring Creek, Blaine Spring Creek, East Fork Gallatin, Gallatin, Grasshopper Creek, Madison, Marias, Missouri, Musselshell, Poindexter Slough, Red Rock, Ruby, Yellowstone

	JAN	FEB	MAR	APR	MAY	JUNE	JULY	AUG	SEPT	OCT	NOV	DEC
Red Quill			••	••••	•							

Rhithrogena morrisoni — size 14, wings=medium gray, body=light reddish brown
Also known as the Western March Brown
Madison

	JAN	FEB	MAR	APR	MAY	JUNE	JULY	AUG	SEPT	OCT	NOV	DEC
Green Drake						••	••••	•••				

Drunella grandis — size 6–8, wings=gray, body=dark olive
Often hatches on the same rivers and at the same time as the Brown Drake.
Big Hole

	JAN	FEB	MAR	APR	MAY	JUNE	JULY	AUG	SEPT	OCT	NOV	DEC
Brown Drake						••	••••	•••				

Ephemera simulas — size 10–12, wings=brown, body=yellowish brown
Big Hole, Culver Pond

	JAN	FEB	MAR	APR	MAY	JUNE	JULY	AUG	SEPT	OCT	NOV	DEC
Small Western Green Drake							••••	••••	•			

Ephemerella flavinea — size 14, wings=slate gray, body=olive
Also commonly called the Flav
Madison

	JAN	FEB	MAR	APR	MAY	JUNE	JULY	AUG	SEPT	OCT	NOV	DEC
Callibaetis							•••	••••	••••	•		

Callibaetis americanus — size 14–16, wings=gray, body=gray
Alder Gulch Creek, Beaver Creek Reservoir, Beaverhead, Carter's Pond, Clark Canyon Reservoir, Cliff Lake, Culver Pond, Dickens Lake, Goose Lake, Hebgen Lake, Lisk Creek Reservoir, Madison, Wade Lake, Willow Creek Reservoir

MAYFLIES

	JAN	FEB	MAR	APR	MAY	JUNE	JULY	AUG	SEPT	OCT	NOV	DEC
Yellow Drake								••••	•••			

Heptagenia elegantula
Yellowstone
size 14–16, wings=straw yellow, body=yellow

	JAN	FEB	MAR	APR	MAY	JUNE	JULY	AUG	SEPT	OCT	NOV	DEC
Pale Morning Dun								••••	••••	••		

Ephemerella infrequens and *Ephemerella inermis*   size 14–18, wings=pale gray, body=pale yellow
Armstrong Spring Creek, Beaverhead, Benhart Creek, Big Hole, Bighorn, Big Spring Creek, Blaine Spring Creek, Cliff Lake, Gallatin, Grasshopper Creek, Madison, Missouri, Poindexter Slough, Red Rock, Wade Lake, Yellowstone

	JAN	FEB	MAR	APR	MAY	JUNE	JULY	AUG	SEPT	OCT	NOV	DEC
Ghost Fly								•••	••			

Traverella albertana
Yellowstone
size 10–12, wings=cream, body=light cream

	JAN	FEB	MAR	APR	MAY	JUNE	JULY	AUG	SEPT	OCT	NOV	DEC
Trico								•••	•••			

Tricorythodes minutus   size 18–20, wings=dark gray, body=very dark olive (appears black)
Beaverhead, Benhart Creek, Big Hole, Bighorn, Blaine Spring Creek, Clark Canyon Reservoir, Gallatin, Grasshopper Creek, Hebgen Lake, Madison, Missouri, Musselshell, Poindexter Slough, Yellowstone

	JAN	FEB	MAR	APR	MAY	JUNE	JULY	AUG	SEPT	OCT	NOV	DEC
White Fly								••	••••	••		

Ephoron album
Yellowstone
size 12–14, wings=white, body=white

	JAN	FEB	MAR	APR	MAY	JUNE	JULY	AUG	SEPT	OCT	NOV	DEC
Tiny Blue-Winged Olive									••	••••	•	

Pseudocloeon sp.   size 22–24, wings=gray, body=olive
Beaverhead, Benhart Creek, Big Hole, Bighorn, Blaine Spring Creek, Poindexter Slough

STONEFLIES

	JAN	FEB	MAR	APR	MAY	JUNE	JULY	AUG	SEPT	OCT	NOV	DEC
Skwala			••••	•••								

Skwala parallela
Dearborn, Smith
size 10–12, wings=dark veined, body=olive

	JAN	FEB	MAR	APR	MAY	JUNE	JULY	AUG	SEPT	OCT	NOV	DEC
Salmon Fly						••••	••					

Pteronarcys californica   size 4–6, wings=dark veined, body=orange
Big Hole, Gallatin, Madison, Yellowstone

	JAN	FEB	MAR	APR	MAY	JUNE	JULY	AUG	SEPT	OCT	NOV	DEC
Little Olive Stone						••••	••••	••				

Alloperla sp.   size 14–16, wings=dark veined, body=bright olive
Beaverhead, Madison, Yellowstone

	JAN	FEB	MAR	APR	MAY	JUNE	JULY	AUG	SEPT	OCT	NOV	DEC
Golden Stone						••••	••••	••				

Calineuria californica   size 6–8, wings=ginger veined, body=golden
Big Hole, Madison, Yellowstone

	JAN	FEB	MAR	APR	MAY	JUNE	JULY	AUG	SEPT	OCT	NOV	DEC
Yellow Stone							•••	••••	•			

Isoperla sp.   size 14–16, wings=yellow veined, body=bright yellow
Also known as the Little Yellow Stone
Beaverhead, Bighorn, Madison, Red Rock, Yellowstone

TWO-WINGED FLIES

	JAN	FEB	MAR	APR	MAY	JUNE	JULY	AUG	SEPT	OCT	NOV	DEC
Midges	••••	••••	••••	••••	••••	••••	••••	••••	••••	••••	••••	••••

Diptera   size 14–28, midges come in most colors
Various species
Hatch everywhere and all year
Midges are especially important on rivers during the winter months and on high mountain lakes all summer.

INDEX OF WATERS

INDEX

**Design & Layout
Q Communications Group
Helena, Montana
Composed in
Stone Serif & Futura
Printed on Joy White Offset
(acid-free) by
Thomson-Shore, Inc.
Dexter, Michigan**